About the author

I grew up in Bedford and attended Bedford School, which I left with little idea of what I wanted to do. After a brief flirtation with farming, I got a job at RAE Bedford as a scientific assistant. That introduced me to sea trials in aircraft carriers and brought a few flights in military aircraft. I soon decided to become a pilot and joined the RAF. Thereafter followed the adventures I describe. Civil flying brought me to Llanbedr in Meirionnydd, where I have lived since 1988 with my wife, June, and where I enjoy walking in the hills of Snowdonia.

Cover photograph

This dramatic, airborne photo (reproduced by kind permission of Mrs Gillian Cooke), was taken in the Ogwen Valley of Snowdonia in the spring of 1978. A camera was mounted beneath the tail of a Gnat trainer aircraft and operated by the late Richard Cooke from the Gnat's rear cockpit. The Hawk was piloted from the front seat by the author and had to be flown in very close line astern on the Gnat. The photo was chosen for the RAF pilot recruiting campaign, where it appeared in a double page spread in the Telegraph Sunday magazine of 23 July 1978.

ADVENTURES IN AVIATION

Wg Cdr Roy Gamblin AFC

ADVENTURES IN AVIATION

Vanguard Press

VANGUARD PAPERBACK

© Copyright 2020
Wg Cdr Roy Gamblin AFC

The right of Wg Cdr Roy Gamblin AFC to be identified as author of
this work has been asserted by him in accordance with the
Copyright, Designs and Patents Act 1988.

A CIP catalogue record for this title is
available from the British Library.

ISBN 978 1 784657 98 7

*Vanguard Press is an imprint of
Pegasus Elliot MacKenzie Publishers Ltd.*
www.pegasuspublishers.com

First Published in 2020

**Vanguard Press
Sheraton House Castle Park
Cambridge England**

Printed & Bound in Great Britain

Dedication

I dedicate this book to those who did not survive to tell their stories as I have been lucky to do. Thirty-five pilots, one navigator and one soldier, all of whom I once knew well, died far too early in violent circumstances. Almost all of the airmen died in fast-jet crashes. The soldier was murdered by one of his own men. Six of the thirty-seven lie in graves in the two Christian Cemeteries near Muscat. May they all rest in peace.

Acknowledgements

I should like to thank all those friends and relatives who, over many years, have urged me to write a book about my unusual experiences over forty years as an aviator.

Chief amongst all those must be the late Mr Nick Smyth of Llwyngwril, Meirionnydd, who was my amazingly adept proof reader for all the articles I wrote and which formed the seeds of this book. Near equal to Nick must be the late Mr Michael Keall of Caldecote near Cambridge, my English master at Bedford School, who instilled my foundations for the language and imbued me with enthusiasm for creative writing.

I am sad that neither Nick nor Michael lived quite long enough to learn that I finally made it to a book.

Last but not least, I thank my dear wife, June, who has supported me magnificently through this project, as she has throughout our past forty-eight years of happy marriage.

Contents

1
AN AVIATOR'S FIRST STEPS

I suppose that the first decision of any significance that I took in my life was at the age of fifteen and a half when I decided one day that I'd had enough of being a schoolboy. I wanted to get on with real life and to see the world. I had also begun to yearn for an improvement in finances beyond my very limited pocket money and the meagre earnings from a pushbike-borne newspaper round. So, rather precociously, in March 1960, I told my shocked parents and a greatly disappointed headmaster that I would be leaving Bedford School following the O-level exams that summer. Unfortunately, the burgeoning taste for adventure and the lust to travel hadn't yet condensed into any identifiable ambition as to how to achieve my aims. Apart from wanting to upgrade from pushbike to motorbike as soon as I reached the minimum age of sixteen, I hadn't got much of a clue as to what I actually wanted to do after that. I guess I had a pretty short-term focus. There was certainly no hint of a business plan or mission statement.

As advertised, I left school immediately after the last day of the exams, ostentatiously displaying my new sense of independence of the system. It didn't last more than one day. A rather angry headmaster summoned me back under threat of expulsion since there were still two weeks left of the summer term. I returned meekly and somewhat chastened. After the formality of completing the last fortnight, I left school properly on the final day of term and soon took a temporary job on a farm to help with the harvest whilst waiting for the results of the 'O' levels. It was a glorious late August and early September and I worked hard and long, under the hot daytime sun, sometimes continuing into the late evening dark under floodlights, manhandling the heavy sacks of grain on the combine harvesters as well as baling then stacking the heavy straw bales. I was shown how to drive the Massey-Ferguson tractor with its towed baler and, to my absolute delight, was soon allowed to go solo on baling operations. It was a healthy and satisfying experience, in the fresh air, under the summer sky, exercising my body and my mind in an exciting, new and free environment with the sounds, smells and sights of farm machinery and the grain harvest all around me and actually *driving* a tractor! I was enjoying farming so much that, in a flash of inspiration and having seen an advert in a newspaper, I sent off for application papers for a three-year farming apprenticeship in Canada.

In early September my sixteenth birthday came along and I immediately invested £15 of my hard-earned farm wages into buying not one, but two, very second-hand, 1,000cc Ariel 'Square Four' motorcycles. One of my machines was unroadworthy and the plot was to use it as spares for the other. In those days such big bikes were normally bolted to a sidecar containing a mother or a granny and, often, a young boy in the boot. In much earlier days, I had enjoyed being the young boy in the boot on weekend expeditions into the countryside with my grandparents and their Harley-Davidson and sidecar. This time I planned actually to ride the bike, and without the attached people carrier.

I'd had a very small amount of experience off the public roads with a school friend's various motorbikes but, in common with most at that time, no training whatsoever. The nearest I'd been to any faintly useful experience before taking on the big motorbike was simply a fair number of years riding the pushbike back and forth to school every day, and on the paper round. Nevertheless, with a brand-new set of L plates, a new provisional licence and no helmet, I was soon whizzing rather inexpertly but very happily around the then quiet roads and lanes of rural north Bedfordshire, haphazardly learning how to ride the Squariel as I went, usually in my shirtsleeves. What with the tractor and baler and now the powerful motorbike, I had taken the very first steps in acquiring a lifelong taste for driving big, noisy machines — and preferably fast ones.

The 'O' level results arrived two days before my birthday. Mine were not sparkling but were followed soon after, surprisingly in view of my end-of-term bad conduct, by a generous invitation from a now kindly headmaster suggesting that I ought to come and have a chat about my future. I dillied and dallied then decided indifferently that I had nothing to lose by having a chat. It was also an opportunity to flash my newly acquired Squariel around. So off I went one afternoon, arriving windswept from the slipstream, to prop my big, hot, shiny bike nonchalantly against a large tree in front of his house — the bike's stand was inoperative. He didn't take much notice of the Squariel but he did persuade me convincingly, over a very pleasant tea, not to risk wasting my education and my life. At his suggestion, the school's careers master soon visited me at home and suggested that he would see if the personnel manager at the nearby Royal Aircraft Establishment (RAE), Thurleigh, might consider finding a suitable position for me. I had hinted that my greatest inspiration at school was in physics and mathematics — and I had also done well in those subjects in the 'O' levels — so I thought that some sort of scientific career might be a good wheeze. At around the same time, it all went quiet on the farm as the grain harvest finished, the weather turned colder and damper and I was put onto hoeing peas. There was an awful lot of peas — almost as far as I could see. My enthusiasm for agriculture, in the quiet cold rain and the muddy pea fields, began to shrink rather faster than it had grown. The Canada idea got swiftly dumped.

Happily, within a few days I was called to an interview at the RAE with the personnel manager. I was successful and was then told to report next to the security officer, a Group Captain Snaith. I later discovered he was the same Leonard S. Snaith who, as a flying officer, had been a member of the Schneider Trophy Team when Britain had won the trophy outright in 1931. He was also the father of a classmate at school. The group captain took something of a chance by supporting the offer to me of a position as a scientific assistant in the Naval Air Department (NAD) at RAE Bedford on the airfield at Thurleigh. That was to be a surprisingly big step up from driving a tractor or the Squariel — let alone hoeing peas. I was very soon to become acquainted with much noisier, faster and significantly more interesting and versatile machines.

The role of NAD, under Dr Bill Stewart at that time, was to provide facilities for certain flight-testing aspects of British, Commonwealth (and occasionally foreign) naval aircraft and to test and develop various ship-borne take-off and landing aids and devices. For take-offs, or 'launches' in Fleet Air Arm terminology, the department was equipped with two steam catapults, one that was flush with the paved airfield surface and the other raised some fifteen feet above it. For landings, there was a section of runway with arrester cables, coupled to hydraulic braking devices, that were engaged by the large hook hanging down under a naval aircraft's tail, the aircraft either having landed just before the cable or having accelerated first along the ground to a pre-calculated high speed. The very important deck landing Mirror Sight, invented by a Royal Navy officer, had been developed and tested at Bedford in association with these arrester systems and was becoming the standard landing aid on carriers worldwide. An aircraft carrier's pitching and heaving motion produced a tricky challenge for carrier pilots, who needed to maintain a stabilised, constant angle of approach down to the deck to avoid exceeding the aircraft's structural limits on touchdown as well as to ensure a successful arrester cable engagement. The Mirror Sight consisted of a curved, aft-facing, gyro-stabilised mirror onto which bright lights were reflected. This gave a 'meatball' of light for the pilot to follow, in relation to other adjacent coloured lights to warn him when the aircraft was too low or too high. The Mirror Sight enabled the pilot to achieve the correct descent angle to the deck despite its pitching and heaving motion. Before the Sight came along, a crewman had stood to one side of the flight deck landing area and had signalled to the pilot with flags to indicate whether the approaching aircraft was too high or too low. 'Flying the Meatball' was easier and more accurate for a carrier pilot.

As well as testing aircraft and devices at Bedford itself, NAD was responsible for planning and conducting ship-borne trials on aircraft carriers of the Royal Navy and on those of certain other foreign navies, including for example Argentina (Veinticinco de Mayo), Australia (HMAS Melbourne), Brazil (Minas Gerais), France (Clemenceau) and India (INS Vikrant). Within the department was a small section responsible for recording and analysing test data, particularly the high-speed photographic film taken of aircraft during catapult launches, on approaches to the flight deck and during arrested landings. As well as the film, an accelerometer operated within the test aircraft, along the fore and aft axis during each take-off and landing, to provide further data. The instrument was linked to a revolving drum of recording paper that gave important readings of acceleration and deceleration during launch and landing respectively. I was to join that small analysis section as its most junior member.

Much of my new work had to take place in a semi-dark room within NAD, after the data had been collected from flight tests, painstakingly analysing the high-speed, black and white negative film of launches and approaches, frame by frame. For the approaches, I had to calculate — from the rate of change of image size — aircraft speeds in relation to the ship and then, in particular, the rates of descent right down to touchdown. The calculations were not straightforward since the camera was placed obliquely to one side of the landing area and the ship pitched and heaved up and down as already mentioned. There were no computers for my calculations. Equations, a set of log tables and a slide rule were the tools. From the analyses, I had to produce various tables and graphs that depicted the precise flight paths and performance parameters. Although work in the analysis room was often long and tedious, and well away from the outdoors that I loved, there were plenty of other distractions to sharpen my appetite and to keep my interest thoroughly alive right from the first day there. RAE Bedford at the beginning of the 1960s was home to some of the most interesting experimental and operational aircraft of the post-war years, flown primarily by the resident test pilots under their chief, Commander Pat Chilton RN, a veteran of World War II and the Korean War, and sometimes by visiting operational pilots. Part of the deal in my new job was that I had to attend an Ordinary National Certificate course in Mechanical Engineering at Mander College in Bedford on a day release basis. Much more excitingly, I was also expected in due course to accompany the full test teams for periods of seaborne trials in aircraft carriers, where the most modern of naval aircraft were to be found in a milieu throbbing with action. It was an extremely exciting prospect for a young boy just out of school.

Before the nautical tales, perhaps I should first tell a little more of the environment at RAE Bedford and at NAD, and then describe in more detail the particular activities and especially the carrier trials.

Experimental aircraft were operated by Aeroflight, the main test flying centre at the south-western corner of the airfield. The aircraft resident in 1960-62 included: the supersonic Fairey Delta 2 with its pre-Concorde 'droop-snoot'; the Avro 707 delta wing development aircraft for the Vulcan; the very noisy VTOL (vertical take-off and landing) Flying Bedstead; the even noisier VTOL Shorts SC1 with its four lift engines and one engine for forward flight; the low-speed Handley Page 115 trying out an early wing-shape for Concorde and the Shorts SB5 low-speed development precursor to the Lightning — effectively a 7/8 scale, single-engine, P1 Lightning. Across on the north side of Thurleigh at NAD, we were heavily involved mainly with the Blackburn NA39 — the prototype Buccaneer — as well as lots of ongoing work with the De Havilland Sea Vixen, Supermarine Scimitar, Fairey Gannet, and occasionally with the Hawker Sea Hawk and Bréguet Alizé from the Indian Navy and the French Navy's own Dassault Étendard. These aircraft, the British ones today evoking memories of several long-dead aircraft design and manufacturing names, were the bread and butter of daily life on and over the busy airfield at Thurleigh. They provided huge interest to a lad of only just sixteen years, working up very close to many of them from the outset. It was to become even closer within a very short period.

I soon became familiar with my duties at NAD, including running out to change the accelerometer recording paper in the various naval aircraft that turned up at the airfield for repetitive runs using the land-based catapults or arrester-gear. The instrument was usually installed behind a hatch in the belly of the aircraft, or in one side of the fuselage, close to the centre of gravity. This meant that I had to work swiftly but safely under or beside the aircraft as the pilots waited with their engines running after disconnecting from the arrester cable following a cable engagement or before taxiing onto the raised catapult. As soon as I received the signal, I would rush out, open the hatch, change the paper, secure the hatch again and then rush back to my station by the camera and watch the next landing or take-off. This was thrilling stuff and I was careful never to trip over! Under test conditions, the combined system of arrester gear and aircraft was often operating close to its limits. For landing trials, the aircraft were often at high weights and sometimes offset from the centre-line, so that they would often whip noticeably from side to side during the deceleration. We were always in a protected position in the event of an arrester cable snapping, which was thankfully rare because a steel cable lashing through the air can make a nasty mess of a human body — it had happened at sea on carriers.

For launch trials on the raised catapult at Bedford, much of the work was to do with establishing minimum launch speeds for various aircraft weights and configurations. A trial would typically start with the raised catapult set to launch the aircraft off the deck at a ten to fifteen-knot margin or so above its estimated minimum launch speed. The speed would be progressively reduced on successive launches until finally the aircraft would sink slightly off the end of its run from the raised catapult. The minimum launch speed was then defined as just above the sink value! Inevitably, there were occasions where all did not go along with the pre-calculated values and an aircraft, launched necessarily in a nose-up attitude, would wobble or sink swiftly down onto the runway ahead of the catapult. I grew to admire the skill of the pilots as they accelerated away from their various 'situations' then often, once a safe speed had been obtained, snapped on the bank and turned sharply downwind into the circuit to land and make another launch. All this catapult launching stuff at close range made for a very noisy, high-vibration environment, with rapid accelerations of aircraft at full throttle accompanied by sharp emissions of steam from the catapult track. I revelled in playing my small part in these dynamic and exciting events.

I had been at NAD for only six months or so when I was asked if I would like to fly in a Sea Vixen as an observer. I could barely believe it. My senior colleague in the section flew often as a flight test observer and I guess our manager, Gerry Suggett, decided it was time the youngster had a go so that he could be called upon occasionally to do the job as a back-up. Up to that time, I had flown only once in my life — as a passenger on a pleasure flight in a 1930s De Havilland Fox Moth off Southport Sands when I was about ten years old. The step up to flying in the Sea Vixen was like going to the moon. I was to fly with the chief test pilot himself, Commander Pat Chilton, a very kindly man who took me patiently through all I needed to know. I had been fitted up with the full kit of flying overalls, helmet, oxygen mask, ejection-seat leg restrainers and so on and Commander Chilton drilled me in the procedures for operating some of the equipment at the observer's station and for ejection in the event of a serious emergency. The view from the observer's seat, below and to the right of the pilot was not brilliant. To the left one could see only the pilot's legs and a small number of his instruments. To the front lay the observer's mysterious instrument panel and to the right lay the best view of the outside world through a small window. A further, smaller window was in the overhead hatch through which I had entered the aircraft rather gingerly. Well, the views maybe weren't that great but the experience of flying in such a machine was just brilliant. The sensation of acceleration on the take-off run, the radio exchanges between the pilot and air traffic control, the aerodynamic noise, the sounds and smells of the pressurisation, engines and electronic gear and the sights of the world rushing past the small window to my right all added up to the most exciting adventure of my life to that point; the first flight in a powerful aircraft. I became immersed in the total experience and began to feel almost as if the machine was an extension of myself. The curtain had been lifted on a totally new and unique world, revealing so many novel sights, sounds and sensations that my mind was kept utterly enthralled.

The expansion of this thrilling experience continued soon into sea trials aboard each of the aircraft carriers HMS Ark Royal, HMS Centaur, HMS Hermes and the INS Vikrant (formerly HMS Hercules). All the sea trials took place in Lyme Bay off the south coast of England and began with the team taking a train trip down to the Royal Naval Dockyard, Portsmouth, to embark on the carrier. The experience of working on, and in an aircraft carrier is strikingly unique. Between operations, huge lifts open up in the flight deck, fore and aft, to take aircraft back and forth from the hangars below. When flying operations are underway, the ship steams at high speed into wind to enable relative launch and landing speeds to be kept to as low a value as possible. So, the first difference is that everything takes place on the flight deck in at least a strong breeze. Then there is the very confined space within which aircraft must manoeuvre, spreading or folding their wings as they taxi whilst following the marshallers precisely. Among the closely packed aircraft, other flight deck crewmen — wearing coloured tabards with letters or numbers to identify their role — scurry about busily preparing aircraft for their next flights, refuelling, replenishing and re-arming. They work against a background of jet noise and wind noise and around aircraft starting up, manoeuvring onto the catapult or disengaging from the arrester cable after landing. A strict discipline is required by all who take part in order to maintain a high level of launch and landing efficiency and to minimise the ever-present risks of mishap. It is amongst the ultimate examples of teamwork at its best.

On the catapult, the Flight Deck Officer (FDO) signals to the pilot whilst a crewman attaches a hold-back strop between the deck and the underside of the aircraft. Further forward, a third crewman attaches a steel hawser, the bridle, around the catapult shuttle and hooks it to two rearward-facing hooks on the underside of the front fuselage. On a signal from the FDO, the shuttle is moved forward a few feet under steam-pressure and jacks the aircraft up into the launch attitude. A further signal, then hydraulic arms in the deck extend to raise the thick steel-plate of the jet blast deflector (JBD) behind the aircraft. With the JBD in position, the FDO rapidly waves a small flag to signal the pilot to throttle the engines up to full thrust — the noise and vibration can be sensed through much of the ship. Finally, after a last quick check within the cockpit, the pilot raises his hand in salute to indicate he is ready for launch. The FDO drops his flag arm rapidly to the deck and crouches down low. Within a small retractable viewpoint poking up from the flight deck, the catapult controller initiates the launch. Pre-calculated, very high steam pressure is applied instantly behind the shuttle; the hold-back shear-link breaks under the strain and the aircraft roars off down the catapult track accelerating rapidly, then off the bow of the ship and up into the air as the bridle is left behind. The high-speed, heavy shuttle hits a water-deceleration device just below the catapult track whilst the aircraft accelerates rapidly away out of sight or turns downwind for a landing into one of the several cables strung across the aft flight deck.

Well, that's what usually happens. Unfortunately, on 31 August 1961 — a fine summer's day in Lyme Bay — I witnessed what could happen when something went badly wrong. Unusually, I was watching from behind the ship's captain and his assistants on the bridge in the island of HMS Hermes for the first launch of the day of a NA39. In the aircraft were pilot Lieutenant Commander 'Ossie' Brown and Blackburn's flight test observer, Mr Trevor Dunn. The aircraft left the catapult normally on launch but was then seen to pitch up to a much higher than normal nose attitude. Immediately, Hermes' captain swung round to 'Flyco', the commander flying in his adjacent bridge annex, and snapped, "Should that aircraft be in that attitude?"

"No, sir," responded Flyco without a pause. The captain immediately ordered full astern on the ship's engines as the NA39, now in what looked to be a nose-up attitude of about forty-five degrees (but which we later measured — from the launch film — was twenty-eight to twenty-nine degrees) and still at very low speed, dropped its left wing. The aircraft's cockpit canopy flew off and, almost simultaneously, the quick-thinking captain barked, "twenty degrees starboard!" to the helmsman. Stunned, I felt the full vibration of the ship's engines straining to slow it as I watched the aircraft, nose-low by now and with the left wing still down, hit the water about five hundred yards in front of the decelerating carrier. The time from launch to crash was probably under twenty seconds. I rushed out of the bridge, down the stairs and out onto the flight deck. There were no other aircraft flying and I joined a small crowd of flight deck personnel quickly gathering along the port side as Hermes drew to a shuddering stop about a hundred yards to one side of the NA39, now floating vertically nose-down with only its clam-shell air brakes at the rearmost end of the fuselage, together with the rear of the tailplane assembly, protruding above the softly lapping water. There was a sudden silence as the ship's engines died and we all stood there staring at this strange sight, willing the two crewmembers of the NA39 to break clear of the sea surface suddenly so that we could all release our tension in a rousing cheer at their escape. It wasn't to be. After what seemed to be several minutes, but was probably much less, the last visible part of the aircraft just slipped down beneath the waves and that was the death of it and our two colleagues.

The details of this tragic event have been imprinted clearly and indelibly on my memory for nearly sixty years. It was the first and, thankfully, last time that I witnessed a fatal aircraft accident as it took place. The NA39 was later salvaged and the subsequent investigation revealed that the wing boundary layer control (BLC, or 'blow') system, that provided a crucial lift improvement at low speed, failed on launch causing the aircraft to pitch up and stall, and that this was probably due in turn to a failure of the micro-switches that initiated the blow after the aircraft's wings were spread.

Sadly, the hurly-burly of carrier operations in the early 1960s meant that accidents of one kind or another were not uncommon. During another sea trial in which I was present, an Indian Navy crewman on INS Vikrant strayed into the prop wash of a Bréguet Alizé running at high power and was blown overboard to land on his head on a gun sponson — he died of his injuries later that day. On another occasion, I was on the flight deck when a Sea Vixen, parked with its wings folded, spontaneously released both under-wing fuel drop-tanks that broke apart as they hit the deck and splashed jet fuel over a wide area. Unfortunately, two crewmen in particular were drenched in fuel and I saw them being carried screaming down to the sickbay with fuel in their eyes and airways. I believe they recovered. More fortunately in my case, the worst thing that happened to me personally was getting a severe bawling-out one day from a Royal Navy officer for wandering across the flight deck without wearing ear defenders. Quite right too, although the bawling-out felt loud enough to exceed the decibels from any aircraft's engines. (There were to be, nevertheless, much later events in my life that wreaked considerable damage to my hearing).

Back at NAD, in due course I felt a growing restlessness with the time spent analysing film in the darkroom and the one day a week in the classrooms at Mander College. I began to yearn increasingly for more time and action in the new-found environments at sea or in the air. I guess it was therefore inevitable that, one day, these new and exciting experiences with aircraft on land, at sea and in the air would steadily draw me to the idea of becoming a pilot. There were two events that provided the final triggers for me to do something about it. The first was when I was offered a flight in the RAE Bedford Meteor Mark 7½ (so called because it was basically a Mark 7 but for some reason had a Mark 8 tail grafted on) with Lieutenant Commander Bernard Holland as pilot and me in the back, where I would get the chance for the first time to handle the dual controls. Lieutenant Commander Holland, like his boss Commander Chilton — both full-bearded Royal Navy officers — was a pleasure to fly with and he allowed me to try some basic manoeuvres. I came back brimming with excitement and overflowing with questions about how the aircraft flew.

The second crucial event was when I saw two Hawker Hunters fly very low and very fast several times across the airfield at Thurleigh, producing that unique and evocative Hunter 'Blue Note' sound (a sort of slightly mournful, wailing note emitted by an Avon-engined Hunter when flying at above five hundred knots or so at low level). After they had landed, I was in the crew room as the two pilots strolled in to debrief their trip over a cup of coffee. I listened, absolutely spellbound by the jargon and the tales they told so casually of flying along the East Anglian coast at low level, their simulated attacks on this bridge and that radio mast, their close-formation manoeuvres and so on. That finally did it. I resolved there and then that I would become a Hunter pilot and would not rest until I did so.

I applied soon to join the RAF and was invited to RAF Hornchurch to undergo the Officer Aircrew Selection Centre process in which I was successful. On 8 March 1962, at the exact minimum allowed age of seventeen and a half, I reported to the RAF Initial Training School at RAF South Cerney, near Cirencester, and joined the Royal Air Force to train as a pilot. Within a few days of arrival, I was despatched to attend the Outward Bound Mountain School course at Eskdale in the Lake District then returned to South Cerney for basic aircrew officer training. On 31 August, a week before my eighteenth birthday, I was commissioned as an acting pilot officer. I could hardly believe that within a few more weeks I would be flying in the Hunting Provost basic jet trainer at No 7 Flying Training School (FTS), RAF Church Fenton near Tadcaster, working towards the first big hurdle — my very first solo flight.

HMS Hermes at High Speed with Buccaneer S2 and Sea Vixens
(Graham Pitchfork Collection)

Sea Vixen for Launch. Note Jet Blast Deflector, Mirror Sight and
Plane-Guard Wessex (Graham Pitchfork Collection)

Buccaneer S1 off Port Catapult, Sea Vixen Taxying to Starboard
Catapult (Graham Pitchfork Collection)

Buccaneer S1 at End of Launch
(Graham Pitchfork Collection)

Scimitar on Approach to the Deck
(Graham Pitchfork Collection)

2
FIRST JET SOLO AND MORE

Author's Foreword: Most of this chapter includes an article written by me over fifty-seven years ago whilst I was still quite intoxicated by the experience of my first solo flight. It was published three months after the event, in the 'Bedfordshire Times' on 15 February 1963, where the editor added these words:

"Acting Pilot Officer Roy Gamblin, an Old Boy of Bedford School, records especially for the readers of this newspaper the experience of his first solo flight in a jet aircraft. He was born in Bedford in 1944 and won a scholarship to Bedford School in 1956. He left Bedford School in 1960 and joined the RAF in 1962, spending the first month at the Outward Bound Mountain School at Eskdale in Cumberland. Commissioned in August 1962, Roy hopes to win his pilot's wings this summer. His ambition is to be a fighter pilot, although his height (six feet two inches!) may prove an obstacle."

By the time Thursday 15 November came around, I'd had some ten hours of dual instruction in the Jet Provost basic trainer. I took off with my instructor, Flying Officer Mike Bond, soon after lunch on the first sortie of the day and we spent nearly an hour flying round and round, taking off, landing and taking off again. After the final landing we taxied back in and, following a short debrief, I rushed off for a quick coffee before the next flight, for which I was due to be briefed by the squadron commander, Squadron Leader Gerry Eades, ten minutes later. A few minutes after the briefing, I was off to do the pre-flight inspection of the aircraft. Squadron Leader Eades joined me as I came back to the cockpit and, as soon as we were strapped in, I started up and taxied out to take off.

The flight lasted half an hour. The squadron commander was constantly criticising every tiny detail, urging me ever towards perfection and accuracy of flying on each circuit of the airfield and on each take-off and landing. We landed finally and, as we taxied back to dispersal again, he went through all his criticisms once more. I was so engrossed in thinking about these that I nearly missed his words, "So now, how do you feel about going off on your own?" I couldn't believe it.

"Okay, sir!" was all I could say.

Before I could realise what was happening, we were back in dispersal and Squadron Leader Eades had given me a final briefing before getting out and going off to watch me from the control tower. A ground crew member strapped up the empty right seat with a cover. After starting the engine once more, I pressed the radio transmitter button and called, "Tango two-three, taxi for first solo!" Tango two-three, the very first time I had used the personal call sign that was to remain with me throughout the rest of my training course. I waved the chocks away and, in response to the marshaller's signals, released the brakes and rolled forward, turning onto the taxiway that led out to the runway in use.

As I taxied along, I looked down at my white-gloved hands, one on the control column, the other on the throttle, and tried to realise what was happening. I was in complete control now. There could be no margin for mistakes. There was nobody there to correct them for me. I knew that, once I was airborne, I would have little time for looking around at the countryside beneath me. There was too much to do and other aircraft to look out for.

I stopped just before the runway and checked all my instruments, my fuel and all the other things that have to be done. Then I called, "Tango two-three take-off!" Permission to take off was given. As I rolled out onto the runway, I took a quick glance at the windsock to ascertain the crosswind so that I would know what corrections to expect on take-off. I lined up, stopped, applied the brakes and smoothly opened the throttle as far as it would go. The jet engine roared up to full thrust and the aircraft strained against the brakes.

Brakes off! — then I was accelerating down the runway, the concrete flashing ever faster under my wheels. I raised the nose-wheel gently off the ground. Within a few more seconds the aircraft had lifted off the runway and I had retracted the undercarriage. I was airborne alone in a jet aircraft for the first time in my life!

I throttled back slightly and climbed away from the airfield, levelling off at a thousand feet before turning ninety degrees to the left. Flying along for ten seconds and turning left again, I was now flying downwind on a reciprocal track to the runway. As I turned, the sun was just disappearing behind a bank of cloud on the horizon. A quick glance at the altimeter told me I was gaining height and losing airspeed very slightly. I made the necessary corrections and looked downwards to see the near end of the runway sliding under my left wingtip.

My wingtip fuel tank started to track accurately along the centre line of the runway a thousand feet below. Directly ahead and below the nose of the aircraft was a railway line along which a train speeding southward was spreading a line of billowing white steam. To my left, on the far side of the airfield, a river scintillated in the last few rays of the lowering sun. To my right lay the industrial haze of Leeds and Bradford.

Downwind checks! Undercarriage down, straps tight, hydraulics and fuel okay, airbrakes in. I called off the checks to myself and, as I finished, I heard the words "Tango eight-two rejoining!" over the radio. My instructor, returning from a flight with another student pilot, was rejoining the circuit right behind me. Now I had his eyes upon me as well as those of the squadron commander in the control tower!

I was leaving the runway behind me to my left and it was time to start turning and descending towards the point where I would touch down. I checked for other aircraft in the area into which I intended to turn and eased the stick over to the left, simultaneously throttling back as I let the nose down. I began descending at right angles to the runway as I came out of the turn. I descended steadily to six hundred feet and then began my final turn-in until I was lined up at four hundred feet with the runway ahead of me.

There was certainly no time for admiring the view now. This was the critical stage — the final approach and landing which necessitated one hundred per cent concentration. The threshold of the runway began to fill the picture I saw from the cockpit. I was getting low. Put on power! Still low. More power!

I came in rather low over the hedge at the end of the runway, chopped the throttle and, as I dropped towards the ground eased the stick back, checking my descent and hitting the runway with a gentle bump and a squeal of tyres. I lowered the nose-wheel on to the runway and felt the vibration as it touched down at high speed. Steady braking brought my speed down as I neared the end of the runway. I was down again — all had gone well. I taxied to dispersal, stopped, shut down the engine, unstrapped and climbed out to be greeted with congratulations from the squadron commander — just as my instructor taxied in, having landed right behind me.

Back in the mess that evening, there were celebrations for myself and three other student pilots who had gone solo for the first time that day, the first hurdle on the long road to a pair of Royal Air Force pilots' wings.

I was awarded my wings at a passing-out parade at Church Fenton in August 1963 and was thrilled to be posted for advanced flying training in the Folland Gnat at RAF Valley on Anglesey. Like so many other pilots, I took to the Gnat right away. I still find it hard to believe that I was flying solo supersonic (albeit in a dive!) only a few months after my nineteenth birthday. I had a very successful course that resulted in my being posted for my first choice to RAF Chivenor for operational conversion training in the Hunter!

On 25 June 1964, two years and three months after leaving NAD, I taxied a single-seat Hawker Hunter F.6 onto the easterly runway at RAF Chivenor near Barnstaple. I opened the throttle to full thrust and felt the kick of acceleration in my back as I released the brakes and tore down the centre line and up into the sky on a brilliantly sunny day for my first solo on the type. I was airborne for fifty glorious minutes, alone in an exceptional aircraft, free to roll, dive and soar around the scattered sunlit clouds, looping and turning in a sequence of high-G aerobatics and exploring the handling of this wonderful machine before returning eventually across the sea, glinting below in the sun, then over the beach and the sand dunes to land back at Chivenor. I taxied in with a huge grin hidden under my oxygen mask. I was still only nineteen and had just become a Hunter pilot. I had taken an aviator's first steps — though I could not have imagined just how many more steps I would yet need to climb.

Author (Back Row Middle) And Graduating Course at Church Fenton in August 1963

3
HUNTERS OVER THE JUNGLE

The Malaysian Federation was formed on 16 September 1963. It comprised the various states of Malaya, plus Sabah (formerly North Borneo), Sarawak and Singapore. During the build-up to the formation of Malaysia, neighbouring Indonesia had raised violent objections to the plans for the new state. Their chief complaint was the incorporation into Malaysia of Sabah and Sarawak on the island of Borneo, where Malaysia and Indonesia shared a long jungle border of over one thousand miles. On the day of Malaysia's formation, mobs ransacked the British Embassy in Jakarta — the period known as 'Confrontation' (towards Malaysia) had begun. Actions soon escalated over the following three years to include guerrilla sea landings in Johore and attacks in Sarawak, Sabah and Singapore. There were threatening flights by Indonesian Air Force bombers over the town of Kuching in Sarawak, air attacks on Malaysian villages in Borneo and paratroopers were also dropped into the jungles of Johore. Confrontation finally came to an end with the ratification of the Bangkok Accord between Indonesia and Malaysia in August 1966. Singapore had left the Federation on 9 August 1965 to become an independent republic under Prime Minister Lee Kuan Yew.

During Confrontation, there was a large defensive presence of British, Australian and New Zealand armed forces, based in Malaya, Singapore and Borneo. Those Army, Navy and Air forces maintained the obligations of the member nations of SEATO, the South East Asia Treaty Organisation. Britain was also a party to a defence agreement with Malaysia which allowed her to maintain bases in the territories in return for guaranteeing their defence. The bulk of the British forces were based on the island of Singapore, where the Royal Air Force had three large and busy airfields: Changi, Seletar and Tengah. Changi was the main transport aircraft base and Seletar had the helicopters and light transport aircraft.

Tengah was home to No 20 (Day Fighter/Ground Attack — DFGA) Squadron, equipped with sixteen Hawker Hunter FGA9 aircraft and two Hunter T7s. Disbanded at the end of 1960 in RAF Germany, the squadron had reformed at Tengah in 1961 in response to a concern that SEATO might have to react to Communist aggression in Laos. 20 Squadron remained at Tengah until the general withdrawal of British forces from the Far East began in 1970. The busy airfield was shared during Confrontation with two resident English Electric Canberra squadrons (45 Squadron with B15 bombers and 81 Squadron with PR7 photo reconnaissance aircraft) and two resident Gloster Javelin all-weather fighter squadrons (60 Squadron and 64 Squadron). At the height of Confrontation, Tengah temporarily accommodated the Canberras of 14 Squadron Royal New Zealand Air Force (RNZAF), a disembarked Fleet Air Arm de Havilland Sea Vixen squadron (for a short period whilst their carrier was undergoing repairs in Singapore), a rotating detachment of Avro Vulcan or Handley Page Victor bombers from the UK or Cyprus and occasional detachments of Royal Australian Air Force (RAAF) Sabre aircraft from their main base at Butterworth near Penang.

Into this busy, exciting, vibrant, colourful, noisy, hot and steaming tropical milieu, a young RAF flying officer arrived sleep-starved at about eight thirty a.m. one morning in the middle of October 1964 after a twenty-seven-hour journey from the UK in a RAF Bristol Britannia troop transport via Istanbul and Bombay. It was six weeks after my twentieth birthday. I was to join my first operational unit, 20 Squadron, having graduated as a teenage Hunter pilot following two and a half years of RAF pilot training, culminating with three wonderful months at the Hunter Operational Conversion Unit at RAF Chivenor near Barnstaple, learning fighter tactics and ground attack techniques as well as getting used to the fabulous Hawker Hunter in the idyllic summer of that long-ago year.

During the last few days before I left the UK, there had been front page stories in the newspapers reporting the actions of 20 Squadron's Hunters against Indonesian guerrillas who had landed in Johore and were being fought on the ground by British troops. I was ready (or so I thought) and certainly eager, to join in the action and adventure with absolutely no thought whatsoever for the dangers. Of course, such thoughts were normal in a young, highly trained fighter pilot, imbued with a sense of invincibility and immortality (perhaps better described as over-confidence in view of his inexperience as an aviator and, indeed, inexperience of life!). However, the reality of the immediate future for me was to be somewhat different. I was very soon to hear that any more action, when and if it came, was to be the province only of the experienced operational pilots on the squadron. Meanwhile, I was to become firmly absorbed for the time being into the ranks of the 'JPs', the 'Junior Pilots', who had yet to complete their in-theatre operational training on the FGA9 before being allowed out against the common foe. I recall, in my youthful naivety, being a little hurt to learn that Her Majesty was not going to make almost immediate use of my newly learned skills, nor even my great daring, by pitching me into battle against any invading air or ground forces at the very first opportunity.

My first taste of 'action' was nevertheless soon to come, but in a manner way beyond anything that I could have imagined, in an environment that was totally unfamiliar and for which I was very ill-prepared and in which I became, on one occasion at least, quite frightened. However, I think I ought first to provide a little taste of what airborne thrills lay in store as the initial weeks and months of training up to operational status unfolded.

The Hunter was of course an absolute delight to fly. I had totally revelled in the training at Chivenor. My very limited ambitions at that time simply did not extend beyond that of being a Hunter pilot, preferably for eternity. I was completely absorbed in my exciting role. The combination of spending my working days flying a fast and agile jet, pointing it frequently at the ground at four hundred knots or more, firing off three inch rockets at targets on the air-to-ground ranges at Asahan, near Malacca, or Song Song Island north of Butterworth, and firing one, two or, very rarely, all four of the 30mm Aden cannons (directly underneath the seat in my high-speed, 6G 'office'), sometimes at ground targets and on other occasions at the hessian 'flag' towed behind a

Meteor 'tug' aircraft, in all cases at very close ranges and, particularly in ground attack strafing, requiring a very quick and sustained application of the full 6G, and occasionally a tad more, to avoid the ricochets, let alone the ground, was just endlessly thrilling and hugely satisfying!

Incidentally, in training on the squadron, we only rarely got to fire the four Adens together for the reasons that it was both expensive and unnecessary other than to prove the system occasionally and to provide each pilot with at least one experience of the multiple effects of firing a full pack. Those effects included tremendous noise and such vibration that circuit breakers popped out all over the cockpit, often in the rear area that was really hard to reach if you were tall or bulky like me. There was also the rapid, eyeball-popping, Newtonian deceleration (in reaction to eighty, nine-ounce projectiles being expelled forward every second at a muzzle velocity of one thousand eight hundred and seven miles per hour), which was matched only in my very much later experiences in 'viffing' with the Harrier. Decelerations in both scenarios were described as like hitting a brick wall in mid-air. When firing four Adens the Hunter lost forty to fifty knots airspeed in what seemed like an instant. I soon imagined that anything more than a two-second burst would have caused the sturdy aeroplane to pop all its rivets — but it didn't when I tried it one day with the full six seconds.

As well as weapons practice, the squadron's routine of training from Tengah naturally included many low-level navigation and visual reconnaissance exercises at two hundred and fifty feet over the jungles of the southern Malayan mainland, with mock attacks on a wide variety of ground 'targets', often bridges, that were always filmed for later analysis on the ground to assess their likely chance of success. Such simulated attack exercises were conducted normally in pairs or fours of aircraft and, in order to provide extended range, often included a high level outbound and return cruise at around thirty-five thousand feet, skirting the Cunims (cumulonimbus clouds) which normally built up to much higher altitudes, by mid-afternoon. Very occasionally, we had the opportunity to make simulated attacks against warships of the Royal Navy. These allowed us the opportunity to make exciting low-level passes across the ships, not always using the most tactical of parameters.

I have some nice pictures of one of Her Majesty's aircraft carriers in the South China Sea, filmed through my gunsight.

In addition to ground attack, the day-fighter role provided much scope for exciting and interesting training too. This began with basic fighter to fighter combat techniques involving just two aircraft, matched one against the other, then progressed up to 2 v 2 or 2 v 4 exercises. In air combat training, we had the chance to practise both basic and advanced offensive and defensive techniques and to improve our abilities to build the essential, mental, three-dimensional picture which enabled us to spot the opportunities early enough to get into a position to 'kill' the other aircraft. Air combat training was usually flown high up above the jungle or the sea and involved much rapid rolling and pitching at high G-force in very tight vertical and horizontal manoeuvres with many rapid reversals, heads swivelling constantly to maintain visual contact with, or search for, the prey. Our G-suits were almost permanently inflated, squeezing the trunk and legs to prevent blood pooling in the lower limbs and body, whilst we enhanced our G threshold (the point at which visual 'grey-out' would occur) by crouching, tensing our stomach and neck muscles as hard as we could, grunting and sweating like mad and frequently brushing rivers of sweat out of our eyes. We had always started off very hot and sweaty anyway on the ground before take-off in the tropical heat and high humidity and the Hunter's cooling system was often not adequate enough to cool us down from the metal cockpit's oven-like ground temperature before the gymnastics began. We returned to Earth frequently dehydrated within, yet soaking wet on the outside, in our thin, green, light-weight, RAAF flying suits that rotted quickly as a result and had to be changed regularly for new ones. Our Australian, fabric, jungle boots, in which we also flew, lasted a bit longer.

One additional reason for sweating so much was that we always flew with a 'treescape' device that was packed into a flat, fabric bag and hung from two buttons on the front upper chest of our thin flying suits, immediately under the 'Mae West' life jackets, where it was protected from our sweaty bodies by its inner, thick layer of polythene. It was a hot, bulky and disliked encumbrance, though potentially of great value. The treescape comprised a hook, two hundred feet of thin nylon rope and a small hand-operated braking device. The philosophy was that any ejection in our theatre of operations was likely to end up with a parachute landing into the tall jungle trees with the most likely outcome of being suspended in the jungle canopy, far above the ground. The treescape was our means to descend gracefully onto the jungle floor, after clipping it onto a branch and separating from our parachute harness. We practised using it from time to time though I never heard of anyone using it for real.

When in air combat as a pair against another pair or four aircraft, it was the main role of a JP to fly as a 'wingman', in loose, swept formation at about two hundred and fifty to three hundred yards from the pair's leader and act as the main rearward eyes of the section. One had to pay prime attention to sticking in the correct distance and angle from the leader as he manoeuvred hard whilst constantly twisting and turning one's neck to the rear to confirm our tails were clear of any threat. It was of course equally important to keep tabs on all the other, 'friendly' aircraft involved. Mid-air collisions could easily occur in air combat training; they did happen in the RAF and were usually fatal.

Fighter v fighter air combat training was one thing, but we also had to train for the possibility of interception and attacks against the Indonesian Tupolev Badger jet bomber aircraft that were a very real threat to Malaysian territory and that had already flown menacingly over Kuching in Sarawak in a show of force. Practice interceptions were carried out using the Ground Controlled Interception (GCI) and air defence radar at Bukit Gombak on a hilltop on the island of Singapore. The GCI controller was responsible for vectoring us into a position behind the 'enemy' aircraft, usually another Hunter, from which a 'guns kill' could be made. Unlike our Javelin colleagues, whose aircraft were equipped with air-to-air missiles, we had only our Aden cannons and so we had to get within about six hundred yards to ensure success. It was a precise process of skilled teamwork for pilot and controller, especially as the initial approach was normally from an offset, head-on position. The timing and execution of the one hundred and fifty to one hundred and eighty degrees turn into the target aircraft's rear sector required great precision by both parties.

However, the Badger had a radar-controlled tail gun so it was not a good idea just to arrive leisurely behind it at the same height and only six hundred yards away. Therefore, a special technique known as a 'snap-up' attack was developed and practised by Hunter pilots to enable us to spend the very minimum amount of time behind the target, having arrived in a shooting position more rapidly and unexpectedly. The technique called for us to be vectored just into the target's line astern, some two to three thousand feet below it, with an overtake speed of about 0.05M. We would wait until we were almost directly below the target, head craned back to see him vertically above, and then ease our aircraft into a climb, changing to a bunt at a suitable point in order to rake the target aircraft with cannon shells as it passed through the gunsight, with the expectation of making the kill on it ideally before the tail gun could be operated when we arrived suddenly behind it. However, all of this exciting stuff still lay well ahead of me when, one afternoon, I was suddenly called to the squadron commander's office, not long after I had arrived.

Confrontation had suddenly become more threatening and it was expected by intelligence staff that the Indonesian Air Force were about to make air attacks on the airfields and other facilities on the island of Singapore. It was known that there were low-level 'blind spots' in the air defence radar coverage from Bukit Gombak towards the Indonesian border just a few miles to the south, south-west and south-east, from which directions enemy aircraft could use the cover of the small, outlying, islands to make surprise attacks on Singapore itself. In an attempt to counter the risk of low-level surprise attack by Indonesian aircraft, a number of visual observation posts (OPs) were to be set up on a couple of the small islands to the south of Singapore, in the narrow strait separating it from Indonesian territory, and those at the south-eastern and south-western tips of the Malay Peninsula. Each OP was to be manned by one RAF aircrew officer, including me, another JP from 20 Squadron plus a JP and navigator from 45 Squadron. Each one of us was supported by five airmen. Our duty was to maintain a twenty-four-hour visual watch and report immediately by radio to Bukit Gombak in the event of any suspected enemy activity so that air raid precautions could be initiated in Singapore. I was to be allocated a team of five Far East Air Force bandsmen from Changi and dispatched to the south within a few hours. It was expected that we would be in our positions for only a few days.

I barely had time to get back to my room in the officers' mess, rapidly throw some kit together and get back to the squadron buildings to be issued with a Sterling sub-machine gun and a small supply of ammunition before the Belvedere helicopter arrived, with my five apprehensive bandsmen already on board (sans instruments, I might add), to ferry us out to the OP in a clearing on the lone hilltop of our own little tropical island barely a mile south of Singapore. We were dropped off along with a large tent, a large radio and several days' food, water and other supplies and left to get on with it. It was about thirty minutes before nightfall and we needed to get the huge tent up before it went very dark suddenly, as it always does in the tropics. By great good fortune, one of my gallant little 'band' had once before erected such a tent so I immediately delegated that to him and another bandsman while I set about finding out what the others could do (apart from making music) and putting together a watch roster and so on. We were on that island for two weeks, supplied regularly by Belvedere. We neither saw nor heard any aircraft but we did have two rather alarming experiences.

The first was in the middle of one early night when we heard, but didn't see, an unlit motor launch approaching the coast of our little island. Several frantic radio calls to Bukit Gombak produced only the information that there were no known friendly naval units in the area. For a very tense hour or so we heard the launch occasionally and we became convinced that the Indonesians could be landing troops to knock out our OP. So, we sat for the rest of the pitch black, warm, tropical night, with our small arms at the ready to defend ourselves. Thankfully, daylight came without the expected attack materialising. Much later in the day we were finally told that our 'intruder' had been identified as a Singaporean custom's launch on anti-smuggling patrol.

The second, rather more scary occasion, was again in the middle of the night and when I was off-watch. I was awakened by a very nervous and frantic bandsman who told me in a faltering whisper that he had heard rustling movements in the undergrowth just into the scrub on the edge of our clearing. This time I really felt that the invasion had come. I grabbed my Stirling and shot out of my camp bed like a scalded cat, whilst trying to be as quiet as I could while the other slumbering bandsmen came to life. After listening to what indeed seemed like furtive rustling for a short while, I decided to attempt to flush out the enemy by firing a burst from my Sterling in the direction of the noises. I figured that, if they'd got that close, we were probably in mortal danger anyway and I might as well take the initiative, start the fight and maybe take a few opponents with me to my untimely early end. Nothing was heard after my first burst, but I gave another one for good measure. This time we all endured a much longer period of very tense alertness until daybreak, when our investigations revealed no sign whatever of any enemy. However, a couple of days later we did find that we were sharing the island with some huge monitor lizards. So, apologies to all animal lovers but I guess I must have given the lizards a severe fright or two although I clearly didn't hit any.

Meanwhile back at Tengah, there had been frantic digging of air raid shelters and other measures taken in anticipation of the coming air attacks. Yet they never did come, so perhaps the valiant presence of my bandsmen and me had tipped the balance and made the Indonesians think twice about chancing their luck against Singapore. However, guerrillas were again landed in November and December of 1964 in Johore near Kota Tinggi and south of Pontian. My operational colleagues were in action against the forces near Pontian on 23 December and again on Boxing Day. In February, March and April, the squadron flew armed escorts for Belvedere helicopters carrying troops into the Kota Tinggi area to operate against the guerrillas. A further landing of twenty-four Indonesian soldiers occurred at the end of May, this time on the east coast of Johore, only seven miles from Changi. Once again, four 20 Squadron Hunters were in action on 31 May when, with rockets and cannon and under the direction of a Forward Air Controller (FAC), they dislodged the enemy troops allowing ground forces to complete the defeat of the intruders over the following days. The JPs of course did not get a look-

41

in on any of this action, although the time was not long off before I'd be on my way to Borneo and closer to the action over there.

Eventually, following my two-week stint in charge of the OP on the little island south of Singapore, and attendance on the Far East Air Force Jungle Survival and Parachute School course at Mersing, I resumed my operational training with 20 Squadron, concluding with two weeks based at the Australian base at Butterworth for air to ground firing on the Song Song island range just to the north of Penang. I was duly declared fully fit for the fray and was dispatched to Kuching in Sarawak to join in the regular border patrols flown by detachments of Hunters from 20 Squadron and Javelins from 60 Squadron and 64 Squadron.

In early 1965, several 20 Squadron Hunters had been detached to Kuching in Sarawak to take over the fighter escort duties (for supply-dropping transport aircraft) from the Javelin squadrons who were often short of serviceable aircraft. The Javelins suffered from structural airframe cracking and from problems with their twin, Armstrong Siddeley Sapphire engines — or Armstrong Siddeley 'time-bombs' as we young wags on 20 Squadron referred to their power plants. Several Javelins were lost in crashes during my two and a half years in Singapore and Borneo. On one particularly spectacular occasion, a Javelin had been scrambled to intercept an unknown aircraft at a few thousand feet above the jungle, just north of the border and between Labuan and Tawau in Eastern Sabah. It turned out that the suspect aircraft was a delayed Malaysian Airways Fokker Friendship aircraft on a scheduled flight from Tawau to Labuan. The passengers and crew in the Friendship had a ringside view of the Javelin, which had completed its interception and identification of the suspect aircraft and had flown past at a safe distance (thankfully), before starting a sharp turn away to signal clearly to the civil crew that they could continue, as was normal practice. However, on that particular day, as the pilot increased thrust, banked away and applied 'G' in the turn, one of his engines blew up and the Javelin continued to roll, upside down, from which position both pilot and navigator ejected (safely). The Javelin continued rolling down into the jungle — no doubt quite a surprise for all the occupants of both aircraft.

I flew for my first time to Borneo as a passenger in a Bristol Freighter (or Bristol 'Frightener' as it was jocularly known) of 41 Squadron, RNZAF. I was a little puzzled before engine start when the Kiwi loadmaster distributed wads of cotton wool to the passengers who promptly began stuffing it firmly into their ears. I thought this might be some corny joke or even some wry antipodean custom. However, the reason soon became clear as the twin engines burst into life with an almighty clattering noise. It took about two and a half hours to fly the four hundred and eight nautical miles from Changi to Kuching. The flight sensation was rather like sitting in a giant metal dustbin whilst a dozen amateur steel band players beat the hell out of it from the outside with metal clubs. The noise for that length of time was totally shattering, even with the cotton wool.

At Kuching, all the working and domestic accommodation was in thatched wooden huts, chit-chats scurrying about the walls, various other creepy crawlies on the floors and ceilings, and full of mosquitos at night. We slept under mosquito nets and burned anti-mosquito coils all night. Armadillos roamed around outside occasionally — shy, armoured hedgehogs from what I saw of them. It rained very often from the huge cumulonimbus clouds that built up over the inland airfield of Kuching by the afternoon.

We flew our low-level patrols as two or three aircraft together and took part in exercises with the Army from their border encampments. At the time of my early detachments to Kuching, and later Labuan, the available aerial maps for Borneo were very poor indeed. Huge areas consisted of little more than a white sheet on which only rivers were marked. There were no terrain contours nor even spot heights shown, although the terrain was often up to five thousand feet above sea level in Sarawak and much higher further north in Sabah. In 1966 better maps became available but, until then, we virtually made our own as we went along. Pilots would come back from low-level flights into the hinterland or along the border, having spotted some previously un-noted significant terrain feature, and plot it on the master map on the crew room wall. We others would then transfer the data to our own personal maps. I still have these nostalgic mementos.

Although the border areas were generally better marked on the maps, the border itself often did not conveniently follow the terrain. So, accurate navigation along the border was very difficult, yet it was essential because, particularly in western Sarawak, it seemed the Indonesians had sited their air defence guns very cleverly just on their side of the bits of border opposite where the terrain was most indistinct. So, we had to learn the trickiest bits by repetitive familiarity and initially only from a safe distance. We lost no fighters to ground fire but a RAF Whirlwind helicopter did get shot down in October 1965 on the border south of Kuching after getting too close to one of the Indonesian guns.

We flew low-level navigation exercises along the great muddy brown Rajang and Bateh rivers, the latter with huge jungle-clad mountains soaring to several thousand feet barely a mile to either side of us and ending where the Indonesian border turned from parallel to our track to then cut directly across it in a spectacular, green, mountain-fringed dead end. Clear weather at the mountain ridges was rare, so we usually needed a steep, full-power climb out at the end of the cul-de-sac into cloud to clear the ridge-tops. Wingmen like me had to tuck quickly into close formation before the leader entered the cloud and then be ready to fly through heavy rain, and often hail, bucking about like a wild horse in the turbulence as we fought to stay in close formation in marginal visibility and turned around to return to Kuching, two hundred and fifty nautical miles to the west. We often had to climb to forty-eight thousand feet or more to get on top of the rain clouds. Our oxygen system limited us in theory to forty-eight thousand feet but I saw well over fifty-two thousand feet more than once.

We sometimes flew at low level across a remote plateau, about fifteen miles long by eight miles wide, deep in the interior about one hundred and twenty nautical miles south of Brunei. The plateau rose steeply out of the jungle to over three thousand feet, soaring nearly vertically for the most part like the legendary plateau of 'The Lost World'. On the northern, steepest side were several very high waterfalls, partially blocked in some places by huge, fallen tree trunks. On top of the plateau was a large, brown, laterite clearing with a dozen or more huts, into which scores of brown, near-naked, jungle dwellers scurried quickly whenever we flew across. Later maps named it as Usun Apau. To us at the time it was simply 'The Plateau', a place of awe and mystery almost as ancient as the world itself. And its people, so cut off from the world and whom we regrettably must have frightened out of their wits whenever we turned up, were a total enigma about whom we could only speculate.

My first session in Borneo lasted just two weeks before I returned to Tengah to re-join the ongoing routine training over Malaya. In August 1965, the squadron celebrated its fiftieth anniversary and, apart from the social celebrations on the ground, the occasion was marked by a sixteen-aircraft flypast at RAF Tengah in which I flew as number six. In fact, there were three flypasts. The first was not a huge success really. We attempted to put two waves of eight aircraft each, in two close echelons, separated longitudinally by about three hundred yards and vertically by one hundred feet or so, across the airfield at Tengah. Although we were all very well-practised at flying accurately in echelons of two to four aircraft, eight aircraft in echelon was not at all an easy matter and the half hour or so's practice that we made over the Straits of Malacca before the actual run was clearly insufficient. So, it was a slightly wobbly pair of echelons that made its first and only appearance across the field at about one thousand feet for the waiting admirers. We did much better with the diamond sixteen that we next flew across the airfield. The final 'flypast' was probably the most impressive. We re-formed and flew across at high speed and low level in a 'finger 4' of 'finger 4s', making lots and lots of noise. And we all have a superb photograph from the same day of all eighteen of the squadron's Hunters, with our twenty pilots and about sixty ground staff, all lined up on the ground in beautiful display standard. The party that evening was jolly good too.

On 1 September 1965, two Indonesian Air Force B-25 Mitchells strafed a small Malaysian village close to the border in Sabah and about one hundred miles south of the RAF airfield on Labuan island. As luck would have it, four 20 Squadron Hunters had been sent to Labuan two days earlier to take part in an exercise and so these aircraft were immediately tasked to patrol the border area to deter or shoot down any further airborne intruders.

A week later I happened to celebrate my twenty-first birthday with a training parachute jump from about a thousand feet out of an Argosy into the South China Sea off Changi (the 'Changi Splash'). I remember it vividly, especially the high-speed jet of water up both nostrils as I entered the water — they didn't warn me about that. My sinuses ached for hours afterwards.

Then, on 17 September, a further three Hunter FGA9s, with the second aircraft flown by me, were sent to Labuan to enable the air commander to step up the patrol rate. A further six Hunters flew out to Labuan from Tengah the following day. At the height of the three weeks attempt to deter or shoot down intruding Indonesian aircraft, we flew a continuous daylight patrol along a very large stretch of the jungle border in the north. In order to allow us the maximum time on patrol, each of our aircraft was fitted with two outboard one hundred-gallon drop tanks as well as the two standard, inboard, two hundred and thirty-gallon tanks. Flying at best range speed to and from the patrol areas, and then at endurance speed on patrol along the border, we were able to stay airborne for just over two hours at low level. The snag was that, with the additional fuel weight and full ammunition for the Aden cannons, the runway at Labuan was only just long enough for take-off. We were always very close to the end of the runway as we lifted off the ground.

My first patrol, the day after arriving at Labuan, involved a take-off soon after dawn. It was typical of the many flights that followed on these 'special patrols'. We headed off to the SSE from Labuan, on much the same heading as the runway, to coast in at low level within four minutes after take-off over the mangrove swamps of mainland Borneo and then on to our patrol area a further six minutes and thirty-five miles away. As we flew south over the jungle in the early light of the day and in the gathering heat, steaming mists rose up all around us out of the jungle canopy like huge columns of smoke from many fires. It was a stunning sight in the early morning. The farther we flew, the higher the jungle-covered hills around us also rose, gradually from three thousand feet to four thousand, five thousand, six thousand and nearly eight thousand feet. As we flew on, we climbed steadily with the rising, densely tree-covered terrain. This was home (as I knew from my nights in the Malayan jungle on the survival course) to a cacophony of noisily calling monkeys, birds and other exotic wildlife but including here the Borneo orangutans and the former (and not so former) headhunter tribes. Once on patrol, the terrain largely flattened out and it was only a random glance at the altimeter that revealed that we were actually flying at around five thousand five hundred feet above sea level whilst visually maintaining the usual few hundred feet above the canopy of that immense natural arboretum that shielded the huge zoo. Though unable to hear or see the wildlife from within our aluminium flying machines (apart from very occasional large birds that we usually managed to avoid), I was nevertheless always conscious that it was there. We kept a listening watch instead on the army radio frequency from which we heard occasional, and usually outdated, calls relating to further suspected Indonesian incursions.

In fact, despite these intensive and continuous low-level daylight patrols, often shared with our Javelin colleagues, we never did catch an enemy aircraft. Had we done so, we would have been greatly disadvantaged by the fact that, for political reasons, we were supposed to ensure that any enemy aircraft we might shoot down had to fall on our side of the border so that we should not be accused of incursions into Indonesian airspace. Occasionally, we thought we were on to something and the leader would call "Buster!", whereupon both pilots would select full thrust from the Avon engines, accelerating the aircraft rapidly from the patrol speed of around two hundred and forty knots to whatever we could get, usually around five hundred to five hundred and fifty knots, as we hared off to the reported area, invariably to find it empty of any threat. The period of 'special patrols' continued for about three weeks and, in that period alone, I logged some forty-three hours flying, all at low level above the wide green jungles of Borneo, apart from one three and a half-hour round trip over the South China Sea to Tengah and back to change an aircraft. We normally flew twenty to twenty-five hours a month, so I'd rather hogged it.

I also learned, when off duty, to water-ski over the coastal waters that, as I had seen from the air, were home to giant rays and, as I saw from the beach, a wide variety of poisonous sea snakes that provided me with a great incentive to learn the art of waterskiing quickly and not to fall off.

So the routine continued well on into 1966, normal squadron training from Tengah interspersed with operational detachments to Kuching for patrols over Borneo. In November I flew as a passenger in a RAF Argosy, via Saigon's Tan Son Nhut airfield and then on over battle-scarred Vietnam up to RAF Kai Tak in Hong Kong for a two weeks detachment. Other pilots from 20 Squadron flew four of our aircraft up to Kai Tak via Labuan and the USAF base at Clark Field in the Philippines, at that time an incredibly busy airfield involved (amongst numerous other tasks) in mounting B52 bombing sorties over North Vietnam and the Ho Chi Minh Trail. I flew as number four in the returning formation on the reverse route. When we taxied for take-off from Clark, I had never before seen so many aircraft manoeuvring around on the ground at once. Our formation of four was asked to pull over into a short 'layby' to allow priority traffic to overtake. As last man, I was singled out by the rude, heavily drawling B52 pilot in a hurry behind me when he asked ATC ground control to "tell the Australian fighter ahead to move his ass clear of the taxiway!" I thought briefly about complaining that I was actually British and in an aircraft of the same nationality, but then thought I'd better not. He had rather more pressing matters on his mind and would, no doubt, have given me an earful. The second detachment to Kai Tak was in January of 1967, when five of us flew up to collect the five Hunters of 28 Squadron, which disbanded in that month, and fly them down to join 20 Squadron. On a later occasion I went to Hong Kong with the Royal Navy in HMS Fearless as an air liaison officer during a major air/sea exercise.

In March of 1967, as operational pressures eased and the end of my tour was looming, I took the opportunity to hitch a lift, along with a good pilot friend from my squadron, in a RNZAF Hercules on its way home from Vietnam down to New Zealand for a three-week holiday. We staged via an overnight stop at the RAAF base at Darwin where we met up with the first RAAF Mirage squadron, including a mutual friend from one of the Sabre squadrons that we had got to know so well at Butterworth. Reg Meisner couldn't stop telling us about the wonders of the new Mirage, a very high-performance, single-engine aircraft. I was interested to know whether it was possible to fly a forced landing pattern following engine failure in such a swift beast as this Mirage. I shall never forget the reply, quick as a flash and in the broadest Aussie accent, that "yer had ter gedd a bluddy hoigh key posishun of nighn thaasand feed owver the bluddy airfield and then yer read the bluddy forced-lending instrugshuns on the insoide of the bluddy fice-bloind!")* We laughed for months if not years at this and other examples of Reg's dry wit. In New Zealand, we were put up amongst many 14 Squadron friends at the RNZAF officers' mess at Ohakea where we each managed to get a flight in a Venom. We moved on for a short while by Dakota to Wigram near Christchurch, where another ex-14 Squadron friend was by then flying as an instructor and where each of us managed to get a flight in a Harvard. Finally, we flew back to Singapore from Auckland in a VIP RAF Britannia that had turned up to drop off the chief of air staff of the time, another Kiwi. Quite a busman's holiday but we did take in a great deal of the countryside on the ground as well.

I had not fired a single shot in anger throughout Confrontation (except with my Sterling at the wildlife as already mentioned) but neither had most of my colleagues, since there were very few instances of our Hunters being in action against ground targets and none at all against air targets. However, I do think I can claim the 'distinction' of flying the last operational Hunter flight over Borneo. I was 'specially selected' for a 'secret mission' in July, immediately before we finally withdrew our Hunters from Borneo when Confrontation approached its end in the August of 1966. The air minister at that time was Lord Edward Shackleton, son of the great explorer Ernest Shackleton, and he'd apparently had a long-running dispute over many years with a friend as to whether the main accepted peak of Mount Kinabalu (thirteen thousand four hundred and fifty-five feet, and ninety nautical miles north-east of Labuan), which the noble Lord had climbed, or a nearby peak on the same mountain that the friend had climbed, was actually the higher. I was dispatched in an FGA9 from Tengah to Kuching on 20 July, briefed by Lord Shackleton and the Kuching station commander in the latter's office, stayed overnight, flew a couple of very low-level passes the next day over each of the two peaks en route to Labuan — whilst checking my altimeter very carefully — refuelled and returned to Kuching to present the noble Lord with the happy news that he was right — the difference was about seventy feet. After another night-stop, I returned to Tengah along with the two other last Hunters to leave Kuching. The 'special mission' had taken two nights, four sectors and exactly five hours flying. I doubt whether this exploit ever got recorded in the official annals of the time, but it did in my log book.

In May 1967, shortly after a most enjoyable five-day air exercise when I was detached with the squadron to a tented camp at the airfield of Gong Kedah in the north-east of Malaya by the beautiful tropical beaches up there, I returned to the UK to take up my next job as an instructor at the Hunter OCU at Chivenor. Thus ended my first operational tour, flying Hunters over the jungles of the Far East at a time when Britain's armed forces were very much larger and flying was much less regulated, much simpler and terrific fun. The experience of that first tour in Hunters over the jungle was a fantastic beginning. It became the launching pad from which I then sought the more unusual and more interesting jobs, though not always getting those that I'd planned.

* Lest anyone didn't get it: "fice-bloind" = face-blind. When ejecting from most ejection seats of that time, it was normal practice to initiate ejection by pulling down the handle above the pilot's head, which also brought down a blind to protect his face from damage by high-speed slipstream. Later, with improved helmets and visors, it became standard practice to use the seat-pan handle as the first choice because it was quicker to reach and operate and so less time was lost in initiating the ejection.

Author at RAF Tengah

Hunter FGA9 Armament

20 Sqn 50th Anniversary Line-up

Hunter FGA9 off South Malaya coast

4
ARABIAN FLIGHTS — PRELUDE

We were on the fourth leg of an eight-sector, four-day, delivery flight from the British Aerospace factory at Woodford, near Manchester, to Kaohsiung on Taiwan. We'd reached the top of our climb after take-off from Dubai in our BAe 146 Series 300 and would soon be coasting out overhead Muscat, the capital of the ancient Sultanate of Oman, to set course across the Arabian Sea to the next refuelling stop at Bombay. I strained forward from the left-hand seat to look over the aircraft's nose, trying to see if I could recognise anything on the ground below and ahead of us. It had been nearly twenty-five years since I had left that exotic and fascinating desert country. The conditions in this mid-January of 1995 gave us fairly clear visibility from the four-engine jet but all I could see at first was a jumble of jagged, buff-coloured peaks, snaking wadis and a looming, widespread and very unfamiliar metropolis of white and dun-coloured buildings. Nevertheless, the memories came flooding back from over twenty-five years previously:

"A kaleidoscope of scenes: ancient forts; proud and colourful tribesmen armed with daggers and ancient rifles; sweltering humidity along the coast in summer and dry but searing temperatures inland; driving for miles in open-topped Land Rovers across the dusty desert plains; primitive conditions everywhere. Landing on hastily improvised airstrips to lift out casualties; straining for height in the tall mountains of the north to reach a high airstrip; free-dropping supplies from thirty-five feet above the ground in a Beaver; hearing the news of an army colleague murdered by his own men; helping to rescue a downed fellow pilot and then destroying his abandoned Piston Provost aircraft. Changing over to the new Strikemaster jets and going into action in them for the first time; coming under enemy fire on the ground and in the air; frequent uncertainty, sometimes fear ... often great danger; exceptionally

challenging flying; always great comradeship — with Arab and expatriate alike."

Gradually, as we got closer to Muscat, and just before the area disappeared for good below the nose of our aircraft, I thought I could just make out the outline of the old Bait al Falaj runway, with its distinctive kink at the south-western end. The runway had long since been absorbed into the new metropolis, yet its outline could just be recognised, pointing in its familiar fashion towards the wadi along which...

"I had several times clawed agonisingly slowly for height after take-off in a heavily laden Sultan of Oman's Air Force (SOAF) Dakota, engines straining and protesting in the searing summer heat, before setting course for Salalah in the Southern Oman province and war zone of Dhofar, over three hours away. In the Piston Provosts or the Beavers, climb performance along the wadi had not been much of a problem. However, when we first got the Strikemasters, we had quite a different problem in trying to persuade the garrison commander at Bait al Falaj to cease the routine dumping of army food-waste on the 'municipal' rubbish tip just off the end of the runway. That hadn't been much of a threat to the slow, piston-engined aircraft but the faster, single-engined jets would not have fared at all well if they had ingested one or more of the scavenging ravens, which circled the tip in ever-increasing numbers as the news of the good pickings had spread widely amongst the South Arabian avian community."

My reminiscing was interrupted by the pilot in the right-hand seat, my colleague — Chief Test Pilot Al McDicken — flying as co-pilot for the first two sectors of the day. "Penny for your thoughts," he ventured in his soft Scots brogue.

"Well," I began, "it would take a long time just to cover even a fraction of what's coming back to me."

"Have you spent much time in Oman then?" he enquired.

"Yes," I replied. "I was there for nearly two and a half years at the end of the 1960s as a loan service pilot in the Sultan of Oman's Air Force (SOAF) during the Dhofar War."

"Really!" he said. "That must have been exciting."

"It certainly was," I replied and then, without thinking, added: "I reckon I used up several of my nine lives there, including getting shot down twice." Al looked at me in some shock, tinged, I suspect, with more than a little disbelief. "Well," I faltered, "shot down or shot up — I'm not quite sure how best to describe it. But I certainly got hit quite significantly by enemy ground fire on two occasions and was obliged to land fairly promptly! In each case I was lucky enough to be able to land in good order back at Salalah before either running out of fuel or losing control."

"Tell me about it." he said.

So I did, in the quiet moments during the rest of our delivery flight to Taiwan plus the subsequent stopovers there and in Hong Kong, as well as during some of the return flight as passengers to the UK. I gave just the barest outline of the story, the most incredible experience of my life before or since. Some of it is simply hard even for me to believe these fifty years on — it shaped my attitudes forever in so many different ways...

In 1967, at the end of two and a half years of flying Hunter FGA9 aircraft in the Far East with No 20 Squadron, the RAF had sent me back to the UK to be a simulator and tactics instructor at the Hunter Operational Conversion Unit at Chivenor, near Barnstaple in North Devon. I was told that this was to be a short posting before a likely move to a conversion course on the F4 Phantom which would soon be entering RAF service. After the excitement of operational flying and the warmth of the Far East, a dank winter in North Devon was a huge anti-climax. I also found myself as one of only a handful of bachelors in the officers' mess. The social life for a young bachelor in North Devon was pretty boring in comparison with the hustle and bustle of partying in Singapore, apart from my weekends in the 'big smoke' of London, a long drive each way in those days. I was getting somewhat disillusioned with life in the UK and a posting to Phantoms was not going to get me out of a European winter either. So, when the opportunity arose, I quickly volunteered to join SOAF as a loan service pilot. I wouldn't be doing much partying there either but at least I'd have the sun and some exciting operational flying in a demanding environment, far away from depressing Britain in its cold, grey winter.

Truthfully, there was a bit more to it than that. The negatives had begun to rub off onto my primary duties as a simulator instructor and I had become a bit rebellious towards my superiors. After several mild altercations, my flight commander despatched me one day for an interview with the wing commander. I was ushered into his office and obliged to stand formally at attention in front of his desk. He was a short man and remained sitting whilst my six foot three and a half inches towered above him a few feet away. The gist of his conversation was this:

"I am far too busy to be wasting my time with some stroppy little flying officer like you!" was one of his early comments in response to my excuses for my poor enthusiasm for my duties. It was a huge challenge for me to maintain a straight face at the 'little', but I just about managed to do so.

"However," he continued, "I do understand your frustrations about being away from operational flying. We have an opening coming up for a loan service pilot in SOAF. I think that might be the best option for you — and for me — but I can't recommend that you should go out there as a representative for the RAF until you can first prove to me that you can knuckle down properly to this job."

He had just come up with the perfect option for me. It was a deal. I was suddenly a good boy and soon received a posting notice to SOAF. After barely six months at Chivenor, I just had time to squeeze in a totally irrelevant *winter* survival course in Bavaria — I wanted to learn to ski for my winter breaks from Oman! — before scuttling down to the Army School of Aviation at Middle Wallop in Hampshire to learn to fly the Beaver. This was to be just one of the four aircraft types that I would come to fly for the Air Force of Sultan Said bin Taimur, the then ruler of the Sultanate of Muscat and Oman.

My course of flying with the army began in the most informal way. I found myself early one Friday evening, at the Army Air Corps (AAC) airfield at Middle Wallop in Hampshire, standing on the doorstep of Major Alan Calder, to whom I was due to report the following Monday morning. I thought I'd extend the journey up from Devon to Middle Wallop to first spend a weekend with the then love of my life who had a flat not far from Russell Square in Holborn. It was fairly important both to a smooth weekend and to a good start with the army that I should establish exactly what time the major would like to see me on the Monday morning. I rang the doorbell twice before the front door of the army married quarters house opened to reveal an unassuming figure, clad only in a towel against the cold February evening and looking at me in a friendly way even though he'd just stepped out of his shower. I hadn't exactly made an appointment to call but the guard on the gate had phoned his wife to say I would be there in a few minutes.

"I'm Flying Officer Gamblin, sir," I announced. "I'm due to start a conversion course on the Beaver with you next week and I wondered what time you would want me here on Monday."

Totally unfazed at this unexpected intrusion, Major Calder replied after only a moment's hesitation, "Ah yes. Can you come to Germany with me on Tuesday? Have you got a current passport?" I was puzzled.

"Er, I think you might have the wrong chap, sir," I said. "I'm the Hunter pilot from Chivenor who's going out to SOAF next month. I have got my passport with me as it happens, but I thought I would be starting a course on Monday?"

"Yes, yes," he said, "but I need to go to Wildenrath next week. I'll see you at nine o'clock on Monday morning. Get yourself some Deutschmarks over the weekend and we'll set off on Tuesday for Germany. We'll do some of your course on the way there, or on the way back." I said my farewell, folded myself back into my red MGA hardtop (the 'London bus') and set course for Holborn and a weekend of joy.

On the Monday, after the briefest of ground school technical study, I flew a forty-five-minute familiarisation trip under the tutelage of the very affable Mr Peter Mackenzie, a retired service pilot then working as a civilian instructor for the AAC, who gave me a most pleasant introduction to the delightful little Beaver. On Tuesday we duly took off, with me as a passenger, for the two-and-a-half-hour flight across the Channel and on to a wintry Germany. We flew at nine thousand feet and around ninety-five knots. This seemed to me a very unfamiliar and unsuitable altitude and speed at which to fly. In recent years I had become accustomed to flying usually at two hundred and fifty feet above ground level (agl), mostly at four hundred and twenty knots and mostly over the Far Eastern jungle, where often we did not make full allowance for the one hundred and fifty feet trees when establishing our two hundred and fifty feet agl. Or, occasionally, it was a respectable Mach 0.85 or so at levels around thirty-five thousand feet on long-range transits. At nine thousand feet in a European winter, the Beaver was chugging slowly along in icing conditions and I soon became fascinated with the large and rapid build-up of ice on the wing strut just forward of the window of the adjacent passenger door. I could also see the flight instruments from my seat behind the two pilots. The ice build-up seemed to correlate with a slow but steady increase in engine power, accompanied by a very gradual reduction in airspeed. There was some occasional discussion and cursing from my two fellow aviators, Major Calder and Mr Mackenzie, and a few changes in altitude, until it appeared eventually that the icing remained within tolerable limits. After arrival at Wildenrath, it soon became clear that the main purpose of the five-hour return trip to the continent was to allow the two instructors, and me their guest, to top up on duty-free booze and fags, which we all did on that same day.

On Wednesday, it was my turn to fly upfront for the leg back to the customs airfield at Manston in Kent and then on to Wallop. Most of this trip was spent with Major Calder explaining to me the intricacies of the totally unfamiliar Decca navigation system. Fascinating to be sure but totally irrelevant too, since I think I recall correctly that the system was not fitted to the Sultan of Oman's aircraft. At last, on Wednesday afternoon back at Middle Wallop and again on Thursday morning, we got down to the business of pounding the circuit and for the first time I was able to learn and practise take-off and landing procedures. As we adjourned for a nice lunch after the Thursday session, Major Calder asked me: "Well, are you happy to take the aircraft off for a session on your own after lunch?" I pondered for a short while and thought that I hadn't had much of a look at such useful things as stalling and forced landings but I supposed I would manage — I'd got about twenty hours in Chipmunks and reckoned there were sufficient similarities between the two tail-wheel types. Just one important thing did occur to me though: "Yes, fine, sir," I said, "though I haven't yet had a go at starting and shutting down the engine!"

"Oh, that's no problem," said the major. "Just do it all carefully from the checklist a couple of times out on the parking area. Give me a shout on the radio if you should need any help, then when you're happy, whiz off for a couple of circuits." I did exactly that and solo'd in the Beaver that afternoon. I had only three more days' flying with the AAC but in that short time I flew over eleven hours of intensive instruction and practice in field landings and forced landings, the real meat of the course. This was wonderful fun. After several years of roaring around at very high speed and 6G in a Hunter, I now had a friendly little aircraft that I could plop down into the fields of Hampshire and stop to chat to the farmers. I did exactly that several times, in suitable meadows where such arrangements had been made. I thoroughly enjoyed my introduction to bush-flying techniques with the AAC. I learned the basic but vital skills of assessing unfamiliar, off-airfield landing areas. In the following years, those lessons matured into a very finely tuned sixth sense that served me very well for landing on and taking off from often hastily prepared, emergency, desert strips in support of the Sultan's army on operations against the communist-backed rebel forces in Dhofar, the southern province of the Sultanate of Muscat and Oman.

I arrived in Arabia in the early March of 1968. I was twenty-three years old and had been promoted to flight lieutenant just days before departing. The temperature and humidity were quite comfortable at first. I discovered unexpectedly that I could initially travel only as far as Bahrain, where I had to wait for several days until the British diplomatic staff at the Political Agency there had been told that a 'No Objection Certificate' had been signed personally by Sultan Said bin Taimur himself, as was the procedure at the time. The Agency was then able to give me a visa for a single journey (only) to Muscat. Oman was very much a closed country in those days and the Sultan, no doubt together with his British advisers, approved each and every individual before allowing him into the country. The first sixteen pages of my passport of the time are filled with entries recording each passage in and out of Oman and certain neighbouring countries. Most of them are in Arabic script and I have no clue as to their meaning except the half a dozen with the English translation: 'Must report to the Police Office within forty-eight hours of arrival'. After issue of my visa I hitched a lift in an RAF Argosy down to Sharjah where a SOAF Beaver, flown up from Bait al Falaj by Flying Officer Mike Webb, who was to become a very good friend and comrade-in-arms, came to fetch me. Mike had been instructed to show me as many as possible of the various coastal airstrips and their associated landmarks that I would need to recognise in the near future. We set off in the middle of the morning on the three-hour-five-minute-flight around the coast to my new home at Bait al Falaj.

Mike did his very best, initially from the seven thousand feet or so at which we were flying, to point out a number of landing strips along the way. My unpractised eyes found it almost impossible to distinguish the strips from the surrounding desert, so we dropped lower and lower until eventually, at about three thousand feet, I began to learn to recognise the subtle signs of difference. We landed in the mid-afternoon at Bait al Falaj ('camp on the falaj' — the falaj system was the old underground water distribution network constructed during the Persian occupations hundreds of years before and still very much in use). The airfield was set in a flat bowl surrounded by bare rocky hills. The runway was distinctly quirky, the like of which I had never seen before nor since. The first and last third was laid in concrete with the middle in graded and compacted fine gravel. However, there was a variation of several degrees in the orientation of the two concrete bits! Some said this was a mistake by the ground-based engineers who built it; others said it was deliberate to take account of clearances from adjacent terrain. Whatever the reason, it didn't present any problems to us desert fliers who, as I was yet to learn, had far more tricky take-off and landing places to deal with and, unlike what I had seen so far on the flight down from Sharjah, it certainly could not be mistaken for virgin desert!

Squadron Leader Alan Bridges, the lean and suntanned Commander, Sultan of Oman's Air Force, (CSOAF) came out to greet me as we clambered out of the Beaver in front of the SOAF HQ building. He was to be my boss for the next twenty-seven months and a good friend for many years after. I was joining a very special little group of serving RAF pilots and one admin officer on loan to SOAF, each nominally there for eighteen months and unaccompanied by their wives — though all but two of us were bachelors — except for CSOAF who was accompanied by his two young children and his lovely wife Lillian and who served for two and a half to three years. We totalled nine pilots and we had nine aircraft, four Beavers and five, armed Piston Provosts. We all shared a craving for adventure and for exciting and demanding flying, of which I found there was plenty to come. I was introduced to the pilot whom I was replacing, who was leaving in a few days and whose 'bait' (room, in this case) I would be taking over. Flight Lieutenant Jules Brett was a highly affable, somewhat eccentric officer. Like most of us airmen and soldiers in Oman, he had a thirst for the unusual and the exotic. He had previously served with the British Antarctic Survey, also flying Beavers. He was also quite innovative. He had adapted the noisy, 1960s air conditioning unit in his bait to channel the cold air along a suitably proportioned wooden box that held about six cans of beer in line before issuing its cooling vapours to the room. The cold beers were a godsend for which I remained grateful every day that I was to spend in the north of Oman, especially after the weeks down south at war in the province of Dhofar, where there was no air conditioning and where the humidity was up to one hundred per cent in the summer heat under the 'khareef' (cloud) of the two to three-month south east monsoon season. But all this, and very much more, was to come later. For the moment, I had some in-theatre training to complete. First of all to come was my familiarisation with SOAF Beaver operations in the north and then a conversion to the Piston Provost T.Mk 52, before being despatched down south on active operations against the enemy in Dhofar.

First time on Finals at Bait al Falaj

Beaver Loading in Oman

Provosts over Hajar Firing Range

5
NORTHERN OMAN

I began my in-theatre familiarisation in one of the four Sultan of Oman's Air Force (SOAF) Beaver aircraft on 15 March 1968, the day after arriving at Bait al Falaj in northern Oman. (For the reggie spotters, the aircraft were XR 213, 214, 215 and 216). The Beaver AL1 was powered by a 450HP, nine-cylinder, Pratt & Whitney Wasp Junior engine with a two-blade propeller. Its maximum speed, in a dive, was one hundred and seventy-three knots and, cruise speed was up to one hundred and ten knots. It carried seventy-six gallons of fuel giving an endurance of three hours. Each SOAF Beaver was painted white with a red stripe along each side, together with a red propeller boss and front edge of the engine cowling. The red emblem of the Sultan's Armed Forces, a belted Khunja (Omani dagger) with crossed swords, was emblazoned above and below each wing and on each side of the fin. Manufactured by de Havilland Canada, the four aircraft had been delivered to SOAF in 1961 to replace the single-engined Pioneers with which SOAF was first equipped on its formation in 1959. By the time I arrived in March 1968 the Beavers had established a solid and reliable record as sturdy, versatile, desert workhorses. They were used for transport of passengers and freight, casualty evacuation, spotting and reconnaissance, supply dropping (by parachute from two hundred feet or by free-drop from thirty-five feet) and general communication. The army regarded them pretty much as large airborne Land Rovers.

The Beaver could carry up to five passengers, including one in the right-side pilot's seat, or up to eight hundred and seventy-four pounds of freight with a full (five hundred and forty-eight pounds) fuel load to meet the maximum all-up weight of five thousand one hundred pounds. It followed that the passengers had to be fairly lightweight, and without much luggage, or fuel had to be reduced. So, a more typical passenger load was three or four, depending on how much kit they required to take with them. In the freight carrying role, a further one hundred pounds or so of payload could be gained by leaving behind the seats and some other minor items. The large port-side access door enabled reasonably bulky loads to be carried such as a forty-four-gallon oil drum or a donkey (sedated!) and its handler.

After a few checks of my flying skills and an area familiarisation with CSOAF, I was let loose on my own on the second day in XR 213 for my own brief tour of the local area and a couple of circuits. There were no airways, no air traffic control, no restricted areas nor anything else to interfere with totally free access to the airspace. The only small exception was the custom not to fly at low level over the Petroleum Development Oman (PDO) complex, with its numerous large oil storage tanks, on the coast at Saih al Maleh (later renamed Mina al Fahal) to the north of the airfield. So I took a wide sweeping tour, first to the south across the dry rocky hills and wadis, looking down on their brown, lifeless roughness, before turning northwards over the sea and along the coast past the little town of Muscat, with its white buildings clinging to the rough and rocky hillocks and its twin sixteenth-century forts (Mirani and Jalali — the Jail) guarding the harbour entrance. Muscat was a walled city with the only land entrance via huge guarded gates. To signal their imminent closure at dusk each day, a cannon was still fired from one of the forts. Thereafter, until dawn, access to the town was granted only to those carrying a lantern that had to remain lit whenever the holder walked within the walls.

I flew onward, chugging along happily and alone in my Beaver just off the coast, past the modern PDO oil tank farm and looked down on a little sheltered beach further along. I would come to swim year-round there, in its warm waters and to water-ski once again, as I had done so often in Borneo and Singapore when last overseas. I pondered about the adjacent PDO complex and on how the oil being newly shipped from there was producing the income that would enable the sultanate to waken slowly from its long desert sleep of hundreds of years. Omani oil exports had begun so recently, only nine months before, on 27 July 1967. I had already realised that it was to be a very special privilege to explore this ancient country before it would really begin to modernise. Finally, I flew inland again with the mountains of the Jebel Akhdar in the distance, before arriving back at the airfield to practise a few circuits before the final landing.

The following day I set off with another mentor, Flight Lieutenant John Ross, for the first of many scheduled flights along one of the three regular routes to outlying villages and army bases in the peaceful north of Oman. The three schedules were named Red/Green, Red/Sand and Blue to match the beret colours of the three regiments of the Sultan's Army and of the Oman Gendarmerie (OG). The Muscat Regiment (MR) wore red berets, the Northern Frontier Regiment (NFR) — green, the Desert Regt (DR) — sand and the OG — blue. Each regiment and the OG were responsible for maintaining the peace in their particular sectors of northern Oman and were staffed by British officers, some on loan service like the RAF pilots in SOAF, whilst others were former British Army or Commonwealth soldiers on contract. During my stay in Oman there was only a handful of Omani officers in the army and they were of very junior rank. The troops were a mixture of Omanis and Baluchis. Baluchistan (a large area of SW Pakistan, SE Iran and S Afghanistan) had a long history of providing mercenary soldiers to the Sultans of Oman. The Baluchis were originally an Iranian people who moved into the area in the tenth century AD. The Baluchi enclave of Gwadar had been owned by the Sultans of Oman for one hundred and seventy years until it was sold to Pakistan in 1958.

My Red/Green schedule covered two days and five hours ten minutes flying and introduced me to the desert airstrips at Bid-Bid, Rostaq, Izki, Nizwa, and Saiq where we spent the night of the first day. After calling briefly at the MR HQ at Bid-Bid, the route took us westwards towards Rostaq and past the entrance to the long, wide Wadi Sumail which led to the small towns of Izki and Nizwa. Along the Wadi ran the one hundred and seventy-two-mile-long oil pipeline from Fahud, in the interior of the country, to the new tanks at Saih al Maleh. We flew onward, leaving the wadi entrance on our port side, and landed on the good level airstrip at Rostaq, a small village with a very old fort that lay at the base of the high Jebel (mountain) behind it. After offloading freight, we climbed away some half an hour later along a narrower valley to the south-east and passed another ancient fort at Awabi. Here, at a later date, I was to enjoy a conducted tour by local tribesmen and to share a meal of goat and rice with them on a dusty floor within the building. During our flight across its flanks, the Jebel Akhadar itself — the 'Green Mountain' — soared to nearly ten thousand feet on our starboard side. We were just able to clear a high saddle between two lower peaks before dropping down into the Wadi Sumail for Izki and Nizwa, where there was yet another fort, this one with a distinctively shaped, large, irregular, round tower.

From 1957 to 1959, a tribal rebellion in the Jebel Akhadar region had been suppressed with the aid of British air power, troops and special forces. At that time, the fort at Nizwa and targets around the village of Saiq, high up on the plateau of the Jebel, had been attacked by RAF Venom aircraft, one of which had crashed on 30 August 1958 whilst attacking targets at Al Ain near Saiq.

An important part of the Red/Green schedule was the series of 'Saiq lifts' in which the Beaver was used to ferry freight of all kinds up to Saiq from Nizwa. The only land communication to Saiq was a rough and tortuous donkey track that took many hours to negotiate. The shuttle up to Saiq by air took less than twenty minutes return flying time. The freight comprised food (including fresh fish and dates from the coast), ammunition, petrol in jerry cans, mail and a host of other items as well as occasional passengers.

After take-off from Nizwa at one thousand six hundred feet we climbed at maximum performance with full boost, clawing steadily up to Saiq at five thousand eight hundred feet then cut the power right back to land on the rough dusty strip on the plateau. The strip was a short distance outside the little village that consisted of a couple of dozen buildings clinging to the side of a gorge on the edge of the plateau. All around the buildings, on green terraces set against the background of the bare rocks of the Jebel in various shades of brown, lay terraced gardens in which fruit and vegetables of all kinds grew prolifically in the milder temperatures, irrigated by channels from mountain springs. Our return flights down to Nizwa, accomplished mostly at idle power and within just a few minutes after take-off along the bumpy Saiq strip, were often loaded with fresh produce from the Saiq gardens — bound for Muscat. John showed me the ropes for the first couple of lifts and we then alternated for the next four. Five or six lifts were the normal requirement and at the end of the sixth, we clambered out at Saiq, secured the aircraft for the night and left it under the guard of a couple of soldiers, whilst we were driven off by our army host officer in the resident Land Rover — it must have struggled up the donkey track at some stage! — for a pleasant and simple dinner and a sleep in the coolness of the high settlement. I would soon learn that in the hotter months it was a true delight and a very welcome relief occasionally to spend a night at Saiq, when temperatures could be a mere thirty degrees C, in stark contrast to the forty-seven degrees C or more encountered at Nizwa during a July day.

As we bounced off in the Land Rover over the dusty and rocky plateau to the officers' mess, a pleasant little white building at the edge of the settlement, we made a small detour to where newcomers were usually taken on their first visit. I was taken to the grave of the pilot who had been killed in 1958 in his Venom. The wreckage still lay a short distance away. Following the crash, the local people had placed his remains respectfully into a crack in the side of a small rise in the ground, then sealed the fissure roughly with stones. After the Jebel Akhdar War had ended, an RAF Padre had been flown in to conduct a burial service. The grave had then been cemented over and marked by a cross raised in the mortar. I remember standing for a few moments in the dwindling sun at this quiet and poignant site, in silent thought about that unknown, fallen, fellow pilot from over ten years previously. I was soon to be in action in similar circumstances. That would be mostly over the mountains at the other end of Oman, but I would be doing my best to avoid the fate of my unknown comrade whilst still trying to do my duty properly. He, no doubt, had also striven to do just that but had lost his life in the process.*

After returning from the Red/Green schedule, I was given an introduction over a couple of days to low-level flying in some of the very much narrower wadis through which we could operate the Beaver, culminating in a couple of quite long, low-level navigation exercises, dual and solo. That was terrific fun and was flown at truly operational heights. That meant as low as one could safely go whilst still being able to navigate and hurl the little Beaver around the bends, standing it on its wingtips and often over-banking to keep it down when the ground fell away downhill. Apart from the thrills, it also had a deadly serious purpose. We often needed to fly the Beaver at ultra-low level in Dhofar, especially in the summer monsoon season when the khareef came down to just above the ground for most of two or three months. The Beaver had to get through to the troops, below the low cloud but in amongst the hills and wadis, to re-supply them and to lift out casualties. There were to be very many occasions in the near future on which I would further hone these skills that I was then learning for the first time at very low level in the north, and without the cloud. The monsoon was coming within a couple of months and I would be tested to my limits when cloud and ground came often, at the same moment, exceedingly close to my little aircraft.

The other main reasons that aircraft need to fly low on operations over hostile territory are of course to avoid detection by radar and to reduce the chances of being seen visually for long enough to be hit by enemy ground fire. That is why we trained in the Hunters at four hundred and twenty knots and two hundred and fifty feet. However, in Oman, there was no radar anywhere, let alone in the hands of the rebels in the south. Moreover, in our slow little Beavers and Provosts and faced in Dhofar, initially at least, only with enemy small-arms fire, it was usually easier and safer to fly out of range of the ubiquitous Kalashnikov semi-automatic rifle, i.e. above one thousand, five hundred to two thousand feet when weather permitted.

With this initial low-level training complete and another Red/Green schedule under my belt, that I operated on my own for the two days and which included a medical evacuation (medevac) flight back to Bait al Falaj, I was just to have time for Alan Bridges to take me round the Blue schedule route and introduce me to supply dropping before I began my conversion to the armed Piston Provost. The Blue schedule took in a number of stops northwards along the coast from Muscat and then inland along the Wadi Jizzi from Sohar on the coast to Buraimi, the beautiful green oasis that lay on the border between Oman, Saudi Arabia and the then Trucial Oman States (now the United Arab Emirates). It involved about two hours flying each way with a stop for an excellent breakfast, courtesy of the Oman Gendarmerie's tiny officers' mess at Buraimi. The first stop was at Seeb, in those days a short, smooth, natural airstrip — today Oman's large and busy international airport — then to Suwaiq and next to Sohar. Scattered along the entire coastline, fish could be seen drying in the sun on the flimsy racks of the boatmen who had brought them ashore.

I had learned my way around the desert and mountains of northern Oman and had flown some thirty-six hours in the Sultan's Beavers in less than three weeks under the hot Arabian sun. That alone was a great improvement in my fortunes compared with the dank, dark, Devon winter where I was lucky to get sixteen hours a month as a part-time Hunter pilot cum simulator instructor! To be in the air for so much time was unprecedented since my days on 'special patrol' in Hunters along the jungle border of Malaysia and Indonesia. In one particular three-week period in late 1965, I had ratcheted up an unheard-of forty-three hours flying in the Hunter, the usual rate being around twenty to twenty-five hours per month in routine squadron training. In Oman there was so much more time to be had in the air. I also enjoyed greatly the extra thrills that came from operating over the raw, hot, desert environment, where there were no air traffic constraints whatsoever and where I was accomplishing something really productive with my aircraft, against a geographical and cultural scene that had barely changed in two thousand years or more. I was truly *operating* an aircraft, not just training in it, nor carrying out endless patrols that never included the chance to use for real the skills that I had spent so long practising. These facets made up the core of the attraction for those of us who volunteered to join SOAF for real operational flying. The next step on that path was to learn to fly the armed Piston Provost before flying south to operate it and the Beaver in the war zone of Dhofar in southern Oman.

The two-seat Hunting Percival Piston Provost was the RAF's basic trainer from 1953 until it was replaced by its derivative, the Jet Provost, at the end of the decade. I had completed my own basic training on the

Jet Provost T3 and T4 at Church Fenton in Yorkshire from 1962 to 1963. Over three hundred and thirty Piston Provosts were delivered to the RAF. They were powered by the 550HP, nine-cylinder, Alvis Leonides radial engine and had a maximum take-off weight (MTOW) of four thousand four hundred pounds. Armed export versions of the Piston Provost (Mk 52 or Mk 53) were supplied to Burma, Iraq, Ireland, Sudan, Rhodesia and Oman (Mk 52). A total of nine had been delivered to SOAF, beginning in 1959. When I arrived in 1968 there were five remaining in service (WV475, WV476, WV678, WV501 and XF 907), two others (XF 682 and XF 868) had been destroyed in accidents, another (XF 688) had been written off and one (XF 683) had been cannibalised for spares.

The Mk 52 version had an increased MTOW of five thousand three hundred pounds; it carried a Browning .303 machine gun in each wing and under-wing armament options of eight twenty-four-pound anti-personnel bombs plus four, three inch high explosive rockets, or two, two hundred and fifty-pound bombs. It also had an extra, twenty-seven-gallon fuel tank (in the rear of the cockpit!) to supplement the two twenty-nine-gallon wing tanks, giving an endurance of over three hours thirty minutes. Like the trainer version, the Mk 52 could and did fly with the hood open, a very useful feature that I shall return to in a moment. It took off at sixty-five to seventy knots, landed at eighty to eighty-five knots and could be dived to two hundred and fifty knots (very steeply!). The Provost was a very easy aircraft to fly. The swing on take-off as power was applied was easily manageable and all other aspects in flight were quite benign. However, in the searing heat of summer over the Arabian Desert and high up in the mountains, performance was barely adequate to do the job. Bombs were released typically in a sixty degrees dive for optimum accuracy but the aircraft typically took five minutes to climb back up to the height at which a further dive could be commenced for another attack! That gave an already elusive enemy plenty of time to disappear in the cover of the scrub in the Dhofar hills. It was also not much better than the performance of the various little biplane aircraft that were operated on the North-West Frontier in the 1930s, but what an outstanding and unique experience of that earlier period of aviation history this was for a recent jet jockey!

My conversion to the aircraft began with a couple of dual trips, of about an hour each, before I took off on my first solo on type just eighteen days after arriving in Oman. There followed a mixed bag of training exercises: formation flying, air to ground weapons training, instrument flying (for the three months' monsoon season in Dhofar!), low-level flying and navigation. There was also a bit more practice supply dropping for me to do in the Beaver but the most interesting dropping of various kinds was that done from the Provost during weapons training.

Strafing in the Provost, with its two .303inch machine guns, and rocketing in a twenty degree-dive were very straightforward and not unlike what we did in the Hunter but of course at much lower speeds and therefore at closer ranges to the target. Dive-bombing, in Stuka fashion, was a new skill to learn. Bombs were dropped in a sixty degrees dive as already mentioned, but the method and technique were quite novel to me. The idea was to approach the target initially at about three thousand feet, flying the aircraft such that the target was tracked just off to the left of the nose until it almost reached the wing leading edge. At that point one dialled in a handful of rudder trim, rolled quickly left to about one hundred and fifty degrees (or more) of bank and pulled the nose down quite hard to enter the steep dive; it looked and felt to be near vertical. Then one rolled the wings level so that the aim-point of the gunsight was placed at about five o'clock to the target. As the speed increased to the release value of one hundred and eighty knots, the sight was allowed to drift leftwards (as the aircraft became directionally in trim again) and upwards, ideally to coincide with the target at the release altitude of one thousand, two hundred feet. I practised all of this first with the SOAF flight commander, Flight Lieutenant Don Angus, and then on my own on the SOAF firing range in the Hajjar Bowl, not far by air from Bait al Falaj. There was one more piece of air to ground delivery to master. The Range Safety Officer (RSO), a fellow SOAF pilot, usually drove the one hour or so out to the range with an assistant in a Land Rover well before breakfast so that practice weapons attacks could be made in the relatively calm, smooth conditions of the early morning air. It was important, therefore, that one of the later-departing attack pilots would first collect the RSO's breakfast from the officers' mess kitchen, suitably wrapped and protected for air-drop from a Provost with open hood at about thirty feet and ninety-five knots. It was usually fried egg sandwiches and later, as an RSO, I always looked forward hungrily to this novel way of having my breakfast served to me, with eggs still warm, in the dry and rocky Hajjar Bowl.

The Provost training was interspersed with a few more Beaver schedules that I enjoyed immensely, both for the novelty and challenge of landing on the short strips and for seeing so much of this fascinating new country close up on the ground. Much of it had simply and truthfully not changed since biblical times. The photographs of the ancient forts of Awabi and Rostaq, together with that of the Omani children at Rostaq village, convey an idea of the scenes. One return trip that was particularly memorable was the long flight up to the Musandam Peninsula at the far north of Oman. The Peninsula guards the south coast of the strategically vital Strait of Hormuz through which so much of the world's oil supply is still shipped. It is Oman's close proximity to such a crucial supply line, as well as its own sources of oil, that has made the country so important to western interests. In the late 1960s, the British government was quietly but effectively supporting Oman against the communist-backed uprising in Dhofar where I was soon to have a small part in the fight. At the end of the Musandam Peninsula, the surrounding sea breaks jaggedly into the landmass to form a series of large, highly irregular and wonderful, flat calm and wide inlets. I gazed down at them with my waterskier's eyes from two thousand feet and thought how fantastic it would be to skim across those mirror-like waters behind a fast speedboat. A quick look at the area on Google Earth today suggests that the area is, amazingly to me, still very much undeveloped. If that is truly so, it remains a secret paradise-in-waiting for waterskiers.

Suitably qualified and practised in the Beaver's operational roles and in air delivery of the various weapons and breakfasts from the Provost, I was signed up for my first visit to Salalah in Dhofar and set off one late April day in a Beaver with the boss, Squadron Leader Alan Bridges, via a refuelling stop at the RAF base on the island of Masirah, for the five-hour flight southwards. By then the temperature had begun to rise daily into the upper eighties. This was planned to be a short stay of just a week. It was spent getting to know the operational areas a little and included landings in a Beaver at one of the most difficult strips up in the Dhofar mountains, Helal. By the end of my first six weeks with SOAF I had clocked up an amazing eighty-three hours in the air on a wide variety of tasks in the two aircraft types. I felt truly ready for action. However, for the moment I had to wait patiently for just a few more weeks, flying Beaver schedules and a few more Provost flights in the tranquillity of the north, before being called down to Salalah on 1 June for an action-packed three months of operational flying...

Some years ago, I was researching the final resting places of the small number of my army and air force colleagues who had been killed in action during the Dhofar War, mostly after I had returned to the UK in 1970. I discovered by chance that there had been a recent proposal to bring in the remains of the 1958 Venom pilot at Saiq (whose name was revealed to me for the first time as Flight Lieutenant Owen Watkinson of 8 Squadron, RAF) to one of the Christian cemeteries in Muscat. I found out that the people of Saiq had refused to allow his remains to be moved. "Allah had sent him to this spot," they had said, "and it is still our duty to look after him."

Author with Beaver at Nizwa

Rostaq Fort Northern Oman

Weapons Close-up

6
ACTION IN DHOFAR

Salalah, capital of the southern Oman province of Dhofar, sits at Latitude seventeen degrees north and longitude fifty-four degrees east. The town and airfield are set midway along an east/west coastal desert plain, with the town immediately alongside the sea. The plain forms a crescent about sixty miles long and about ten miles wide at the centre. Along the northern edge of the crescent, the Qara Mountains rise quite steeply to between four thousand and five thousand feet.* Frankincense grows in these mountains. Further east from the crescent, the Samhan Mountains reach to about seven thousand feet. In 1968, there were no metalled roads anywhere in Oman apart from about three miles into Muscat in the north; the rest of the country was accessed by desert tracks — few were even graded.

In the late 1960s the Sultan, Said bin Taimur, lived closeted in his palace in the then very small Salalah town. He had hardly ever ventured out following an attempt on his life some years previously. His son, the Sandhurst-educated Sultan, Qaboos (who died on 10 January 2020), lived with him and also left the palace only very rarely — usually to meet visitors at the airfield which lies immediately to the north. The airfield was staffed by RAF personnel under a RAF squadron leader. However, its main purpose, apart from being a staging post for occasional RAF Argosies and a Gulf Air Fokker Friendship that called from Bahrain every fortnight or so, was to provide fuel and airfield facilities for the resident detachment of SOAF aircraft. There was even an air traffic controller, who used an ACR7 radar to talk us down to the runway in the monsoon season. After 1964, when the local uprising against the Sultan had escalated into open attacks on both Sultan's Armed Forces (SAF) and RAF facilities, SOAF had maintained a detachment of one Beaver, two Piston Provosts and three or four pilots at the airfield. The SOAF detachment supported SAF in its struggle to prevent the rebellion from gathering momentum and from increasing its support from communist backers across the border in South Yemen.

The uprising had first begun in the early 1960s amongst the Jebali ('mountain-folk') tribesmen in the hills and mountains of Dhofar. Jebalis speak a language quite different from the Arabic of the Bedouin and other lowland tribes of South Arabia. 'Jebali' — or 'Shahari' — is closely related to the ancient South Arabian 'Himyaritic' language that was displaced by the North Arabian speakers who brought Islam to South Arabia in the seventh century AD. The Jebali people looked different and dressed differently when compared to other Omani Arabs. They seemed to be a little darker and their features resembled Ethiopians or South Indians. In contrast to the long flowing white robes worn by most Omani men, the Jebali men normally dressed in a wazir, an oblong cloth wrapped around their waists and extending down to their calves, with a bare torso above. The women, however, in strict Islamic custom, were totally obscured in their black robes and each wore a heavy, black leather, beak-like face mask with only a thin slit through which to see.

The Jebalis had for a long time regarded Sultan Said as an oppressive ruler. Dissent was fuelled by the increasing presence of American oil prospectors whose activities had begun to affect the tribes of the hills and plains. Under their leader, Mussalim bin Nafl, the uprising crystallised into the Dhofar Liberation Front (DLF) in 1962. By 1964 there were incidents of sabotage and sniping at oil company trucks along the only vehicle route out of the plain, the 'Midway Road', a rough track that climbed up from the Salalah plain north of the airfield and wound through the mountains to Midway, some forty miles inland, then an oil prospecting camp in the desert and now the major Royal Air Force of Oman (RAFO) base of Thumrait. In August 1964, a RAF truck was blown up by a landmine, killing the driver. It was that incident that sparked the increased counter-insurgency activity by SAF. With Yemeni support, the rebel movement soon mutated into the People's Front for the Liberation of the Occupied Arabian Gulf (PFLOAG). It took a further eleven years, until December 1975, for the counter-insurgency war against PFLOAG to be won, by which time the Sultan had been deposed by his son, Qaboos (on 23 July 1970 — six weeks after I had left the country). By the end of the war, the tiny air force of nine pilots and nine aircraft that I had known had expanded to include a squadron of ex-Royal Jordanian Air Force Hunters, AB 205 helicopters and a range of other fixed-wing transport aircraft, as well as the new BAC 167 Strikemaster jets that began to arrive halfway through my twenty-seven-month tour. Back in 1968, little was I to know but my forthcoming service in Oman was to cover a large part of the period in which the rebels were able to increase their activities and SAF were to lose ground.

I landed at RAF Salalah on 1 June 1968 in a SOAF Beaver that I'd flown down from Bait al Falaj in northern Oman to change over with the resident Beaver. Within days I was busy ferrying passengers and supplies to SAF troops operating against rebel tribesmen (the 'Adoo') in the Dhofar Mountains. On one early flight, I took with me in the right-hand seat Lieutenant Colonel Mike Harvey, CO of the Northern Frontier Regiment, which was the 'duty regiment' down from the north when I first joined the fray. The three regiments, Northern Frontier, Muscat and Desert, rotated duty in Dhofar every nine months. In the back of the aircraft was a diminutive Baluchi sergeant whose name was Habibullah. He was my air dispatcher for the mission, which was to drop supplies to the troops involved in Operation Guruma, one of many SAF attempts to round up Adoo in the hills. I was to get to know both of these soldiers well. Colonel Mike had a sound understanding of the capabilities and limitations of our little Beaver and Provost aircraft and we got on well together throughout the period that I worked for him as one of his SOAF Tactical (SOAFTAC) pilots and later as Officer Commanding (OC) SOAFTAC. Sergeant Habibullah was one of the bravest men that I've ever had the good fortune to fly with. In the months and years to come, he was frequently on duty in the back of my Beaver as I hurled it around, often barely above the ground when we free-dropped supplies to the troops and, occasionally, also flying at the same time only just below the khareef of the late June to early September** monsoon. Habibullah was attached to the aircraft only by a single safety lanyard fastened to the floor and his job was to throw the stores out of the left side of the aircraft, from which the door had been removed before flight, on my command.

A normal human being would have become air-sick quite quickly, during the often violent manoeuvres; almost anyone else would have been quick to complain. Habibullah's faith in his pilot (or, far more likely, in his maker) was apparently without bounds. On the ground, I was often invited to share a cup of chai (tea) with him and we chatted about all sorts of things. I became privileged to count him as a friend as well as a fellow aviator and comrade-in-arms.

For the first two weeks at Salalah, I was employed mainly in the Beaver, ferrying troops and supplies to Midway, Janook and Habrut, all of which were quite easy landing strips. Midway in particular, out on the flat, hard desert to the north of the Qara Mountains had — by Beaver standards — a very long, level, wide landing strip that had been cleared to accept aircraft such as the Fokker F-27 that had supported the earlier oil-prospecting camp beside it. By 1968 the camp was deserted and had been vandalised by SAF troops. Janook, on the very edge of hostile territory, was much shorter and rougher. It also lay some forty miles away, but to the west of Salalah and only just north of the mountains. It was okay for a Beaver but not quite long enough for a Provost though, in a much later incident, a colleague did manage to force-land a Provost there successfully when the area was unmanned by SAF troops. As his leader, I was directly involved in his rescue. I will return to this story in a later chapter.

Habrut, ninety miles west north west of Salalah, was an Omani fort and airstrip by the wadi that marked the border between Oman and the People's Democratic Republic of South Yemen (PDRSY) and was quite unique. The airstrip was easy enough, on flat gravel in the floor of the wadi. The little white SAF fort sat on the high rim of the east side of the wadi, just a few minutes away by Land Rover. Habrut was totally in the middle of nowhere except that it faced a near-identical fort on the opposite, PDRSY, side. It was a stand-off situation that I could compare, in one aspect at least, to the much more sophisticated Checkpoint Charlie in Berlin or the demilitarised zone border posts between the two Koreas. In all three cases, opposing sides sat and watched each other through binoculars and dutifully recorded every tiny movement of the opposition. There was just one more significance at Habrut; it was across this long border that the guerrillas were transiting frequently and virtually without hindrance, ferrying arms and supplies from their Communist Chinese sponsors in the PDRSY. Those supplies included British mortar bombs kindly left behind by our departing British forces when they were withdrawn from Aden in 1967. I was, quite soon, to undergo the distinctly ironic and alarming experience of being mortared on the RAF airfield by bombs originating in Britain.

SOAF Beaver operations in Dhofar included the occasional, very unpleasant task of recovering dead and wounded soldiers to Salalah following ground action against the Adoo, or after the not infrequent accidents to desert convoys from the north. The Beaver could be set up with two stretchers by taking out the mid and rear right seats. We usually flew with the stretcher kit dismantled but available in the rear of the cabin and it was a fairly simple matter, if an unexpected casualty evacuation (casevac) was necessary, to remove the two seats and rig the stretchers and poles, bunkhouse fashion with one above the other. On one such occasion, I was scrambled in a Beaver to the site of an accident that had occurred to a SAF convoy over one hundred miles away on the gravel plains to the north-east. The convoy was en route from Muscat to Salalah and had been travelling with several long-wheelbase Land Rovers and about a dozen three-tonners with supplies and relief soldiers. To avoid each other's thick dust trails, the vehicles were always strung out in a loose line abreast or echelon formation on a constant heading for hours at a time. Although the plains were flat and relatively smooth, just occasionally there was a very soft patch or a very rough patch. On that day, an inattentive driver had hit one such rough patch and his truck, with twenty-five soldiers aboard had turned over. There were many casualties, dead and wounded, but the signal that came in from the convoy to scramble the Beaver for a casevac flight gave no further details apart from the approximate position.

I set off alone from Salalah, not knowing what I might find. After about forty minutes flying, I spotted first the huge dust trail that clearly indicated the major part of the convoy that had resumed its drive across the flat desert towards Salalah. I followed the rear of the dust trail and then the fresh vehicle tracks a short distance across the desert floor, to where a group of two Land Rovers and the crashed truck were parked alongside a hastily cleared strip for me to land on. After the usual low, slow fly-by to check the strip carefully for hazards (as I had first learned over the green fields of Hampshire during my AAC course at Middle Wallop), I landed and taxied up to where I saw the casualties had been collected for evacuation by air. There were two serious stretcher cases and five less serious, but still urgent, 'walking wounded'. After the airstrip had been quickly prepared, the dead and lesser wounded had been sent on in the other trucks. They would not reach Salalah for nearly eighteen hours because the last part of the journey was a time-consuming and perilous crossing of the Qara Mountains where Adoo ambushes were becoming frequent — it could not be done by night. It was quickly clear that I would have to make two flights to evacuate the seven casualties and so I set about removing two seats and rigging the two stretchers. I had been working for about ten minutes when I became aware that I was starting to feel distinctly weak and light-headed. It was in the middle of a very hot day, deep into the desert, with the temperature probably around fifty degrees C or more. In that parched ultra-dry atmosphere, in comparison to the humidity of the coastal plain, I wasn't aware of sweating and was concentrating on the task in hand. I stopped suddenly and stepped out dizzily from the extra heat of the aircraft cabin, tottering into the shadow of the Beaver's wing to seek shelter for a few moments from the blazing, merciless sun. Without a word, a young Baluchi soldier stepped forward and offered me his water flask. He'd spotted the rapid onset of dehydration. I was at first reluctant to accept his precious water. "It's okay, Sahib! We have! We have!" he said, pointing at the crashed truck and then I spotted the jerrycan of water. I drank deeply and freely and within a few minutes was able to carry on. It was a salutary lesson in how quickly dehydration could set in. The rest of the casevac operation went well and I was sure to carry an adequate supply of water with me on the second flight.

My other aircraft during those early months, was of course, the simple Provost. It was easy to fly, fairly reliable, rugged and lacking only in climb performance and speed. On the rare occasions that there was a problem, it was usually unique and always a surprise, though that could be said of many aircraft. One not so unique 'surprise' that happened to me more than once, especially in my early days in action, was forgetting to change the fuel feed over manually from the auxiliary tank, behind me in the cockpit, to the main tanks in the wings. We would generally take off with the fuselage tank selected, so that we could use up that fuel first, for two reasons. The primary reason was that the aircraft was technically 'non-aerobatic' with fuel in that tank but we needed full aerobatic capability to carry out ground attack manoeuvres. Secondly, since we were always at risk of being hit by small-arms fire from the Adoo, it was a good idea to minimise the amount of fuel with which we shared the cockpit! However, it did take forty-five minutes or more to use up that fuel and, since the contents gauge was on the tank itself and therefore out of sight of the pilot, it was very easy (when often busy at that stage of flight) to forget about the changeover. Aviation 'Law' prevailed and it was often the case that the first and last fuel reminder was issued by the usually trusty Alvis Leonides engine. It would cough quite obtrusively as its fuel supply faltered. If at low level or diving at the ground — which was what we spent a lot of time doing — it was necessary to reach down and back quickly for the changeover cock and, even more swiftly, select it to main tanks. The engine would then emit only another petulant cough or two before happily resuming normal service.

Provost ground attack and other operational flights in Dhofar were typified by long periods of inactivity and short periods of intense flying. We usually flew in direct support of troops in contact with the Adoo or as 'top-cover' (loitering overhead or nearby) in anticipation of contact being made. On some pre-planned operations, we were kept at ten minutes readiness on the ground, sometimes for interminably long periods. Then there were occasions when an ambush or other contact occurred outside of pre-planned operations and we were scrambled from whatever situation we might have been in at the time. On one rare incident of an unexpected dawn scramble, after dashing from being asleep in my bed and having paused only to throw on my desert boots, flying suit and holstered pistol, I noticed that my trusty Airworks Services engineer — who was helping me to strap into the Provost cockpit — was still in his pyjamas! Mostly our flights took place by day as we had no night capability, although later on I was instrumental in developing a limited night-attack capability after we had converted to the BAC 167 Strikemaster. A typical daytime operation was that on which I first found myself over a three-day period a few weeks after my arrival in Dhofar.

In standard fighter ground attack fashion, we usually operated as a pair of aircraft to provide the mutual tactical support of two pairs of eyes. On the first day of Operation Granite, SAF troops aimed to secure an area in the mountains just south of Janook to where we had steadily been flying in troops and supplies for the preceding several days. Since the operation was to begin before dawn, we were placed on alert from an hour before sunrise as the area of likely action was some thirty minutes flying time to the west. Halfway through the morning, a signal was received by radio-telegraphy (there was no direct, ground-to-ground, voice-radio contact with troops in the mountains) that simply said, "Scramble," and gave one of several pre-planned position references. I and my colleague paused only long enough to register the position before we raced outside from our small crew room and dashed the thirty yards to our readied and waiting pair of aircraft, jumped into the left-hand seats, strapped in rapidly, fired up the engines and taxied quickly out to the runway for take-off on the northerly strip. Pre-start and pre-take-off checks were minimal in such a simple aircraft. We were airborne in formation, leaving a long dust cloud along the unpaved runway, within five to ten minutes of first seeing the signal being decoded from Morse by our SAF signallers in an adjacent room. Straight after take-off, we turned hard left to the west as I moved out into a more comfortable position, some three hundred yards in echelon on my leader and climbed, with the sun already high behind my left shoulder, steadily and slowly along our route and up to six thousand feet, which was about two thousand five hundred feet above the estimated ground level in the area to which we were heading. It was very hot initially in my Provost, which had already brewed up greatly on the ground in the morning sun, but, as we gained altitude, it was very nice to be able to cool down a little in the lowering temperature.

Once we were within about ten minutes of the troops, my leader made direct radio contact with the Air Control Officer (ACO), a British SAF officer whose platoon had last been in contact with the Adoo until about half an hour before our arrival. He believed that a small band of rebels were holed up some five hundred yards away, just around a bend in a wadi that he understood to be a cul-de-sac. He gave us simple directions by using an orange T-shaped cloth panel laid on the ground and estimating the range to the target area. Normally with a pair of aircraft we would have attacked as near simultaneously as possible, and from different directions, to present a less easy target to the Adoo. On this first time for me, and as often subsequently proved the case, we were each constrained by the terrain to follow much the same direction. So we carried out the pairs attack, using guns only, but with only about ten degrees separation between us. That was the best we could do to make ourselves a slightly more difficult target. We saw nothing of the enemy but, at the request of the ACO, made another couple of attacks along the blind wadi before climbing to circle overhead as top-cover whilst the SAF troops moved forward to search and clear the area. The clearance phase took a long time and there was no sign of the rebels, who had vanished, perhaps climbing out of the cul-de-sac or perhaps just well-hidden in the extensive brush of frankincense and other bushes that covered these hills. After nearly an hour over the area, we returned with minimum fuel to land at Salalah via a short radar approach to the runway after two hours and thirty minutes in flight. The monsoon had begun and the cloud base was already down to about one thousand feet on the approach. For the first time, I noticed the angry sea below and the spray from the surf crashing on the beach, as it would do for the next ten weeks while the cloud lowered week by week.

In the afternoon, after another scramble to an area adjacent to the morning's operation, I was on my own in a single aircraft and was unable to get below the weather to attack. The next day saw me airborne on four separate occasions on the same operation, three for pre-planned top-cover and the fourth a scramble to strafe suspected enemy positions. My flying log book reveals that I was 'in the saddle' for a total that day of nine hours and twenty minutes. That was absolutely gruelling both in the hot air above the searing desert to the west and on the ground at cloud-covered Salalah in the stifling hot, one hundred per cent humidity during the short turnarounds. I had time on the ground only to refuel, take a pee and grab a long drink of water and maybe a sandwich then off again for the operational area. At the end of the day I was exhausted and, after dinner and more than a few beers, I collapsed into my hot sweaty bed to try and sleep in the high temperature and high humidity of the monsoon — there was no air conditioning. That time it was easy. On some later occasions it became very difficult, especially, but thankfully rarely, under the noise of incoming or outgoing mortar rounds. The third day saw only one flight, a pre-planned attack on suspected Adoo positions around a waterhole in the mountains and on which we used guns, rockets and bombs.

The particular operation that I have described had me flying fourteen and a half hours over seven flights within two and a half days. It was to be typical in principle of the scores of occasions that followed over the next two years. We mostly attacked guerrilla targets that could rarely be seen. Only once, during a day-long battle by the coastal fort of Marbat at the extreme east of the Salalah plain, did I have a clear view of the enemy in the open. Apart from that, I had the task of destroying an abandoned SAF fuel dump where the Midway road began its descent down to the Salalah plain. That was rather spectacular and the smoke could be seen clearly from the airfield for the rest of the day. I was also obliged to attack the disabled Provost on the ground at Janook that I mentioned earlier, to prevent the ammunition being harvested by the enemy.

By the end of August, I had completed three months' operations — some eighty-five hours in the Beaver and forty hours in the Provost — against the Adoo in Dhofar, much of it in the sweltering one hundred per cent humidity and occasionally drizzly monsoon conditions. I returned to Bait al Falaj for a very welcome break in the peaceful, cloudless, hotter but still very humid north. Unexpectedly, but to my pride and delight, Squadron Leader Alan Bridges, the Commander SOAF, had decided to appoint me as his flight commander and deputy at Bait al Falaj until I returned to stay once more at Salalah some five weeks later. The second surprise was that, as his deputy, I was instructed to get checked out quickly to fly the first C-47 Dakota that had recently arrived, along with our first four contract pilots. I was allowed three days off, spent the next two days in the relaxation of flying the regular Red/Sand Beaver schedule around the Jebel Akhdar, and then began my 'conversion' to the Dakota.

*Just as I had found a few years earlier when patrolling in Hunter FGA9 aircraft along the mountain border in Borneo between Indonesia and the newly formed Malaysia, the available maps in Oman were also barely adequate. There were extremely few spot heights shown and absolutely no contours whatsoever; only rough hill-shading covered with statements such as 'Maximum elevation in this area is believed to be one thousand three hundred metres, possibly one thousand six hundred metres, falling to north and south'. Not at all helpful!

**From June to September each year, the Qara Mountains are covered in moisture-laden cloud. As a result, they are heavily vegetated, and for much of the year are actually green and lush. In fact, when the monsoon suddenly lifts in September, there is abundant, emerald-green grass to be seen in the area immediately adjacent to the interior desert where the hills slope down to the gravel plains beyond which lays the huge Empty Quarter. The bright green grass turns quickly brown under the still-fierce sun within just a few days. (It was from Salalah that the famous explorer, Wilfred Thesiger, set out on his unique crossing of the Empty Quarter).

A Baluchi Lieutenant of the Northern Frontier Regiment of the
Sultan's Army. At Janook in Dhofar

Sgt Habibullah, In-Flight Despatcher

Armed Provost at Salalah(B)

7
DAKOTA INTERLUDE

The first of two C47 Dakotas, along with the first contract pilots to come to Oman, arrived in SOAF in July 1968 and was put straight into service, ferrying supplies and soldiers from Bait al Falaj in the north to Salalah in the Dhofar war zone. From that year on and for the next two years, the tide was unfortunately turning slowly against the Sultan's Armed forces (SAF) and in favour of the Adoo, the rebel tribesmen who had risen against Sultan Said bin Taimur a few years earlier.

During the June to September summer monsoon season, the khareef often lay low above the hills of Dhofar where the Adoo set their ambushes against SAF. It made the already perilous land journey, on the only track across the Qara Mountains surrounding the Salalah plain, even more dangerous and unpredictable. Within a year or so, that land route was to be cut off completely by increased Adoo activity. Sea freight to Salalah always had to cease during the monsoon. That was a consequence of the rough surf that raged against the beach-heads and at the tiny port of Raysut by the western edge of the crescent, near where the mountains come down to the sea. Prior to the arrival of the first Dakota, the only other lifelines into Dhofar from the north during the monsoon were the weekly Gulf Air F27 service and an occasional Beaver shuttling back and forth on a five-hour flight each way via a refuelling stop on the island of Masirah. The four SOAF Beavers were otherwise kept very busy on local flights within Dhofar or in the north. The Dakota really arrived in the nick of time, just as the re-supply effort to SAF in Dhofar had to be stepped up.

A week after returning from Salalah, I was airborne in a Dakota with Flight Lieutenant 'Lec' Mintowt-Czyz, an irascible but highly likeable Polish veteran of World War II and the Berlin Airlift. It was my first introduction to flying a twin-engine aircraft, yet the training was to be carried out entirely within route sectors to and from Salalah and elsewhere. We could not spare the precious aircraft for dedicated training trips — there were therefore a few more surprises to come! We began by flying the Dak down to Salalah for a night-stop before returning to the strip at Azaiba, close to Seeb.

Unlike the northern base airfield of Bait al Falaj, that lay in a bowl surrounded by bare, brown, rocky hills, nearby Azaiba was on the flat gravel plain by the coast. So it was a much better place for flying out heavy loads, as there were no obstructions to the Dakota's ponderously slow rate of climb after take-off in the heat of the desert day.

CSOAF only required me to gain co-pilot status on the Dakota, so that I could at least claim some knowledge of it when acting as his deputy supervisor of flying in the north before returning to Dhofar where, within a few months, I was to command the SOAF Tactical Detachment there. My 'conversion' was therefore greatly limited and I came to fly only about eighty hours total in the aircraft within my twenty-seven-month tour, the larger part taking place in that September of '68. Nevertheless, it was a privilege to fly such an already iconic aircraft. The first-ever Dakota had flown thirty-three years earlier in 1935, nine years before I was born. Interestingly, the actual aeroplane that I flew had played a unique part in aviation history. This, the first of our two Dakotas to arrive and registered just as '501' in Oman, was even then very venerable. It had the previous distinction of serving in 1944 (the year of my birth) with the 2nd Allied Tactical Air Force before becoming the personal aircraft for General Dwight Eisenhower. Following subsequent service in the Mediterranean after the war, it had eventually been transferred to the re-formed German Air Force from where it had been loaned to Chancellor Adenauer. It arrived in Oman still largely endowed with its VIP interior, although the seats had been replaced with the utility variety more suitable for local soldiers. The rest of the smart fittings didn't last long either.

I did all of the early flying in the Eisenhower/Adenauer Dakota with Lec who had some very particular idiosyncrasies in his attitude to aviation; he was not actually an instructor. My successful familiarisation with the aircraft occasionally owed as much to my own finely-honed survival instincts as to his very informal, and occasionally quite irregular, methods of showing me 'the ropes' (literally on one occasion, as I shall explain!).

The first thing I had to learn was that Lec, as an old Dakota hand from way back, had a particular disdain for the use of the aircraft checklists. He didn't believe he needed them and, most of the time, he was right. However, as a new boy to the Dakota and without the benefit of any ground instruction on the aircraft whatsoever, I certainly did depend on the checklist, most of the time. This dichotomy of basic operating habits did lead us to the odd minor clash. It only approached something more serious when, one day after arriving at Salalah, Lec left the cockpit for me to do the final tidy-up after engine-shutdown. Meanwhile, he had clambered out and whizzed off to the control tower to berate the tame RAF air traffic control officer for some minor linguistic misunderstanding between the two of them during our earlier approach to land, as was his habit. Following the checklist to the letter, I ended it by confirming with the engineer outside that the wheel chocks were in place and then released the pneumatic parking brake. After an unhurried lunch in the familiar surroundings of the small RAF officers' mess at the airfield, we drove back in an open Land Rover to the aircraft as Lec switched suddenly into great-hurry-mode as he saw that the aircraft was loaded and waiting only for us. I'd seen this before a couple of times. He asked me to do the walk-round external checks quickly whilst he leapt into the aircraft to do the paperwork and prepare for our return to the north. I'd spotted that an engineer was at hand to the left of the nose for start-up and that the port chock had already been removed, but that was fine as the aircraft was on level ground and the starboard chock was in. I'd got as far round as the starboard engine when, totally unexpectedly, the port engine burst loudly into life and the aircraft lurched awkwardly to the right before suddenly stopping again after a few yards. I guessed what had happened. I got in and shut the main door on the port side, aft of the wing, and 'climbed' up the sloping floor of the cabin to the flight deck to find Lec in a mild rage, swearing non-stop and almost incoherently at nobody in particular. "I left the bloddy parking brake on!" he ranted. "Who bloddy took it off?"

"It was I," said the co-pilot, feeling a little hurt that his assiduous use of the checklist was being scorned in this way. We got airborne a few minutes later without further incident and his rage petered out within moments of my confession. Nevertheless, I felt it wise to wait an hour or so into the flight northward before I felt I could recommend, once more, the beneficial effects of using a pre-start checklist to pre-empt such a problem in the future. In view of my new status as Deputy CSOAF, whilst also Lec's young pupil, it required as much tact as I could summon.

I'd flown nearly fifty hours in the Dakota before I could finally persuade Lec that I needed to have a go at asymmetric handling, especially as I'd never done any such thing in my flying career to that point and so that I could be properly signed up as co-pilot. We had of course been flying with passengers all this time. For the sake of the passengers as well as for each of us, I had long thought it would be handy for me to be able to fly safely on one engine if he or the aircraft, or both, should become incapacitated for any reason. I had in mind one particular reason. Despite strong hints and even exhortations, almost to the point of pulling rank on this sage, much older and very experienced pilot, I could never dissuade him from flying the normal transport pilot's straight-in approach to the runway from eight miles and two thousand five hundred feet. That always had us dipping at slow speed (actually, *any* speed in a Dakota *is* slow!) to less than one thousand feet over the Adoo-infested hills to the north of Salalah airfield, where I had already had to dodge the bullets frequently in the Provost for much of the previous three months. I wondered daily in the Dakota how long it would take the enemy to spot this habit of making ourselves such an easy target before they might reward us right up our backsides with a burst or two from their 7.62mm semi-automatic Kalashnikovs — or, worse, the 12.7mm Shpagin that we'd heard they'd recently acquired.

Lec finally capitulated and, on 24 September at Bait al Falaj, I got my very first, and only, one-hour training trip on type during which I was introduced to asymmetric flight techniques. The trip was not without amusement. I think it was Lec's first attempt for a long time at instructing in asymmetric flight or, perhaps, instructing in anything. He was rightly keen straight away to instil in me firmly the first principle of reacting to an engine failure, i.e. to apply rudder to oppose the actual yaw, rather than in the possibly wrong direction if one should react solely and incorrectly to flight instruments or to an incorrect call from the other pilot, or whatever. That mistake has, of course, led to the loss of many an aircraft, especially during training. It still does so, but far less frequently than in the 1960s or earlier. So, once established at a safe height, Lec warned me that he would close the throttle on one engine and that I was simply to keep the aircraft wings level and on the same heading. So far so good — I thought I could handle that okay but the accompanying instruction had me wondering a bit. He told me to shut my eyes so I couldn't see which engine he was 'failing'. Now, I thought that might be jumping the gun a bit for the first attempt — doing it with my eyes shut? Well, maybe when I'd reached his age and level of experience but not on lesson one, surely! Anyway, I did blindly (!) as I was told, if only to prove my point. When that exercise didn't work out too well at all and we'd recovered from the ensuing, mildly aerobatic, excursion, he decided to cover the throttles with a map in one hand whilst he 'failed' an engine with the other hand. All then proceeded admirably well. He signed me up that very day in my logbook as a Dakota co-pilot at last. I'm still very proud of having that minor qualification, even compared with those that were then already in my logbook for high-speed jets and my later advances to include QFI (qualified flying instructor), VSTOL (vertical/short take-off and landing) four-engine jets, Category 3 all-weather approach, test pilot, CAA (Civil Aviation Authority)-authorised examiner and various other qualifications and experiences that accumulated over the subsequent years. In fact, it is quite truthfully the *only* co-pilot qualification that I was ever awarded!

I had at least one more apocryphal experience in the Dakota with Lec. We didn't have a great spares package with the first aircraft and it was difficult to equip both our main operating airfields with a spare for every part that might be needed. One item that gave us quite a lot of trouble in the early days was the engine starter motor so we'd soon got down to only one spare starter. Aviation 'Law' (known elsewhere as 'Sod's Law') led to us being at Salalah one day with a starboard starter failure whilst the spare starter was over five hundred miles away at Bait. "No bloddy problem!" says Lec. "We'll do a bloddy rope start!" Now, I was well-familiar with rope starting the engines of speedboats for water-skiing but I couldn't imagine how any man could manage such a feat on the big three-bladed, fourteen cylinder, 1200HP Wasp engine, especially as it was too heavy and just too high off the ground actually to hand-swing the prop sufficiently to start the engine. Well, Lec had been around, as I mentioned, and he'd used his particular technique many a time at Tempelhof and elsewhere. As he explained it to me, my eyes got ever wider. I was soon to witness it being used successfully and by no means for the last time. It was basically rather simple. The idea was to get a long thick rope, in which a knot of a sufficiently critical size could be tied such that it could be wedged between two of the prop blades, with the free rope taking a few turns around the boss to turn the prop assembly until the knotted end finally slid radially, outwards and away, as the engine, hopefully, started. The other end was attached to a Land Rover, parked span-wise, pointing away from the aircraft in front of the outboard wing section. The final and crucial piece in this magnificent scene of aeronautical choreography was a suitable system of signals and actions between the three human players, pilot (Lec), Land Rover driver and ground engineer. It seemed to me that the process also depended on a fair modicum of faith, good luck and expert timing, especially from Lec who had to switch on the magnetos not too soon and not too late and from the Land Rover driver who had to do a very smart racing start without stalling his own engine. I had horrible visions of the rope not releasing and either breaking, to flail the fuselage to bits, or dragging the Land Rover back into the prop to decapitate the driver. But no, it worked like a dream, every time!

Now, lest anyone thinks I am poking fun at Lec, I must assure them that is not my real intention. It is the situations that I make light jests about, not the man. He was a very shrewd, highly competent and vastly more experienced pilot than me at that time. He stayed in Oman throughout the remainder of the Dhofar war, after two of his three Dakota colleagues were lost in action in a Caribou (the replacement for the Dakota) that crashed due to enemy action on 19 May 1971, and for a very long time after. Under the new Sultan Qaboos, he was to lead the formation of the Omani Royal Flight and was its chief for many years.

The second Dakota arrived a year later in August 1969 and both aircraft gave sterling service until August 1970. However, they were only a stopgap until replaced by Skyvans and Caribous. I was fortunate enough before leaving Oman both to enjoy a demonstration flight in a Skyvan from Bait al Falaj, along with a Shorts test pilot, and to see our first Skyvan arrive there days before my departure. However, before we get to that point, there are other tales to tell of Arabian flights in Oman. I will return over the next two chapters to more about Provost and Beaver operations and, finally, to the introduction and operation in action of the country's very first jets, the BAC 167 Strikemasters that began to arrive in mid-1969.

Postscript: *Twenty-four years later, in 1992, as a training captain and production test pilot for the Civil Aircraft Division of British Aerospace (Bae) at Woodford, I experienced one of those rare and bizarre twists of fate. I was flying back as a passenger from Gatwick to Manchester, out of uniform, after visiting the CAA on BAe business. I found myself allocated a seat next to a young first officer in uniform. We got chatting and he told me that he flew for Monarch and was on a positioning flight to operate a service that evening. I explained that I was also a pilot, with BAe. After a while chatting about airline flying, I mentioned that I had flown first in the RAF for some twenty-two years. "Oh!" he said. "Were you ever in Oman? My father flew there for many years." The young pilot was Pash Mintowt-Czyz, the son of Lec, whom I heard from Pash had, sadly, died a few years earlier. It was a fortunate meeting in more ways than one as Pash was able to supply me with the photograph of rope starting the Dakota. Without that, I suspect that many would not believe the story!*

Dakota 501 At Azaiba - Northern Oman

Rope-Starting Dakota at Salalah!

8
DIVERSIONS, DALLIANCES & DHOFAR DANGERS

My relaxing interlude flying the Eisenhower/Adenauer Dakota back and forth from Northern Oman to Dhofar, and once to Bahrain and back, was soon over. After five weeks in the peaceful north, I was back down at Salalah and in action again. It was early October 1968 and the monsoon cloud (khareef) in Dhofar had cleared from the mountains around the Salalah plain. The brush on the hillsides and in the wadis had grown thicker. The Adoo and SAF were stalking each other afresh. It was a very busy few weeks in the air, flying the Provost and Beaver on operations in support of SAF, including reconnaissance, resupply, a casevac, a lot of top cover, and a few ground attacks on the elusive rebels. I returned to the north once more on the last day of the month in the right-hand seat of the Dakota. I was then able to enjoy a proper rest of just over a week, including a very pleasant stay of a few nights in Dubai which, at that time, boasted only one or two quiet little hotels and a couple of restaurants. The next few weeks back at Bait al Falaj, until my long Christmas leave was due to start, soon passed by in the leisurely scheduled Beaver flights around the Jebel Akhdar and along the coast northwards, then inland to Buraimi Oasis. There was also an introduction to firing the newly arrived Swiss Sura rockets from the Piston Provost. The more accurate, high-speed Sura was to be the standard weapon that we would use on the BAC 167 Strikemasters when they arrived in mid-1969. Until then, they would first replace the old three inch rockets of 1939–45 design that we were still using on the Provost.

On the magic day of 5 December, I left Oman for a full six weeks' leave, returning first to London and my home town of Bedford before flying out to the Austrian Alps for a wonderful two weeks' skiing. It was so refreshing after the excitement and tensions of nearly four months at war in Dhofar, not to mention the many general privations in Oman at that time. We had no air conditioning in Dhofar. During the monsoon season, we even had to switch on a small heater (!) in our wardrobes to help stop our clothes from mouldering and rotting in the perpetual high temperature and near one hundred per cent humidity. There were no hotels and no restaurants anywhere in Oman. During the very rare days off in Dhofar, our recreation centred on the RAF swimming pool at Salalah. In the north we waterskied from the SAF beach on the one day off per week. In the evenings in Dhofar we had mainly the tiny RAF mess. Very occasionally, we were invited to dine with the resident regiment at their base of Iskander (the Arabic word for 'Alexander' — he really got around!). The army base had its own airstrip there that we used frequently for picking up or dropping off troops and supplies in the Beaver. However, social trips to Iskander had to be under armed escort across the plain in open-top Land Rovers, their floors sandbagged optimistically against the threat of landmines. Sometimes in the north, a kindly civilian or two would invite one or two of us to dinner in the town of Muscat. The Cable and Wireless manager and his wife showed us particular kindness and provided excellent food. For a very short time in the north, I was most fortunate to befriend a beautiful Dutch girl, a teacher at the Shell Oil complex at Saih al Maleh, before she was transferred to work in Brunei. Then, in the latter part of my tour, I enjoyed a longer and very pleasant friendship with an American nursing sister, one of just two who worked at the country's only, tiny hospital in Muscat run by American missionaries. Otherwise, the opportunities for a young bachelor to enjoy himself socially in Oman were pretty thin. So the two long Christmas leaves that I had during my tour with the Sultan of Oman's Air Force (SOAF) were a chance to throw myself into a hectic and welcome round of skiing, partying, disco dancing, and nursing the inevitable hangovers.

At the end of January 1969, I left the cold, snowy Alps and flew back to the very pleasant warmth and dryness of the South Arabian 'winter'. When outdoors and gazing skyward, it felt and looked little different from a clear mid-summer's day in the UK. However, everything on the ground was brown, yellow and very dusty, instead of lush and green. Within a week, I returned once more to the war in Dhofar to use the new Sura rockets in anger for the first time, as well as carrying out a demonstration of our ground attack capabilities for HM the Sultan in person, on one of his extremely rare excursions out of his palace. I was also significantly involved in 'capturing' a suspected enemy gun-running launch — a short tale that may be of interest.

It started one day when I flew across to Iskander in a Beaver to collect the British Army commanding officer (CO) of the resident Northern Frontier Regiment and his relief, the CO of the incoming Muscat Regiment. We were to fly a tour of the operational areas. The idea was for the outgoing boss to give the incoming one a handover brief during the airborne tour. It included a landing out west at a SAF base in the badlands. With all that done, it was decided we'd return to Salalah just off the coast. This was, as much as anything, to admire the magnificent huge cliffs that descended majestically — and almost vertically — for one thousand five hundred to two thousand feet into the sea at the edge of the mountains to the west of the coastal plain. We'd been flying back offshore at around one thousand five hundred feet for about twenty minutes when we spotted a motorised dhow heading towards the coast in a remote area and about two miles out to sea. Having decided to approach for a closer look, we saw the boat alter course rapidly to adopt a route parallel to the shoreline. A radio call back to Salalah soon revealed that there was no expected marine traffic in the area. It was decided that the launch should be regarded as unauthorised and must be 'arrested' and shepherded back to Salalah. That was going to be difficult from the air in a Beaver. A couple of passes, air-intercept style, showed no sign of activity on deck and absolutely no inclination from the boat to follow my attempts at indicating the course onto which I wanted it to turn. With the agreement of the two colonels, I flew straight back to Salalah, leapt straight into the ready Provost that I'd called for on the radio, and set off again for the errant mariner and his launch. This time it took only a couple of bursts of my twin .303inch machine guns across the bows to persuade the captain to turn for Salalah. However, the job entailed three hours of flying because, in my absence, he had headed off further away from Salalah and kept having a go at wandering off again. There were a few more judicious and steadily closer bursts from my guns to put him back on track again, until one of the two Sultan's Navy dhows could finally intercept him and escort him in to port at close range. The airborne arrest was duly logged as the first of its kind.

Talking of guns, at all times in Dhofar we pilots carried personal side-arms — a pistol and a dozen rounds. In the Beaver there was also space to carry a Sterling sub-machine gun (SMG) and a couple of clips of ammunition. The carriage of personal weapons conveyed only a very small sense of security were one ever to have the bad luck to be stuck on the ground in contact with the Adoo, especially if alone. Even less assuringly, we also carried what was known as a 'Goolie Chit', a certificate in English, Arabic and the local Jebali language, that proclaimed one as a loyal servant of the Sultan for whom a substantial reward would be paid if we were returned to Salalah, unharmed, i.e. with 'goolies intact'. Since any meeting on the ground with the Adoo could well occur after ordnance had been fired at them from a Provost, it was unrealistic for us to put any faith in the usefulness of the Goolie Chit, whatever the price that might be offered from the Sultan's coffers. The general line of thinking was that it would probably be a less painful death to use our last bullet on ourselves. Thankfully, since I didn't rate my chances very highly against trained Adoo guerrillas armed with Kalashnikov AK-47 assault rifles and I had serious doubts as to whether I could actually shoot myself, even in extremis. I came vaguely close to that situation on only two occasions. Once was when I was obliged to stay overnight with my aircraft on a rough strip in hostile territory, guarded only by a few soldiers whilst we waited for a returning SAF section that had been ambushed by the Adoo and were carrying a badly wounded casualty to evacuate to Salalah. We had expected that they would reach the strip within a few hours after nightfall. Landing there in the dark in rough terrain was out of the question so I had landed in the very last minutes of daylight to await them. With the aid of Land Rover lights and a few flares, I could fly off in the dark with the casualty. When the returning soldiers were greatly delayed, I had little option but to remain and try to sleep, guarded by the others but very uneasy indeed, beside the precious Beaver. The aircraft — as well as me, its driver — was a potentially tempting and easy target to the Adoo.

I got airborne at first light to remove the aircraft from the possibility of Adoo attack and also to provide a radio link to the party struggling in with the casualty. It transpired that he had died much earlier during the night-time journey so I had only a badly smelling corpse and his mourning brother for company on the return to Salalah. It took very few hours in the high temperature and humidity for a body to begin to decompose noticeably.

The other potentially close call with the Adoo on the ground was when I was talked into landing on a strip in broad daylight for yet another casevac. Despite my firm conviction that it was not the correct place, a SAF officer on the ground assured me repeatedly by radio that it was. Having landed, I heard a faint radio call apologising that I had indeed been directed to the wrong place and, worse, was in the path of a retreating band of Adoo! I was too furious to be scared but took off like a startled grouse, expecting at any moment to come under a hail of bullets! But I didn't, thank heavens.

In the air, oddly, the Beaver never seemed to get hit by enemy small arms (SA) fire. Although we always operated to minimise the chances of being hit, by flying either very low or above SA range, it seemed the Adoo didn't even try to fire on the aircraft. We wondered whether it was our red and white colour scheme that gave us the sanctity of an apparent air ambulance, in which role we did frequently operate as I have said; or maybe it was for some other fathomless reason. Even later, after some senior bright spark at SAF HQ had decided that our Beavers should be painted in dark camouflage colours (which made them ten times easier to spot from the ground against the bright background light!), the Adoo still seemed to leave the aircraft alone. In the Provost, it was a rather different story in that we were frequently fired upon, although without being hit that often. I guess that, with the obvious indications from the Provost that it was indeed a direct threat to Adoo life and limb, it would have been a very brave or very stupid guerrilla who would not shoot back, unless he risked giving away his position unnecessarily to the Sultan's soldiers. On one occasion I was at Salalah when a very frightened Provost pilot returned with his aircraft absolutely peppered with SA fire, yet it was still flying and he himself was totally unscathed. Much later on, and after we got the 167s, the Adoos' aim seemed to have improved and I had a couple of very hairy incidents when my aircraft were hit quite significantly, as I will describe in the next and final chapter of events in Oman.

1969 was an exceptionally busy year in Dhofar. I was to spend a total of just under six months there in that year alone as the tempo of the war heated up significantly. The Adoo grew bolder in their attacks upon SAF and on the RAF airfield at Salalah where we were based. The attacks were mostly by night, often using the mortar rounds left behind by British forces who had departed Aden some two years earlier. On one occasion, we were required to evacuate our tiny force of two Provosts and two Beavers hurriedly to the airfield at Midway (now Thumrait) after such an attack early one night, as there had been an intelligence report of a further large-scale attack on the airfield. The attack never came but we had a very interesting time landing at Midway, relying almost entirely on moonlight and the dim lights of one Land Rover. The Adoo later carried out their first daylight mortar attack on Salalah airfield, for which they must have been given more accurate and comprehensive intelligence than we'd received! They caught us all out in the open one afternoon, in the midst of refuelling two Strikemasters and whilst a Beaver was being towed across to the protection of the mortar pens. By that time, I had been put in command of the SOAF detachment at Salalah. The Beaver in question got fairly well peppered with shrapnel and, unfortunately, the Airworks engineer in the cockpit, riding the brakes, collected a significant piece in his neck. I was the first to reach him after the attack stopped, my knees and elbows grazed from 'biting the dust' as I had heard the unmistakeable sound of the first of the eight shells whistling down to explode loudly around us, but otherwise unscathed. The engineer sat frozen to the aircraft seat and could only say: "Sorry Boss! Sorry Boss! I think the aircraft's been clobbered!" When I told him not to touch his neck due to the risk of dislodging the foreign object there, he nearly fainted in fear. With a bit of help, I got him out and drove him swiftly around to our army doctor who removed the shrapnel, patched him up and we had him in the bar in less than an hour. He — and the rest of us — barely stopped talking for hours afterwards. We had all come very close indeed to being killed or seriously injured.

There came a time when we all began to get very twitched up about these attacks on the airfield. It was 'protected' only by a long and flimsy perimeter fence patrolled by very young and very old Askaris, irregular tribesmen equipped with old — sometimes ancient — rifles. In due course, the British government helped us out by flying in a 'Green Archer' mortar-locating radar which was linked in to our own mortars that could fire directly back at the accurately plotted Adoo position. It was a great idea, and a considerable comfort, but a real sleep-wrecker as we desperately tried to recover for the next day's operational flying whilst lying there with eyes wide open, trying to work out whether the deafening explosions at three o'clock in the morning were from incomers or from our own outward fire. We anticipated the possible need to leap instantly from our beds with pistol or SMG in hand lest the explosions were heralding a storming of our flimsy perimeter. It was made worse by the Askaris firing off rifle volleys into the darkness at nothing in particular, whoever was doing the mortaring. That did as much to frighten us as any skulking bands of Adoo who might have been bent on invading to polish us off.

As the time grew closer to replace the Piston Provosts with brand new BAC167 Strikemaster jet aircraft, our ageing Provosts (and even the newest!) seemed to tire very rapidly. Two particular incidents illustrate their accelerating dilapidation. Both involved the same pilot, Flight Lieutenant Rory Downes, a fine colleague who had joined us from a tour on Air Defence Lightnings and who therefore had no ground attack experience until coming to SOAF but acquitted himself very well. Rory turned out to be both unlucky and lucky. His first dash of bad luck in Dhofar was during an attack in a Provost using a pair of two hundred and fifty pound bombs. At the point of release in the sixty degrees dive, the starboard bomb had released okay but the port bomb had failed to come off the rails, leaving him with a sudden and significant asymmetry in drag and weight. In such a situation, it was necessary to pull an emergency release handle — whilst ensuring that the aircraft's bank angle should not exceed forty degrees — or the bomb could hit the fixed undercarriage! Rory swiftly pulled the handle. It jammed at first then came fully away in his hand together with a nine-inch length of broken, rusted cable! With some difficulty he managed to land at Salalah, very gently and having used copious amounts of opposite rudder and aileron to keep the port wing up as the speed reduced to touchdown. He was lucky that the bomb did not become dislodged in the latter stages of the approach as that could have been disastrous.

The second piece of bad luck was doubly more serious. Rory, my wingman on this occasion, and I had been scrambled to provide top cover over the mountains to the west for a SAF operation in progress. His aircraft had failed to start, so I set off alone whilst he got help from the engineers to start the engine. He followed me about ten minutes later then, suddenly, just shortly after I had arrived on task over the troops, he called me in emergency to say that his engine was overheating badly and that he was unable to maintain altitude. I advised him to jettison all his weapons and turn back to Salalah. He did that but the deteriorating engine prevented him from flying much further. There were two other choices; we had all discussed such a situation many times before. First, he could turn south and bale out as far out to sea as possible and hope that the Sultan's navy in one of its two slow dhows could pick him up before the Adoo got to him in a boat. Ditching with the Provost's fixed undercarriage was not recommended. Otherwise, he'd have to turn north and find a flat area clear of the mountains and put the aircraft down there or, if not possible, at least bale out over the easier terrain and reduce the chance of breaking a leg on landing.

He chose the forced landing and was fortunate in being able to reach the deserted SAF airstrip at Janook, lengthy enough to land a Beaver but not a Provost — in theory. Nevertheless, he pulled off an excellent landing, virtually without engine power, and managed to come to a halt without damage in the rough area well beyond the end of the strip. By radio, I had told the SAF commander on the ground below me what was happening and they had agreed that I should fly across to Janook, about ten minutes away, and provide top cover for him, since his need was greater than theirs at the time. I arrived just in time to see Rory emerge safely from his cockpit and set off at a run towards a small area of high ground. He got there okay. His training kicked in automatically and he launched off a flare to show me where he was, then came up breathlessly on his emergency SARBE radio to tell me that was an awful mistake as he'd just advertised his position to the world! I agreed!

I'd also been busy on the radio to Salalah and had discovered that the only available Beaver was taxiing out for an air test. I ordered it to be diverted immediately to Janook to pick up Rory, and flat out please. Our troops on the operation not too far away had also sent a fast recce team in Rory's direction but the need to be alert to ambush and post scouts en route meant they would take an hour or more to reach him. As I flew top cover overhead, straining my eyes at the ground for any signs of Adoo activity, Flying Officer Barry Fullerton — the brave Beaver pilot — screeched onto the airstrip twenty-five minutes later, scooped up Rory and the rescue was done. The next priority was the downed aircraft with its two machine guns and full load of .303inch ammunition. Many of the Adoo had .303 rifles and would have welcomed the gift. By radio link through Salalah to HQ in the north, it was agreed that I should destroy the aircraft and its ammunition since there was no chance of getting an engineering party in to fix it in such a dangerous area and there were anyway only two or three weeks left before the Provosts would be withdrawn from service. So, with a very strange feeling indeed, I turned my attention to the bizarre task of trying to destroy Rory's Provost that had so gallantly kept going long enough for him to land it without damage, hardly an hour previously.

I strafed it; I rocketed it and I threw several twenty-five-pound fragmentation bombs at it, all in an attempt to get it to blow up or at least to burn as happens so easily in the films. It didn't happen. It didn't want to die. After one further flight out to the stricken aircraft to try again to blow it up with another load of rockets, unsuccessfully, all further attempts were abandoned for that day. I returned the next day in the Beaver, after the strip had been secured by SAF troops, with an explosives expert, two soldiers and a quantity of plastic explosive (PE) and detonators. They packed the PE around the sad, tired, badly wounded aircraft, wired it up and we all retired to a safe distance to watch its spectacular but very miserable final demise in the hot and arid desert. XF 907 had bitten the dust after less than three years' service over the desert and mountains of Oman — it had been the last to arrive in August 1965. I guess the bits might still be there these fifty years on. But her pilot had survived, had been rescued and lived to fly for many more years.*

My last weeks with the two remaining Provosts at Salalah were spent in action almost every day. The tempo was frantic as contacts between SAF and the Adoo became more frequent. The first three BAC 167 Strikemaster Mk 82 aircraft reached Salalah at the end of May, together with several new pilots already checked out on type. I flew the very last Provost, WV 501, back up to Bait al Falaj on 2 June 1969, to take a short break in Beirut before beginning my own conversion to the new jets a couple of weeks later.

After his tour in SOAF, Rory Downes joined Britannia to fly Comets and, by the early '90s had risen to become the chief pilot of Air Europe at Gatwick.

Author with Friendly Forces at Mawaffaq

Strikemaster at Salalah - note the proximity of the hills beyond

9
JETS INTO BATTLE

The introduction of BAC 167 Strikemaster Mk 82 jets into service with SOAF began in mid-1969. It was the first significant increase in air power since SOAF had been formed ten years earlier. It was therefore a big stride forward in turning the fortunes of Oman towards winning the war against the communist-backed PFLOAG rebels in Dhofar, the Adoo. Winning that war undoubtedly set Oman firmly on its path of successful development to become the strong, stable and prosperous country that the world has known since 1976. A strong and stable Oman has helped greatly to secure safe access for the world's oil tankers on the crucial shipping routes in and out of the Arabian Gulf.

There were of course several other decisive factors that helped SAF to win the war: the overthrow of Sultan Said bin Taimur by his more enlightened son Qaboos in June 1970; the introduction into SOAF of more advanced transport aircraft and helicopters from the same year; a better strategy for defeating the rebels on the ground and — so very little known — help from the BATTs, the British Army Training Teams, the thinly disguised cover name for the British SAS presence in Oman.

The arrival of the Strikemasters — '167s' as we referred to them — was the first of all these events. SOAF was eventually to receive twenty-four 167s, replacing the four Piston Provosts that were left after the deliberate destruction of XF 907. The 167s multiplied SOAF's firepower and effectiveness by a huge factor. At a typical low-level cruise speed of two hundred and forty to three hundred and sixty knots, the jet was two to three times faster than the Provost and could arrive from Salalah and be on station over the troops in ten minutes, rather than the twenty-five minutes it took its predecessor which 'cruised' flat out at only one hundred and thirty-five knots. Moreover, the 167 packed a much greater punch with its 32 Sura rockets — or 16 Suras and two, five hundred and forty-pound bombs — as well as its two FN 7.62mm machine guns. The high-speed Suras were more accurate and gave the opportunity for far more attacks per mission than was possible with the maximum of six (usually four) old, three inch rockets carried by the Provost. The effect on the Adoo — it was learned much later — was demoralising. They had much less time and chance to escape after their customary hit and run attacks on the SAF troops. The tide was about to turn back in favour of SAF.

I began my conversion to the 167 in June 1969, after another long spell in Dhofar. It was nice to get back into a jet. The aircraft handling was very easy and familiar. I had trained to get my RAF pilot's wings on the similar Jet Provost some seven years previously. It was good to have a more comfortable cockpit and a reasonably good air conditioning system to keep the 'office' markedly cooler than the searing forty-five degrees C temperature outside the aircraft in flight at low level. Though frankly, after getting airborne, it took quite a while before the cooling system began to make any inroad into the furnace-like conditions inside the cockpit that had brewed up as the aircraft sat on the ground under the blistering, high sun of the Arabian summer. The temperature in the cockpit of a parked aircraft could quickly rise to dizzying levels. I often remembered my father, who had serviced Hudsons in Aden during much of the Second World War, telling me that you could fry an egg on an aircraft wing on a hot day. I never really believed him until, much earlier in my tour in Oman, I had scorched the skin on my bare inner forearm a few times when carelessly dangling it over the Provost cockpit sill with my sleeves pushed up. That was enough to convince me quickly — so I didn't bother with the egg.

As well as the faster Sura rockets that I had tried out earlier in action with the Provost, the 167 came with a better gunsight that improved the aiming of all our weapons. The new aircraft also had some token armour-plating, including around the fuel recuperator (under the rear of the cockpit section) and directly under the cockpit floor, below the pilot's seat — a thoughtful and comforting enhancement. The presence of a Martin-Baker ejection seat was another reassuring feature in the circumstances in which we operated, provided — of course — that one could have some control over when and where one might use it. An unexpected arrival by parachute into an enemy-held area would not be a good idea at all — more about that prospect later.

Within a few flights, I had become totally at home in the 167, including in weaponry, instrument flying, navigation and formation flying. So, a few weeks later, I set off alone down to Salalah, via Masirah Island, to deliver a brand-new jet that had arrived only days earlier from the UK. On the second leg, cruising happily along in a shiny new, cool cockpit at over thirty thousand feet, the new aircraft began to spoil the good impression that it had so far created with me. I began to suffer a string of successive and apparently unrelated electrical failures, none of which could be fully resolved by use of the emergency check lists. The situation became really quite confusing and I began to get more worried when control over the pressurisation system failed and I had to descend to a level where I began to eat up fuel at a much higher rate. I was able to make a short radio call to Salalah to report that I had a complex electrical failure before the radio packed up on me as well. Although it was the monsoon season, I was fortunately able to make a visual approach — all my navigation aids had gone — and landed safely with very little fuel remaining to keep the engine running. The cause of the problem was quickly guessed by the chief engineer from Airworks Services (who happened to be at Salalah on a visit to his men) though he didn't tell me until he'd confirmed it. There was a manufacturing fault. The part of the airframe to which the main earth of the electrical system was affixed had been painted over instead of being left as bare metal. How that had got through production flight testing and the long series of ferry flights from the UK, just to take a bite at me over the remote and scorching Arabian Desert, I could never understand.

I returned briefly to the north, for another few weeks, to introduce three other pilots to weaponry on the 167 and to fly some delightfully relaxing Beaver schedules. There was also a round-trip to Salalah and back in the Eisenhower/Adenauer Dakota, before taking up the reins once more in command of SOAFTAC at Salalah. This time I had an enlarged team of pilots including several of the new contract officers, all of whom were considerably older than me but who readily (and thankfully from my perspective) accepted my tender years and adapted well to their new environment. There followed an unusually quiet period of four weeks in which SAF consolidated after its retreats in the middle of the year. During that period, 167 operations were confined largely to reconnaissance flights and it wasn't until mid-September that I fired the first shots in anger from one of the new jets. Then, once again, live engagements with the enemy remained sporadic for yet more weeks. However, there was plenty of trade in reconnaissance, top cover and numerous scrambles from ground alert. Meanwhile, re-supply and casevac activities with the Beaver continued unabated until I returned once more to the north in mid-October for a couple of months, before going off on my second midwinter leave over Christmas and New Year in the UK and in the Austrian Alps. This all turned out to be the quiet before the relative storm to which I returned at the beginning of January 1970.

One of the problems facing SOAF was that, despite the arrival of the shiny new jets, we still had no night attack capability. Having begun to take an occasional pasting by day, the Adoo wouldn't take long before they began to attack outlying areas by night. With the approval of CSOAF and the SAF commander in Dhofar, I decided early on to see what we could do to redress the gap in our capability. I had acquired some experience of flying in formation by night in Hunter FGA9s of 20 Squadron from Singapore, only two or three years earlier. The aim there had been to develop the capability for several aircraft to take off and fly in formation to a target at night prior to a dawn attack, or to recover back to base by night following a dusk attack. Neither I, nor anybody else in SOAF at the time, had any experience whatsoever in carrying out actual attacks by night, for which one really needed the capability to drop flares to illuminate the target area. Nevertheless, I thought we should see what we could do and so I set up a simple trial to ascertain some parameters that we could follow, should we be called upon in extremis, in order to support our friendly forces with air attacks on the Adoo by night. Using just a single aircraft at first, the initial requirement was to devise a system for a pilot to locate a target position by means of a line of two or more lights on the ground, at a fixed reference distance apart and pointing at the target, with an estimated distance from the last light to the target given over the radio from the friendly forces on the ground. By day we were well accustomed to a similar method using a T-shaped orange panel and a distance given by an air control officer, a British Army officer on loan to SAF (as were we RAF pilots on loan to SOAF), or a British or Commonwealth contract officer.

On the evening of 9 January, I put these procedures into practice on a small trial with a very limited degree of success. Forty-eight hours later, the Adoo kindly obliged by attacking the Wali's (village headman's) fortified house at Taqah, on the coast about twenty nautical miles east of Salalah and I was able to put what I had learned in my trials into practice. By a strange series of coincidences, I had flown a Beaver into Taqah on the day of the trial, with an interpreter, to brief the irregulars who defended the house, as to how they might direct an aircraft to carry out a night ground attack should they themselves be attacked by the Adoo. They would need to set out the lights as described and then give directions in Arabic via the army base at Umm al Ghawarif, the SAF HQ in Dhofar, who would in turn relay the details in English to the 167 pilot via the control tower at Salalah. Oddly, enemy were then sighted in daylight on the tenth, north of Taqah, and I carried out an attack on that area. When the time came after dark on the eleventh, it seemed the Adoo were playing right into our hands. A call came through at about seven thirty p.m. for us to scramble to Taqah, so I thought I should give it a go and quickly got airborne in a 167 with another pilot beside me in the cockpit. The cumbersome communications procedure meant that the chances of success were not high, though I imagine my jet roaring around at low level by night must have frightened the Adoo as much as the limited ordnance that I felt it was worth expending in their general direction. Anyway, for that or for some other reason, something went wrong on their side because it appeared that they failed entirely to fuse correctly every one of the rocket propelled grenades (RPGs) that they fired at the house — or they were too close for the fuses to arm in time before impact. On the following day, in the early morning after a SAF patrol had secured the area and the local airstrip, I flew out in a Beaver with an army colleague to find several RPGs embedded, but unexploded, in the western wall of the Wali's house. There were no confirmed casualties on our side, although significant bloodstains at a suspected RPG firing position indicated that friendly SA fire from the house did find an Adoo or two.

Later on, and together with another pilot colleague, Flight Lieutenant (later Wing Commander) Tony Hughes-Lewis, I extended the trials and we were soon able to carry out a pre-planned, two-aircraft, night raid in conjunction with the Sultan's Navy who landed troops after our attack. The operation was in response to intelligence reports that senior members of the Adoo were sheltering by night in a building close to a small coastal village to the west of Salalah. Once again, the results were uncertain — although we must by then at least have begun to deter the Adoo from thinking that they were safe from air attack by night. There were a couple more attempts to use this very limited new night attack capability but further development had to await the later arrival of equipment for delivering target illumination flares. They did arrive just in time for me to carry out flare-dropping trials in the north, only a month before my tour came to an end but too late for me to use them in action. (Five years later, on secondment to a Royal Norwegian Air Force F5 Squadron, I became thoroughly familiar with night attack practices using flares, both as an attack pilot and as a flare dropper).

For the rest of my time on operations in Dhofar, until I left there finally on 28 March 1970, the tempo increased markedly and I was in action either in the 167 or the Beaver almost every day for three months. This was the time when we began to be mortared more frequently and to see the Adoo having success at hitting our new 167s with SA fire. Unfortunately, I was to star in two of the more serious airborne incidents. Over the period, it seemed that the Adoo were becoming more adept at hitting the 167 than the much slower Provost. I put this down to one or both of two factors. Firstly, it was known that a number of the Adoo had been trained in China or North Korea by courtesy of their Chinese sponsors across the border in South Yemen. I believed they had been well instructed in the art of putting up a SA 'barrage' in front of an attacking aircraft as it pulled somewhat predictably out of a dive attack and when it was therefore at its closest point to the ground. I had read that this tactic was used to some degree of success against American aircraft over Vietnam. Anyway, that's how I got hit on both occasions! Secondly, I believed that the faster attack speed of the 167, when compared to the much slower Provost, actually worked to our disadvantage in this respect as we had a larger radius of turn and so could not 'jink' as effectively directly after the initial pull-out. Having been hit and having recovered to land at Salalah, as was the case in both of my events, a third factor to our disadvantage then came into play. Whereas the old Piston Provost was an extremely simple aircraft that could usually be patched up in a few hours, the more sophisticated 167 had a much larger area of its planform in which a hit could cause secondary damage. That often meant a repair scheme had to be devised by the manufacturer in the UK and, sometimes, special materials or spare parts had to be flown out to us. So, until faster battle-damage repair procedures were devised, we soon found that a hit 167 could be out of action for many days on end. My two events serve as examples.

The first occurred on 4 February 1970 when, alone in a single aircraft, I was carrying out an attack in co-ordination with SAF units in the Wadi Jarsis in the foothills barely four nautical miles north of Salalah airfield. Pulling out of the dive, I felt a very distinct but unfamiliar thud and knew straightaway that I must have been hit. I banked immediately and instinctively away from the area and kept the pull on hard to get around the corner as quickly as possible onto a heading for the airfield, whilst I assessed what had happened. It didn't take long to find out. When I came to relax the pull, I found that the stick had jammed in pitch! A degree of back and forth forcing restored some control, although it felt very graunchy as I limped back to the airfield. I had to decelerate without the benefit of any pitch trim and therefore had to hold a quite considerable stick-back force down to the landing. After landing and closing down, I joined the party of engineers and other onlookers who had by now assembled at the back of my aircraft to see that a small, neat entry hole had been made in the rear right fuselage. The bullet had then exited the top of the fuselage, re-entered the lower right fin and re-emerged through a much larger and ragged, final exit hole higher up on the left side of the fin — four holes for one bullet! The fragmenting bullet had meanwhile shattered the elevator trim-tab mechanism and it was this that caused my symptoms. Although the aircraft skin could be repaired quite easily, it took a fair while for spare parts for the trim mechanism to arrive.

The second occasion was apparently more spectacular, at least to my wingman, a contract pilot and veteran of the then recent Biafran War where he'd flown the armed Jet Provosts from which the 167 was directly developed. On 24 March 1970, we had just carried out a co-ordinated pairs attack in an area a few miles further north of my first incident when, once again, just after the bottom of the pullout as the nose came back above the horizon under 5 or 6G, I felt a particularly hard and rather more worrying thud through the airframe. Immediately, my wingman radioed excitedly to me "You've been hit! You've been hit! You're on fire! Eject! Eject!" That was actually a very silly call and I took him to task over it later on the ground. I was well aware that I'd been hit and I was also well aware, quite rapidly, that the aircraft was flying perfectly well and that I had no cockpit warnings or malfunctions of any kind. To eject from where I was at that point would have had me floating down on a parachute behind the Adoo, whom I had just attacked and on the opposite side of them from our own soldiers — a distinctly unacceptable prospect. I doubted very much that they'd have invited me to tea or, if they had, I'd have probably ended up in the pot (or far worse, more likely). My wingman continued his excited and pessimistic speech to the effect that I was on fire and had sprouted a two hundred-yard smoke trail. I ignored him and turned for the airfield since I had no evidence whatever of fire. What I did spot quite soon though was the fuel gauge needle moving steadily, and abnormally quickly, anti-clockwise towards the empty end of the scale.

I discovered after landing that I'd been hit twice in the starboard wing. One bullet had penetrated the integral wing fuel tank. I had been airborne for barely ten minutes after take-off so the aircraft was still feeding off the fuel tip-tanks. The wing tanks were therefore totally full. Even a little 7.62mm bullet hitting the wing and penetrating the skin of the tank was enough to cause a hydraulic shockwave through the fuel. That, in turn, popped a dozen or more rivets in the underside and turned the tank into a colander. What my wingman had seen was a trail of vaporising fuel — there was no fire, fortunately. I was later presented with the bullet — it had lodged in the tank and was found during the later repair. I still have it in a small box in my desk. Again, for the third time in just over six weeks (another accompanying wingman had been hit in the outer wing only three days previously, though with less dramatic effects), an aircraft was grounded for days whilst a repair scheme for the stressed skin of the tank was devised and implemented.

My very last period in action in Dhofar was due to end just four days later on 28 March, so it appeared that my luck had come close to running out right at the end. I was nevertheless to have the last word in my personal battle by jet with the Adoo. On the very morning of my day of departure, in a combined air/sea attack by day with another 167, we bombed, rocketed and destroyed suspected anti-aircraft positions around a coastal Adoo stronghold halfway to the Yemeni border. I then took off alone from Salalah for the last time on a two-hour, direct, solo 167 flight to Bait al Falaj in the north of Oman. "For me the war was over".

By the time I returned to the north, my notional two years tour had been extended twice, by six weeks each time, as a result of the increasing tempo of operations in Dhofar. During the final eighteen months, I had found time for some serious soul-searching as to what I wanted to do next. Initially, I was hell-bent on leaving the RAF at my first option point of eight years' service. I really couldn't bear the thought of going back to the cold, damp UK that I'd remembered from my winter at the Hunter OCU in North Devon and which separated my two tours in warmer latitudes. Moreover, I reckoned that there was nothing the RAF could then offer me that would not be a considerable anti-climax after the recent years on fully operational flying. I had at first thought of pursuing an airline career and had been studying the Commercial Pilots Licence ground syllabus hard for some months in Oman. However, the reality began to dawn that it was much too early to take such a huge downshift away from adventurous flying, so I turned my attention elsewhere.

I had long yearned to take part in aircraft carrier operations, since it was with naval aircraft that my appetite for flying had been whetted straight after school. As earlier described, my first job had been as a scientific assistant in the Naval Air Department at RAE Bedford and at sea in Royal Navy and Indian Navy carriers. An earlier application for an exchange tour with the Royal Navy at the end of my Far Eastern Hunter tour had not been successful and, having just had a Loan Service Tour in Oman, would not have been even considered at this point. So, after weighing up various other options, I fired off an unsolicited application to join the Royal Australian Navy. Carrier flying, possibly an involvement in operations over Vietnam, and continuing to fly in warm climates would be a logical follow-on to what I had become accustomed. I waited a long time for a reply. Meanwhile I had, to my disgust, been 'non-volunteered' by the RAF for the Central Flying School (CFS) Qualified Flying Instructor (QFI) course at Little Rissington. At that time, I couldn't imagine anything more unsuitable for me than becoming *a teacher*!

By the time of the deadline for submitting my decision either to leave the RAF at the eight-years point or to stay in at least to the twelve-year point, a little maturity and a little more realism had begun to kick in. I was also carefully counselled by my excellent boss and good friend, Squadron Leader Alan Bridges (later Group Captain, but unfortunately no longer with us) that a QFI qualification would be a great asset in *any* future aviation role. Reluctantly I acquiesced, agreed to stay and the deadline for submitting my application to leave the RAF at eight years passed by. Two weeks later, after more than six months waiting, I received the most splendid letter from the Australian Naval Representative in their High Commission in London. They offered me a four years commission, probably flying the A4 Skyhawk! It was too late! I returned to the UK, did the CFS course, was posted to Valley where I met my wife and where I had the first of two superbly satisfying tours as an Advanced Flying Training School QFI, flight commander then, later, squadron commander (on Gnats, Hunters and Hawks). I remained in the RAF for a further fourteen years and *then* left for civil aviation!

Of my two years and three months as a loan service pilot with SOAF, I had spent a total of fifty-one weeks in the war zone of Dhofar and had accumulated nearly nine hundred hours on four very different aircraft types. I learned a great deal about flying in a most difficult and raw environment, not at all unlike that which had existed for an RAF pilot in the conditions and aircraft (when seen from the slow and rudimentary Provost) of the North-West Frontier of India during the 1930s. I was frequently in considerable danger and often had to use my skill and concentration to the very limits of my ability. It was a thoroughly exciting, and sometimes very frightening, experience. I learned far more about myself and my own strengths and weaknesses in that twenty-seven-month period than in the rest of my career put together. In fact, coming as it did quite early in my flying career, I believe it prepared me well — in hidden ways that I was only later to discover — for some subsequent, very challenging, flying assignments both in military and in civil aviation. My departure from Oman was accompanied by the significant honour of being awarded the Sultan's Commendation Medal.

In Dhofar, the war continued until the Declaration of Peace signed by Sultan Qaboos in December 1975, though mopping up operations continued for a further three months. By that time, SOAF had grown remarkably in size and capability from the nine pilots and nine aircraft that were there when I arrived in March 1968. Days before I left in June 1970, the first of eight Shorts Skyvans flew in and the first helicopter squadron commander had arrived to await his AB 206 Jetrangers and twenty (eventually) AB 205 Iroquois/'Hueys' (both types licence-built in Italy). The two Dakotas soon left and along came three DHC-4A Caribous. These new aircraft were joined in 1971 by the first of five Vickers Viscounts to do the Bait al Falaj — Salalah supply run and subsequent overseas flights. In 1974, the Beavers were supplemented by eight new Britten-Norman Defenders. In March 1975, King Hussein of Jordan made a gift to the Sultan of thirty-one (!) Hunter aircraft. They arrived over a two-month period and were soon put into operations in the closing months of the war. Today, the Royal Air Force of Oman (RAFO), as it was soon renamed under Sultan Qaboos, is a thoroughly modern force including Typhoon, F16 and Hawk fighters, five types of helicopters, Airbus A320 and C130 transport aircraft.

Sadly, in the early months after I left Oman, I was to learn regularly of the loss of a number of my friends and colleagues from my period in the country. I am considerably humbled by the fact that I survived for long enough — well into retirement — to put together this series of chapters that has given me so much pleasure. It is therefore perhaps appropriate for me to remember some of those who were not so fortunate. These included: Captain Eddie Vutirakis, a contract army officer and formerly of the SAS, who was treacherously murdered by one of his NCOs who defected to the Adoo; Flight Lieutenant Del Moore, a long-standing and greatly valued friend from SOAF and 20 Squadron in Singapore, killed in a crash whilst on a desert patrol in his Strikemaster; Flight Lieutenants Jack Wynne and 'Mac' Macdonald, former Dakota pilots who died together in action when their Caribou crashed in particularly tragic circumstances; Squadron Leader Roger Boyce, formerly RAF Station Commander at Salalah who returned later on contract to SOAF, who was shot down in his helicopter by a missile. Much later, in Northern Oman, Inspector John Milling, formerly a Royal Marines captain on loan to SAF, died in an unexplained helicopter crash. (This event featured in a novel, "The Feather Men", by 'Ran' Fiennes — Sir Ranulph Twisleton-Wykeham-Fiennes — the now famous explorer who was also a colleague in the team of Brits in SAF in the late 1960s).

HAVE NO FEAR — S O A Fs' HERE — !

The Jets Have Arrived!

167s On Alert With 32 Suras Each

10
ARCTIC FIGHTER SQUADRON — THE COLD FLANK OF THE COLD WAR

I suppose it was one of those life-defining moments. The squadron commander had asked me to pop down to his office for a few minutes and I was sat there wondering what it was about. I wasn't aware of anything particular that we needed to talk over. He usually left me well alone to get on with my job of running the flying programme as his deputy. There was nothing unusual happening with our current course of student Gnat pilots. I had a few months left as a QFI at RAF Valley and was looking forward greatly to my next posting. I was off soon to the Buccaneer OCU for a conversion course before joining one of the RAF's Buccaneer squadrons, the posting I had asked for. Earlier in the year, and with great difficulty, I had fought off a proposed ground job at HQ Training Command to help introduce the new Systems Approach to Flying Training. So it couldn't be postings that he wanted to talk about either — or could it be?

"Well," said the boss, "there's good news and bad news. Nothing's definite at this stage but which would you like first?" I was slightly mystified but always preferred to take any bad news first, so I said just that. "Roy," he replied, "There's a problem with your Buccaneer posting. The posters want you to consider an alternative." He looked at me, waiting for the inevitable reaction.

"B...r," I thought, reeling at this significant blow. Just when things were looking great for the future and I'd got my first choice of posting, now some ratbag's thrown a spanner into the works. Well, I had been flying continuously for nearly ten years after finishing my own training so it wasn't at all unusual to pick up a ground job at that stage. "B...r," I thought once more. Someone's clobbered me for that ground tour after all. Fearing the worst, I asked the obvious, "So, what's the alternative, Boss?"

"You've been provisionally selected for an exchange tour with the Royal Norwegian Air Force, on an F5 squadron based at Rygge in southern Norway," he replied. If anyone had been there watching, they'd have seen both of us break into wide grins — but I reckon mine would have been by far the wider. I knew two other pilots who had served earlier in that exchange slot in the RNoAF. It was a very good assignment and it was certainly unique and totally unexpected. Having previously enjoyed the tour as a loan service pilot in SOAF, I could not have imagined that I would get another opportunity to fly in a foreign air force. I needed only a second or two's thought before readily accepting the change. My luck was really in after all and I left the station that evening on a high to break the good news to my wife. We had been married for less than two years and she was thrilled at the news — she had wanted to visit Norway since seeing pictures of its landscape and learning about the country in her school geography lessons.

So it soon came that we set off by ship one day in early August, 1974, from Newcastle to Oslo, together with a few boxes of possessions, a new Saab 95 (duty free — thankfully) our golden retriever dog and a certificate from the Civil Service Commission to say that I had qualified to colloquial standard in the Norwegian language after a ten-week part-time course in London. After docking at Oslo, we drove straight down to our home for the next two years, a well-appointed wooden house near Rygge airfield, by the town of Moss about forty miles south of Oslo on the eastern side of the Oslo fjord. We would rent the house for the duration from the Norwegian pilot who was my opposite number and who was on exchange with a RAF Jaguar squadron. It was an excellent arrangement for both of us.

The RNoAF was equipped with single-seat Northrop F5A and RF-5G models and a small number of two-seat F5B trainers. As well as a helicopter squadron, the base at Rygge had two F5 squadrons: 717 with RF-5Gs in the reconnaissance role and 336 — which I was to join — with F5As in the fighter/ground attack and air defence role. Each squadron had a couple of twin-seat F5Bs for training. The primary role of 336 Squadron was ground attack. In its secondary air defence role, it augmented the Lockheed F104 air defence squadrons based in the north of the country. The dual role was very similar to that which I'd enjoyed on my first tour, flying 20 Squadron's Hunter FGA9s in the Far East. However, there were certainly some significant differences with which I would very soon get acquainted.

My first operational tour had been in the hot and sweaty tropics, flying over the jungles of the Far East where we faced low-intensity operations by Indonesian ground and air forces. After a short spell next as an instructor back at the Hunter OCU at Chivenor in North Devon, I had then spent a twenty-seven-month tour in the dust and exceptional heat (and very high humidity during the coastal monsoon season) of the Arabian desert with SOAF during the Dhofar War, flying armed Piston Provosts, Strikemasters, Beavers and Dakotas. So, the first major difference in Norway was that this was the north flank of the Cold War where the RNoAF, in which I had arrived for my brief and minor guest appearance, faced a very sophisticated potential enemy. If ever war were to come to NATO's northern flank, the massed hordes of Soviet forces in the Kola Peninsula would be the main threat to NATO's Northern Command, and to Norway itself. NATO defence policy in the north recognised the military threat as three-pronged: naval, air and ground. Firstly, in the event of a progressive transition to war between NATO and the Warsaw Pact, Soviet naval forces, operating out of Murmansk and into the North Atlantic via the Greenland-Iceland-UK gap, would pose a significant threat to interdict allied shipping not only in the Norwegian Sea but southwards into the north-east Atlantic and beyond. In fact, even in the uncertain peace of the time, a great amount of activity took place constantly in the 1970s, on the surface, under the sea and from the air, as each side did its best to track the whereabouts and monitor the capabilities of the other's maritime forces.

Secondly, the threat in the air came from the wide variety of Soviet air forces based in the Kola Peninsula. They could also interdict NATO naval forces but, in addition, were able to reach round as far as the UK itself with their long-range bombers equipped with conventional or nuclear weapons. Soviet aircraft in the 1970s frequently probed round the north of Norway and south towards the UK (see Note 1). They were invariably intercepted and inspected by NATO fighters, usually RNoAF F104s out of Bodø or Øerland and then RAF Phantoms (or, in earlier times, Lightnings) out of Leuchars. Thirdly, on the ground, there was the potential for Soviet troops and armour to attack and occupy strategic bases in Northern Norway either directly in the far north-east (where Norway shares a common border with Russia) or via the territories of Finland or Sweden. The likely routes were of course limited by the geography through the mountains as well as by the climatic conditions.

Although in Norway there were further conflict scenarios that acknowledged the possibility of Soviet attacks against southern Norway or in the Baltic, Norwegian defence planners had for some time given priority to preparations for defence against the more likely possibility of attacks in the north. Hence, the squadron that I was to join, though based in the south, had to train for the greater likelihood of being deployed to the north in the event of increasing East/West tension or actual attacks by the Soviet Union. So, a significant part of my flying with 336 Squadron was to be on ground attack and air defence exercises flown out of the far northern airfields of Bodø, Andøya, Bardufoss and Banak, all of them north of the Arctic Circle. So the coming tour, spent often in sub-zero temperatures and almost always over dramatic mountainous terrain and sometimes under a midnight sun or in midday dusk, would complete the climatic trilogy of my experiences to that date — with a number of startling contrasts.

But first, aside from the new potential enemy and the spectacular change of climate and scenery, there was much to do in learning the new aircraft whilst adjusting to the new environment. 718 Squadron at Sola, near Stavanger, carried out all conversion training courses for pilots new to the F5. So after only a few days at Rygge to unpack the boxes and meet some of my future colleagues, we drove off to Kjevik near Kristiansand, at the southernmost tip of Norway, for a one-week technical course and then on around the coast to Sola for my five-week conversion course to the Northrop F5 Freedom Fighter.

Over two thousand eight hundred F5s were built and they saw service with the air forces of more than twenty-two countries, including six NATO nations. The aircraft was quite different to anything else that I had flown up to that point. It was a very fast jet and capable of carrying a greater weight and wider range of armament than I'd seen before. The fundamental difference for me was that it was the first American-designed fighter aircraft that I had even sat in, let alone flown, apart from one earlier familiarisation flight in a RAF F4 Phantom, to qualify for my Mach 2 tee-shirt — still waiting for it, Mike! Although some minor aspects of the F5 were a little negative, most were very positive indeed. A few comments on the aircraft and its systems will reveal some of the main differences that I found in comparison with British-built aircraft (see Note 2).

As a tall pilot, I was very grateful for the extra space in the American cockpit. On the other hand I was rather disappointed with the US-standard safety equipment of that time, from the somewhat pedestrian ejection seat (minimum one hundred and twenty knots at ground level, and a requirement to detach/attach a lanyard manually above/below ten thousand feet to control the parachute delay time — not a patch on Martin-Baker's products) to the flimsy flying helmet and awkward oxygen mask. I never became truly comfortable with the helmet or the mask.

The F5's engines were a novelty in several ways. Apart from one hundred and twenty hours or so in SOAF's Dakotas, I'd flown only single-engined aircraft before arriving in Norway. The F5's twin engines were equipped with after-burners (ABs), a new feature for me and one which gave a rather satisfying, slap-in-the-back punch of acceleration when engaged for take-off or in flight. Unexpectedly, I learned that the ABs could also be used as a very welcome and highly effective hot-relight facility following engine flame-out, an event that I had suffered only in the simulator during my single-engine experience (up to that point anyway!). The technical rationale was that selection of afterburner also lit the igniters in the main combustion chambers. The method was known as a 'Tiger Start'. The Tiger Start came in quite handy for me on several occasions, particularly soon after joining the squadron one day during close echelon formation on my squadron commander when, not just one, but *both* engines flamed out. It was not unusual at low airspeed and high altitude that, if only a little yaw was applied, the long nose section forward of the intakes in the F5 could blank off or interrupt the airflow to an engine. Add a little bit of throttle cycling and a yaw reversal as I fought to stay in close formation at much too low a speed, then it was not too surprising that both engines flamed out. Nevertheless, the trusty Tiger Start had them both going again within seconds, though I wasn't very amused and couldn't quite forgive my leader for putting me in that situation. I think he was testing my mettle quite frankly. On the other hand, he was the boss and I was a guest so I didn't press the issue unduly on the ground after we'd landed. Whilst talking about the engines, I found it quite odd to discover that, although each had a fire-warning system, neither were fitted with fire extinguishers!

The RNoAF F5As had, uniquely for the type, been fitted with an arrester hook and could also be fitted with two or four 'assisted take-off' (ATO) rocket bottles. Both features were for use in short-field operations (e.g. from bomb-damaged runways), though it would be some time before I got to play with those goodies back at Rygge. Oddly again though, there were no anti-skid devices — surprising for fast aircraft that were operated on runways in winter conditions — and no handbrake! I remember once having to hold my feet on the brakes for a long while in a low-weight F5 on a down-sloping taxiway at Rygge whilst waiting for traffic ahead — my legs started to tremble with the prolonged muscle tension!

For me, the very best new features of the F5 were the increased performance and the greater range of armament. Though I had flown in dives at supersonic speeds on many occasions in the Gnat and Hunter, the F5 was supersonic in level flight. Its limiting speeds were seven hundred and ten knots IAS or M1.72 — pretty quick. At high altitude, level and in clean configuration, it could reach a very respectable M1.4. In the air defence (AD) configuration, with two AIM-7 Sidewinder missiles, it would still achieve over M1.2. Later on at Rygge, after flying for a year or more in the usual heavy and 'dirty' ground attack configuration, I had a rare flight in a very lightweight and clean configuration. Even at the abnormally steep nose-up angle that I had selected after take-off, I came within a gnat's nostril hair of going supersonic in the climb! I would not have been at all popular for breaking a pile of windows on the western side of the Oslo fjord had my concentration not just caught up in the nick of time with the extremely rapid acceleration.

The internal armament of the F5 consisted of two 20mm cannon. Though somewhat less impressive than the noise and vibration when firing four 30mm Aden cannon in the Hunter, the much higher rate of fire and nearly double the firing time in the F5 were significant benefits. Moreover, as already mentioned, we could also carry two Sidewinder missiles for air defence so there was something else quite new for me to learn within the procedures for acquiring targets and firing the missiles. In the ground attack (GA) role, the two cannons were augmented by a range of externally carried bombs up to seven hundred and fifty pounds individual weight, 2.75inch or five inch rockets in twin pods of nineteen or four each respectively and the Bullpup AGM12B, a manually guided, air-to-ground/anti-ship missile. The aircraft was also used in the air-to-air target-towing role, when it was fitted with a reel dispenser to tow either a hessian flag or with a dart target for air-to-air cannon firing practice. Lastly, it could carry a dispenser containing up to eight parachute flares for use in the night GA role. The wide range of AD and FGA ordnance and the inclusion of a night GA role, meant that a comparatively large proportion of routine training on the squadron would be taken up with armament practice, the most exciting and demanding part of any FGA pilot's work. It was looking good for the next two years!

My course at Sola was restricted to a basic conversion to the F5, including instrument flying practice to get me an instrument rating on type and basic AD combat manoeuvring training. The six weeks passed by smoothly and uneventfully for me, but rather less so one day for a Dutch F5 pilot who happened to be there for part of the time with a temporary detachment of aircraft from a Royal Netherlands Air Force squadron. I will tell the short story to illustrate a particularly significant and unique aspect of low flying in Norway.

One of the first things I had learned from the Norwegians when I started flying at Sola was Golden Rule number one. You should never, ever, fly below the level of the hilltops on either side of a valley (or fjord) unless you knew, absolutely positively, that there were no cables slung across the valley from one side to the other. Anyone who has visited western Norway on the ground (or on water) will know what I mean. To avoid lengthy diversions for road vehicles, roads are often carved directly through the mountains via numerous tunnels. Fjords or lakes are often crossed via bridges or ferries, Similarly, and to minimise both cost and power-drop, electricity supply lines need to take the shortest route too so they are strung frequently at right angles to the valleys, from one ridge-top to the next, often bridging great distances and so hanging down several hundred feet into the valleys. By contrast, the most tactical route (though not necessarily the shortest) for pilots in their DFGA flying machines, is of course along the valleys at low level where they can practise being shielded from enemy radar in order to achieve both radar and visual surprise. So, aeroplanes and power lines most certainly have a conflict in routing requirements as well as other characteristics and should very definitely not be mixed. All resident and all visiting aircrew were therefore very carefully briefed on Golden Rule number one before their first flight at low level in Norway and then frequently reminded of it. A trip on a boat up particular fjords to see the huge cables dangling down in their clusters could be enough to give nightmares to a low-level pilot for years.

There was one further small aspect of the cable danger which didn't often get mentioned. It was thought hardly necessary, if only the minimum of common sense was applied. Between some of the small, relatively flat coastal islands, cables were also slung across the narrow separating straits. Since the inter-island cables were usually at less than one hundred feet at their highest points, and the supporting pylons could be more easily seen, it would have seemed rather pedantic to make an issue of the matter to FGA pilots who were anyway not supposed to fly below two hundred and fifty feet agl. Well, one day, the errant flying Dutchman that I mentioned whizzed between two islands at less than one hundred feet in a tight turn, enjoying himself greatly until, with a loud bang and an almighty judder, he met the power cable at seventy feet or so. The cable was about two and a half inches diameter. He returned to Sola with a three to four feet length of it embedded diagonally across the intake of his left engine, that engine having coughed violently and stopped as a result of the sprung rivets and other bits and pieces being shoved rapidly down its gullet immediately after the collision. I saw the aircraft taxi in, decorated with its newly acquired cable, and so I was one of the first to meet the pilot after he climbed down out of the cockpit. I knew him from evening sessions in the bar as quite a jolly fellow. We looked together at the cable across the left intake. His manner when he eventually spoke was very, very subdued, but he was lucky to have temporarily lost only his jollity. Had he been flying just a few feet lower, the cable would have taken his head off — and he knew it.

The Norwegians reckoned that, since I was an experienced DFGA pilot, they could reasonably leave my initial weapons training on the F5 in the hands of 336 Squadron. That decision also had the great advantage of allowing my wife and I to drive back across the shorter, mountain route to Oslo and Rygge well before the winter snows arrived in the mountains. I hadn't yet acquired the studded tyres essential for winter driving in Norway! The F5 conversion course at Sola passed by quickly and we were soon on our way back via a night stop at the ski resort of Geilo where we vowed to return for our first New Year in Norway.

Arriving back at 336 Squadron, I learned that the squadron had only quite recently taken up air-to-air firing on the flag and dart targets. I had done quite a bit of this — firing at flags anyway — on 20 Squadron, so I was able to help quite a lot with the general principles whilst familiarising myself with the specific F5 techniques. So it was that the first weapons training that I enjoyed on the squadron was air-to-air firing over the Skaggerak Strait between Norway and Denmark and learning, for the first time, the role of a 'tug' pilot towing the flag and dart targets. The F5 was a very stable weapons platform and the young Norwegian pilots were as keen as mustard to do well in this new activity. The informal competition between all of us was fierce as we strove on each occasion to get as many shells as possible through the target, which was subsequently jettisoned over a grass area of the airfield for each pilot's hits to be tallied on the ground. As with RAF practice, each aircraft on a firing exercise had a dab of a specific colour paint applied to every shell tip which then left a colour trace on the flag or dart to distinguish each individual pilot's hits.

I moved on very soon to the first session of air-to-ground weapons firing on the range at Hjerkinn in central southern Norway. One of these early flights was distinguished by a memorable experience that served to spur me into improving my linguistic skills greatly. As usual, we were operating as a pair of aircraft. I was flying a two-seat F5B, with a weapons instructor in the seat behind me and the wingman accompanying us in a single seater. The weather in the range area was not too good and, flying the leading aircraft, I'd ducked and dived unsuccessfully several times with my number two in close formation before finally finding a small break through which we could split up and have a go at joining the range pattern for our weapons firing. After two or three attempts at getting around the pattern between the clouds, during which time my back-seater exchanged one or two high-speed bursts of chatter in Norwegian with the wingman, it looked hopeless, so I agreed with the instructor that we should abort and return to Rygge. I called the number two back into close formation but got no acknowledgement. Puzzled, and slightly worried, I queried this with the instructor who replied nonchalantly that he'd sent the wingman home a couple of minutes earlier! This would not do, I thought, and set about over the following months to get my Norwegian language skills rapidly up to a far better standard!

The pace of flying with 336 Squadron quickened once I had completed all my air to ground weapons training by the end of November 1974. I was improving my Norwegian language skills steadily too, under the excellent tutelage of the local RNoAF padre who had become a good friend, even though I was not a churchgoer. The next major phase in the squadron's annual training programme was night low-level navigation and night ground attack, in each of which we all on 336 Squadron had little or no experience.

The aim of developing a night attack capability within the RNoAF was to present Soviet planners with another problem, i.e. the fact that we could actually hit ground targets by night with a reasonable degree of success. It was an important capability in view of the very limited daylight hours that existed in winter, especially in the north. Possession and refinement of the option contributed to the overall aim of deterring the Soviet foe. However, we had no terrain-following radar, no night-vision goggles, no inertial navigation systems, no moving-map displays, nor anything else that might help us to fly and navigate at low level by night. We had only the same navigation aids as we used in daytime, i.e. a map and a stopwatch! So, it wasn't surprising that the minimum height for 'low-level' transits was set at one thousand feet agl. Wherever possible every part of the route followed long, wide fjords or flat terrain and each leg had to be planned in meticulous detail. Flying over snow-covered, relatively flat terrain under moonlight was almost like flying in daylight so it was easy to get down to only a few hundred feet. On the other hand, flying below a fully cloud-covered sky at night felt very scary at times. All one could see were the lights of the few towns, villages and road vehicles and I'm sure we all had great difficulty often in getting down even to one thousand feet! The lesser-experienced pilots on the squadron were not introduced to these joys until rather later on.

I had a small amount of previous experience in night close formation. Ten years earlier in the Far East I had done a little night close formation in the Hunters of 20 Squadron, where we developed a capability to carry out dawn or dusk formation attacks on distant targets by including a night transit to or from a target area, but with the attack phase only taking place in daylight. Later, in Oman, I had extended that experience a little more with some very limited night formation and ground attack operations in the Strikemasters as well as a few flights in the Beavers into desert strips with very minimum ground lighting, somewhat Lysander-like I suppose. This was enough to make me a little more comfortable with the night low-level and attack scenario than many of my colleagues. So again, it wasn't surprising that, after a few sorties launching bombs and rockets at targets on the air-to-ground range at Hjerkinn under the light of parachute flares dropped by another F5, I was quickly press-ganged into joining the small number of senior pilots nominated as night 'flare-ship' leaders. That brought the responsibility for leading three-aircraft formations at low level to the point a few minutes before the range, where the two attackers would split off on a longer 'dog-leg' route. The leader meanwhile would continue on to launch his flares at the correct displacement and height before and above the targets to allow the attackers time enough to acquire the targets visually and make their attack as the flares drifted in the wind to create the optimum lighting for the show. That was the theory at least, a tricky bit of airborne choreography under special lighting effects, a little like the pathfinders of World War II except that they dropped incendiaries directly onto the ground.

Now all of this, as you can imagine, had to be worked out very carefully in terms of headings, timings and wind corrections. Clearly, and particularly for the effect on the flight path of the slow-drifting flares after they'd left the aircraft, it was essential to have very accurate information on the wind at the release height and below. Since Hjerkinn was well inland and up-country, such wind information was sometimes considerably less accurate than desired. And so it came to pass one dark night that I drew the short straw when, having made all my calculations before flight, adjusted them as best as I could for in-flight observations of drift and released my first batch of flares in what I believed to be the right place and at the right time, I was aghast to see them eventually drift well away from the target area and even outside the range area! My two attack colleagues were unable to fire their rockets at a target they couldn't see and, much worse, as I was to learn later, the flares managed to drift down into the power lines supplying a nearby cement factory! Somehow, they caused a power failure which shut down the factory and some surrounding habitations for several days. I felt very guilty but the calculations were re-checked on the ground and found to be correct. Inaccurate wind information was blamed and I was thankfully exonerated, thus avoiding a diplomatic incident!

As the winter of 1974–75 came upon us, my wife and I made our plans for our first Christmas at Rygge and the coming New Year break skiing at Geilo. Just before leaving for Geilo, I received the very happy news that I was to be promoted to Squadron Leader on 1 January 1975, so we had two causes for celebration! A Christmas tree was cut fresh locally and set up in our house and we enjoyed a great Christmastime with some of our new Norwegian friends before driving up to Geilo for another conversion course, this time onto the very narrow Nordic skis used for cross-country work and on which you can and do ski frequently uphill! In fact, I soon found that, unlike my own downhill slalom skis that I knew quite well, these slimline skis could be very tricky when used downhill! Fortunately, the brief experience on the ankle-wobblers at Geilo was followed later in the January by another cross-country skiing session. The second session, on which my wife was also able to accompany me, was at the RNoAF's own Winter Survival School at Vesleskaugum, not to be confused with the NATO Winter Survival Course at Spåtind — more of that one later. At Vesleskaugum, we skied on the wider, military, cross-country skis and were taught how to get along on these with rather more success.

You can imagine that winter survival training was something we pilots in Norway all took very seriously. I had already enjoyed the benefit of some winter survival training in the RAF, not least at the RAF Germany Winter Survival School at Bad Kohlgrub in Bavaria, but there was more to learn from the Norwegians who were of course well-seasoned at living outside in winter conditions. Many had cabins up in the mountains that they used year-round. Although the RNoAF had a very capable helicopter rescue service, the chances of having to survive outdoors for at least a few hours, or perhaps overnight, should one have to eject up-country, were quite high. Norway is sparsely populated, mostly quite mountainous and of course the top bit extends well beyond the Arctic Circle. (Curiously, the eastern-most part of the north of Norway lies on a longitude further east than Istanbul. "Not a lot of people know that" (as Michael Caine used to say). Then again, why on earth should they? I just thought in passing that you might like to know. There are a number of mountain and glacier areas in Norway that remain snow-covered year-round and in the winter most of the country is snow-covered for weeks or months at a time.

Although on the course at Vesleskaugum we spent most nights in a warm and well-insulated log cabin, we each had to dig the obligatory snow cave and sleep in it once overnight. At Spåtind, we also spent the obligatory night in a self-dug snow cave but the rest of the nights were in the luxury mountain hotel to which we took our DJs and full mess kit to wear for the dancing and drinking with our aircrew colleagues from many NATO air forces. Well, perhaps I should qualify that last statement. I should make it clear that I didn't actually dance with any of my NATO colleagues. Whereas I was alone, most of the RNoAF pilots took their wives or girlfriends along so, together with other hotel guests, there was no shortage of attractive female partners. After discovering that same fact following my first session at Spåtind, and when I volunteered to return the following year in a 'liaison' capacity rather than as a student, my wife decided she'd better come along to chaperone me as well as to swell the throng of female dancing partners. We both enjoyed ourselves immensely on that occasion when we also saw, for the only time during our stay in Norway, the Aurora Borealis. I must confess that, having drifted into Scandinavian drinking habits by that second winter, I had already been experiencing dramatic visual effects that evening and well before being called outside the hotel to watch the real thing in the dark northern skies. Nevertheless, the Aurora could still be discerned as the more impressive of the two experiences.

In February of 1975 I flew north with the squadron to Bodø, crossing the Arctic Circle for my first detachment to north Norway which lasted two weeks. We flew many low-level navigation exercises in pairs and fours of aircraft, each normally ending in a co-ordinated, formation, simulated attack on a target in the north Norwegian landscape. Sometimes the attacks were carried out in co-operation with the Norwegian army who, after we had navigated to a pre-planned pull-up point, guided us by radio on to simulated targets using forward air control techniques and ad hoc visual reference points, flares or other signalling aids, all much the same as were used in the RAF and in Oman. The backdrop for most of this flying was simply spectacular. I particularly remember flying at low level over the sea to the north-west of Bodø one early day, heading northwards, when I saw for the very first time the chain of tall Lofoten Islands in their dazzling white winter coats. They seemed from a distance like a line of huge and ragged portions of ice cream sticking up above the water. The mountainous islands of Lofoten and those inland in the north are generally much more rugged and sharply scarped than in the south. However, when cloud is about, the hard 'ice creams' or any other mountain tops can merge wickedly together with the cloud to create, sometimes very swiftly, the lethal conditions of 'whiteout' rightly feared by fliers and skiers alike.

Whilst flying out of Sola on my conversion course, I had been introduced at an early stage and in dramatic fashion to 'white-out' when flying one day towards the Jostedal glacier in western Norway. A sudden change of lighting or angle from the glacier caused all visual reference to be lost quite suddenly, prompting a swift pull up from low level to a safe altitude to avoid the cloud that might have a hard centre. This was of course standard practice for an FGA pilot though sadly, over the years, I lost numerous pilot friends and acquaintances who failed to pull up early enough, or vigorously enough, in response to a sudden loss of visual reference at low level. The history of civil aviation is also marked with such tragic events, most relevantly the 1979 Mount Erebus accident in Antarctica when all two hundred and fifty-seven people on board an Air New Zealand DC10 sightseeing flight were killed when the aircraft flew into the mountain in what were believed to be 'white-out' conditions. When the news of that accident broke, I distinctly recall shuddering at the memory of my own first experience of a dramatically sudden 'white-out', five years previously in Norway.

During the remainder of my tour, I spent several, more lengthy detachments in the north. There was Åndøya ('Duck Island') near… (well, near nowhere really, except its local town of Åndenes), where I had the somewhat quirky experience of flying through a snowstorm in the middle of summer, at midnight — in broad daylight! Bardufoss was another, some forty nautical miles south of Tromsø and where the approach to the airfield was along a valley flanked by high mountains, adding a significant extra impetus to ensure very accurate instrument flying during a departure or approach in cloud. Not far to the east of Bardufoss, an imaginary north/south line ran across the country and extended well out over the Norwegian Sea. Above that line, an invisible wall marked the easternmost limit beyond which non-Norwegian military aircraft were not allowed to fly in peacetime. That was a sensible precaution to avoid a diplomatic incident should any other NATO country's aircraft get too close and awaken the Russian Bear. It was a bit of a grey area as to whether the rule should also apply to non-Norwegian pilots per se, even if they were flying RNoAF aircraft. However, since there was only ever one Brit and, in my day, one Canadian at a time on exchange with the RNoAF, a blind eye had customarily been turned towards me and my predecessors going beyond the invisible wall.

That remained so until I unwittingly drew attention to myself one fine day after firing on an air-to-ground range to the east of Banak, another detachment airfield in the north which itself lay well east of 'the wall', so the firing range was yet further east. By that time, at least when flying that far beyond 'the wall', I was particularly careful to speak only in Norwegian over the radio. On this particular day, I'd had some difficulty with the broad accent of the RNoAF range safety officer when he was passing me my scores and so I lapsed into English as I knew he would be better at that than I was at Norwegian. Unfortunately, up to that point, he hadn't realised that an Anglo-Saxon had been loose in the area for a week or more so chose to put in a report to the RNoAF HQ in Oslo. Nothing personal I think — just covering his backside, I guess. Fortunately, the station commander at Rygge, a Norwegian Air Force brigadier who had been directed by HQ to explain why I was there and to ensure that I shouldn't be there in future, chose to put up a vigorous and successful defence on my behalf. He stated that, as a NATO pilot on a Norwegian squadron, I would be obliged just as much as my Viking colleagues to fight Ivan up north as effectively as they themselves would, if it ever came to the crunch, and so I needed to know my way around the likely battle areas just as well as my fellow pilots. Another potential diplomatic incident had been avoided but I, like all of us, had to be very careful with the navigation and, in my case, the tongue.

In all, I spent more than three months of my tour in Norway flying far up north at low level in the arctic winter, enjoying the scenery and the highly varied flying. I enjoyed also the memorable experience on several occasions of witnessing a peculiar arctic meteorological phenomenon known as arctic mist. This occurs when very cold air drifts over slightly warmer lakes and fjords. In calm conditions, moisture from the water surface is drawn upwards in gentle thermals and condenses immediately in the cold air. The total effect, on a crystal-clear day with a very low sun, is to make it look as if the water is giving off multiple, wispy, plumes of steam, ten or twenty feet high, and is really quite spectacular if come upon suddenly after turning around a mountain at two hundred and fifty feet agl and four hundred knots or more.

Down south, there was also much of interest to do and see. We had a minor anti-shipping role and, for the first time, I enjoyed the experience of firing guns and rockets at 'splash targets' towed by Norwegian Navy ships in the Skaggerak, as well as carrying out simulated attacks on the warships themselves there and in the Oslo fjord off Rygge. There were frequent short visits and exercises in our F5s to other NATO airfields, especially in Denmark and Germany and twice to my previous RAF station at Valley for the annual air show. I flew with about half the squadron down to Bavaria for a most enjoyable ten days in May 1975 on exchange with one of the resident F104 squadrons at the German Air Force base of Memingen, where we flew with the 104s in mixed formations. Even neighbouring Sweden, not part of NATO but where we had an emergency diversion facility from Rygge to the Swedish airbase further south at Såtenes, allowed us to make very occasional visits to practise the diversion and to have a look at their Saab Viggens close up. Mind you, the Swedes were awfully coy about letting us see too much. They covered up several instrument displays in the Viggen simulator when I cadged a ride in it.

June of 1975 saw 336 Squadron, together with its sister F5 Squadron at Rygge, tasked with mounting a flypast in commemoration of a famous Norwegian polar explorer, aviation pioneer and founder of the RNoAF (see Note 3) who had died ten years previously in 1965. The plot was to fly across Rygge in a formation that spelled out the distinguished officer's initials. The slight problem was that the deceased gentleman's name was Hjalmar Riiser-Larsen, so that meant we had to form the letters H, R, L, one behind the other. This was not an easy task and we practised first with fifteen aircraft, then twenty-four, before finally settling for eighteen on the third practice as well as on the actual day of the commemoration. I have always enjoyed the rare thrill of taking part in big formations. On these occasions I flew as number five, thirteen and eight respectively and the final result was apparently quite acceptable to the cognoscenti on the ground. At least we avoided any comments like 'broken chair' formations and suchlike that circulated after one of the early practices with inadequate numbers.

In September of 1975, I obtained permission from the squadron to take a pair of F5s to Iceland, another NATO country that was within our range from Rygge via a refuelling stop at RAF Lossiemouth in Scotland. I had never visited Iceland before and was intrigued by what I had read about its unique landscape. With a little effort through the RNoAF HQ in Oslo, I was also able to secure permission for a low-level navigation exercise to have a squint at the scenery within Iceland on the day after our arrival at the USAF base at Keflavik where we were to stay overnight. Leading the pair from Rygge, I set off for Lossie where I decided to wait overnight because the weather forecast at Keflavik was atrocious. The next day, despite little improvement in the conditions, we set off across the sea at high level towards Iceland, eventually landing at Keflavik in pouring rain below a five hundred- feet cloud base. It was so wet that, after engine shutdown, our American hosts kindly towed us into a hangar before we dismounted from our aircraft. Regrettably, the weather was exactly the same the next day, so we had to bin the low-level trip, climb into our aircraft in the hangar once more and set off into cloud a few seconds after take-off in the rain towards Lossie. Well, at least the Icelanders hadn't twigged that there was a Brit in their midst. It was during the 'Cod War' of the 1970s and I wasn't really sure that they would have welcomed me, had I met anyone apart from the resident Yanks at Keflavik. I didn't see much of Iceland until many years later when ferrying ATPs and 146s across the North Atlantic to and from the Caribbean and the Americas, when we used Keflavik and Reykjavik as stopovers.

The final event of great note during my two years guest appearance in the RNoAF was undoubtedly the hard and closely fought squadron air-to-air firing competition in the glorious summer of 1976, just before my departure for the UK. The two-week official competition would see a winner presented for the first time with a very nice silver trophy that had been originally donated to the squadron by my Brit predecessor on his return to the UK two years previously. I naturally thought it was fitting that I should win the trophy and take it back to the UK from whence it had come, if only for the excuse of being able to return and present it to the next winner in Norway at some date in the future! As mentioned earlier, we did our own target towing. It seemed incredibly ironic then that, on the last firing session of the competition, in which I had led the field for some time and had completed my own final shoot but now had only a very narrow margin ahead of the second pilot in the ranking, that I was to tow for my challenger. The tension was enormous as I sat there in my tug aircraft, with the challenger pressing every single attack right down to the absolute minimum range and minimum offset angle to put as many of his shells through the flag as he could. I honestly heard some of the shells going past and that was not on but, in the circumstances, I could hardly complain let alone disqualify the pilot as a tug pilot was empowered and ought to do. As it turned out, he put in a superb score and just beat me to the trophy.

In the closing months of my Nordic adventure, I received a call from the British Air Attaché in Oslo who had the details of my next posting. I was to return to RAF Valley as the deputy chief instructor before taking up command of one of the training squadrons there. I was not best pleased at having to go back into the training world after my operational flying in Norway. I rather hoped that I could pick up where I had left off and go to the Buccaneer. In the event, before I got to Valley, my posting changed to taking over as the OC of the training standards squadron where I was to fly the Gnat, Hawk and Hunter concurrently over a superbly enjoyable and fantastically busy period when the Hawk entered RAF service.

Some time after returning to the UK, we saw Norway and many of our friends there twice more. We took a long holiday from RAF Valley with car and trailer tent in the summer of 1978, when we drove right up to the very top of the country at Hammarfest. In 1984, we were invited back for the thirty-fifth anniversary of 336 Squadron. By this time, one of my good friends from earlier days had taken over as the squadron commander and kindly, and most surprisingly, he arranged VIP treatment for us. We were picked up from Oslo airport and flown down to Rygge by helicopter, to my wife's absolute delight as she'd never been in a chopper before. We were given an airborne tour of the area in which she'd spent her earlier time riding horses whilst I had been zipping around the wider, and wilder, countryside at four hundred and fifty knots and two hundred and fifty feet. After the weekend's festivities, including displays by F16s which by then were replacing the F5s, we were duly helicoptered back up to Oslo for our return flight to the UK. We treasure these and many other happy memories of our time and of the friendships we made when we were the only Brits amongst the Norwegians for two years on an arctic fighter squadron.

Notes:

1. During my tour as an instructor at RAF Valley, we sometimes took part in air defence exercises against RAF bases in Scotland. Our Folland Gnat trainers operated in pairs with Vulcan bombers that simulated Soviet Badgers. The tiny Gnats simulated the Kelt missiles carried by the Badgers and we were 'launched', singly or in pairs from close formation on the Vulcans, against airfield and other targets. We then followed the Kelt missile profile down to low level. There it became a 'licence to wire' (i.e. beat-up) airfields. We could just about achieve five hundred and forty knots at low level (in theory not below two hundred and fifty feet agl), with the slim control column at the forward limit of its range and the aircraft reacting extremely twitchily to the slightest roll or pitch input. This was a refreshing break to the daily work of a QFI and much enjoyed by all of us.

2. I compared the F5 not just with the Gnat and Hunter of my main experience but also to others in which I had occasionally flown, e.g. the Meteor, Sea Vixen, Buccaneer, Gannet, Vampire, Javelin and Canberra, and one aircraft for which I found that I was simply too big — and so was regrettably never able to fly in it — the Lightning

3. The RNoAF was formed in 1944, from the Combined Arms Air Force which in turn had evolved from the earlier Naval Air Force. Larsen was instrumental in developing those air forces.

F-5 in winter

Box of F-5s

Author with F5 and in US flight equipment + Norwegian
hairstyle

11
GNAT FORCED LANDING

Monday, 19 September 1977, at No 4 Flying Training School, RAF Valley, on the island of Anglesey, began in much the same way as any other day at the time. The busy training station was in the process of changing over from the Gnat and the Hunter to the Hawk — the RAF's new advanced jet trainer. I had completed my first sortie of the day, a practice instrument rating test in a shiny new Hawk T.1 for the benefit of one of the qualified flying instructors (QFIs) who, along with many others that year, was in the process of converting to the aircraft for the first time. I was very lucky to have the job of officer commanding the Standards Squadron (OC Stds). My responsibilities called for me to fly all three types concurrently, a fantastic privilege, albeit a very demanding one. The second trip of the day was in a Gnat and was to be a routine, instructional standards check, for another QFI, Flight Lieutenant Mike Hulyer, a former helicopter pilot. Like each one of the small number of helicopter pilots, who had become Gnat instructors, Mike was a very competent operator. His check was to be flown as a close formation exercise in company with another Gnat flown solo by Flight Lieutenant Bill Cope, another fine pilot who, as a group captain, went on to become the Buccaneer force commander during the first Gulf War.

My role was to fly as captain in the front seat of XP 540 whilst Mike in the rear seat practised his 'patter' on me as if I was a student pilot learning close formation in the Gnat for the first time. By then I had spent some four years as an instructor on the Gnat, as well as receiving my own training on it, way back in the early '60s. I enjoyed the aircraft greatly. It was an absolute pleasure to fly, especially in close formation. Even though there wasn't a spare inch in the cockpit after I had strapped in my six-foot-three-inch-frame, I felt very comfortable in it — especially in the front seat with its superb view. With two very reliable other QFIs as my companions, the trip promised to be straightforward, easy and fun. But, the fickle finger of fate was to intervene rather rudely. Unbeknown to any of us, XP 540 was going to have a bad day.

As formation leader, Bill briefed the exercise and I merely needed to add a few short points to meet my requirements as the checking pilot. We were soon airborne from runway 14 at Valley and climbing swiftly to the south east. The sortie proceeded absolutely normally over the northern half of Wales for the first twenty-five to thirty minutes. Mike's patter was just fine and I had the pleasure as 'the student' of doing most of the flying after his initial demonstrations. With such a responsive and agile aircraft to fly, I could not fail to get a thrill out of it on every flight but especially during formation aerobatics. We had completed our required manoeuvres in the close 'echelon' positions, including loops, barrel rolls, tight turns, 'emergency' breakaways and rejoins and had just changed to close line astern on the lead aircraft. Mike was now flying the aircraft as we climbed close behind Bill's Gnat to regain some altitude before starting the next phase in the sequence of exercises. We were in clear conditions at about eighteen thousand feet with blue sky above and full cloud cover way below us. Our two-aircraft formation was in a turn to the right, passing a northerly heading about eight nautical miles east of RAE Llanbedr, the MoD target facilities airfield on the coast near Harlech that we occasionally used for circuit training. I was very relaxed and was enjoying the view of the lead aircraft only a few feet ahead and above us as I waited for Mike to restart his 'patter'.

Suddenly and unexpectedly, I felt a marked deceleration and decreasing engine noise. We dropped rapidly back out of the formation position. My first thought was that Mike had throttled back to clear formation for some reason. A fraction of a second before that, Mike had noticed an AC/DC warning caption (indicating an alternator failure) but, as he had control of the throttle lever, he was the first to realise a second later that the engine had actually quit. He called me on the intercom to say that we had flamed out. Simultaneously, Mike closed the throttle and I instinctively hit the engine 'hot relight' button. Mike then called that he was trying a hot relight, so I left him to it, switched on the standby radio and made a brief 'Mayday' call on 243.0 MHz to say that we had flamed out and were heading for Valley. The call was picked up by Bill, who was monitoring the emergency frequency (standard procedure in formation flight) as were various others. One of these was my deputy, Flight Lieutenant Pete Webb, who was sitting quietly in the 'local' control room in the Valley ATC tower as the duty instructor. Pete told me later that he listened to a very calm Mayday call (I was glad he thought that, because my mind was racing too fast to even think of trying to sound calm). It took a few seconds before he realised from the call-sign that it was me. "S**t" he said to himself. "It's the boss!" He immediately began his own procedures on the ground which included informing the OC Flying, the station commander and so on.

Meanwhile, back in XP 540, 'the boss' had taken control as the unsuccessful hot relight attempt ended after the allotted ten seconds. I turned in a gentle zoom gaining altitude on a north-west heading and began decelerating to the gliding speed of one hundred and eighty knots. Simultaneously, Mike and I noticed that the engine revolutions (RPM) gauge was registering zero. Now this was very odd and not in accord with what should have been. Both of us had firmly believed that the engine had flamed out, rather than seized, since there had been absolutely no engine vibration and the engine had run down in the same way as an engine starved of fuel or flame. We had practised enough with engine failures in the simulator to know the difference. In a flame-out condition, the engine would 'wind-mill' — i.e. it would turn over at low RPM in response to the airflow through the engine intake. In a mechanical failure leading to a seizure, there would normally be vibration and the RPM would be at zero, or near zero. Our reasoning, and the initial actions, had taken place only in a very short span of about fifteen to twenty seconds from the first symptom, so we now began to take in the conflicting evidence and to try to fathom out what was going on.

The next event, within a few seconds, was a HYD (hydraulics low pressure) warning, which appeared to confirm that we had indeed suffered an engine seizure. If the engine had simply flamed-out and was wind-milling, it would be expected also that the idling hydraulic pump would maintain enough pressure to provide power to the tail plane. We now had a more serious condition to confront since, not only did we have a dead engine, we had no flaps available for landing and we would also have to revert to manual control (for ailerons and elevators), using electrical movement of the tail plane, backed up by the small elevators, for pitch control. At this point, I should digress to explain briefly how the three pitch control modes worked in the Gnat.

In normal operation, the elevators were mechanically locked to the tail plane so that movement of the control stick moved the whole assembly hydraulically as a slab. An electrical 'feel trim' was used for pitch trim. In the second mode, the elevators could be unlocked from the tail plane (via a lever in either cockpit) so that they would move directly in response to stick movement, with the hydraulically powered tail plane 'following up'. This second mode was much more sensitive and so the aircraft could be flown without the need for pitch trim due to the very light control forces. Use of this mode conserved electrical power, for example after an alternator failure or flameout. The third mode was manual, where the stick moved only the small elevators, but in order to maintain full control over the aircraft (especially for landing) the tail plane had to be moved electrically (via a standby trim motor using standby trim switches). In manual, primary pitch control was therefore achieved by motoring the tail plane electrically, though slowly, and the stick-controlled elevators were used only for 'fine tuning'.

In the 1960s, the complexities of the pitch control system, including the three pitch modes, two trimming systems, a 'scissors' restrictor, q-gearing and a variable cam, had been highlighted in a number of accidents involving pitch-control problems. Indeed, only instructors were allowed to attempt an actual forced landing in manual and even they, for a period, had only been allowed to practise them to the point of a go-around. Student pilots had to eject if they found themselves with both an engine failure and hydraulic failure. A fairly fool proof drill for entering manual control had been devised — with the acronym 'STUPRECC' — and this had been drummed into the memories of all Gnat pilots until it was instinctive. I can still remember it accurately, some forty-two years and nearly a dozen different types after my last Gnat flight!

So, the HYD warning immediately sparked me off into the **STUPRECC** memory drill:

Speed — below four hundred knots/0.85M

Trim — to the 'ideal' sector

Unlock the elevators (checking two 'clicks', white band and ELEV caption on)

Power (hydraulic) cock off

Raise the guard on the standby trim switches

Exhaust the (hydraulic) accumulators (tail plane first, ensuring small movements so that it 'froze' at the correct angle of one to two degrees appropriate to our 'clean' configuration, then ailerons)

Check operation of the elevators, ailerons and standby trim

Changeover switches to standby

Halfway through the drill I interrupted it to switch off the fuel booster pump and low pressure fuel cock, the high pressure cock having been correctly closed at the end of the relight attempt, an attempt that I was now regretting since that was an incorrect and potentially hazardous response to what by now appeared to be a seizure. Though we hadn't suspected a seizure at the outset.

The memory drills for flame-out and seizure are different in many aspects and we had been obliged to start with the one and switch to the other, so I asked Mike to get his flight reference cards out to make sure that we had completed everything necessary under both drills. We had. Somewhere in the middle of all the action, the emergency centre at West Drayton had answered my call with a triangulated position some five miles to the north of Llanbedr, *which had just shut for the day (!)*, though Drayton were trying to contact them to re-open. I could now turn more of my attention to weighing up the two possible options for landing, limited as they were. Not that I had much time for that as I was also aware that, in the absence of the alternator, the battery was advertised as only lasting for twenty minutes — assuming that it was in good shape to begin with!

We had reduced to the gliding speed of one hundred and eighty knots and had drifted back down to the original eighteen thousand feet. Valley was still about thirty to thirty-two miles away, with a bit of a headwind at medium altitude and a strong crosswind (eighteen knots — the limit being twenty knots) on the only runway that we might stand any chance of reaching. With its very narrow wheel-track and a high-set and highly swept wing, the Gnat was a bit of a handful in a crosswind, more so in manual. The gliding range even to Valley, about one and a half to two nautical miles/per thousand feet in still air, would give us little or no margin for error. On the plus side, there was the fact that the airfield at Mona might provide a last-minute option if we couldn't make Valley, but it would prove a late and cumbersome switch onto a much shorter runway and with a significant tailwind! On the other hand, Llanbedr was not only closed but completely obscured under cloud. The only ground feature anywhere in view was a tiny area on the coast near Pwllheli that was of no use to us at all. Llanbedr was also less familiar and had only one runway direction, 18, that was equipped with a jet barrier to stop us if needed. As I wrestled mentally with the options, Mike told me unequivocally that he thought we'd never make it to Valley. He was probably right but, before we could enter further debate, Drayton mercifully told us that Llanbedr were re-opening so it was there that I decided to go. I wasn't able subsequently to find out who it was that decided to pick up the telephone that day as he was leaving the closed ATC tower, but it's possible he might have saved my life and certainly helped save the aircraft.

With plenty of height in hand now, I flew one orbit overhead Llanbedr in the hope of finding even a tiny break in the cloud cover, but there was none. Terrain rises up to two thousand, five hundred feet a few miles east of the airfield, so all initial instrument approaches at Llanbedr were made from over the sea to the west. With that in mind, and to enable full advantage to be made of the excellent radar facilities at the airfield, a special instrument forced landing procedure had been developed many years earlier. The procedure involved flying from overhead then out over the sea to the west before turning back in under ATC direction to make a 'low-key' position at three thousand feet abeam the downwind end of the runway in use, 18. I hadn't had the opportunity to practise that particular procedure in a long time but, in my job as OC Stds, I was well-practised in visual and other instrument forced landing procedures as well as in manual flying techniques. So I was happy enough to set off initially on the westerly heading from about eleven thousand feet overhead the airfield under ATC direction, still above cloud. Nevertheless, despite the adequate altitude, it seemed a bit unnerving with a dead engine to be heading away from where I planned to land! Around that stage, I had to be a bit rude to a Jet Provost pilot who had come up on the emergency frequency with a lengthy Practice Pan call having failed first to listen out for a while to ensure that there was no actual emergency in progress. Well there sure was, and it took me less than five words to tell him so.

As well as being in manual control, which made the aircraft quite heavy and sluggish to handle, I was also having to fly on the smaller and less accurate standby instruments, the main instruments having failed and 'frozen' at their last reading when the alternator came off line. This was normal for our situation and, to cater for it, all Gnat pilots carried a couple of easily detachable sticky patches, usually on the sides of their flying helmets, from where they could be whipped off and stuck over the otherwise misleading and distracting main attitude and direction indicators. However, we had as yet not had an opportunity to set up the standby direction indicator accurately on a steady heading from the wobbly E2B standby compass, so I warned Llanbedr that our headings were not likely to be very accurate. We were given a correction onto heading two hundred and forty degrees.

It took a long time to get the actual Llanbedr weather. They had after all only just re-opened so that was understandable. Eventually, as we reached about eight thousand feet, we were told there was a cloud base of three thousand five hundred feet over the airfield, which would not give us much margin over the normal three thousand feet low-key, especially if there were any deviations from the ideal three-dimensional pattern. At that point, at around eight thousand feet, still above cloud and about four to five nautical miles out to sea, heading away from the airfield, I felt very uneasy about the total picture that was developing and so I decided to bin the procedure, turn back there and then towards the airfield, dive off the height through the cloud and gain speed to give me as much aircraft energy as I could get for visual positioning once we broke cloud. Llanbedr gave me an inbound heading and I turned onto it.

Meanwhile, apart from checking in briefly on the emergency frequency, Bill in the other aircraft had wisely avoided getting involved in the radio chatter as there was little or nothing he could do to help up to that point. I caught a glimpse of him about two hundred yards away over my right shoulder just before we entered cloud at around five thousand feet, when he chirped up on the radio with perfect timing and gave us an accurate fifteen degrees heading correction to the airfield. I could spare him no time, and barely any thought, and not even a quick glance once we were in cloud, but I trusted his judgment implicitly and so left him to it entirely. However, I knew that he had to be flying as close as possible to me to maintain visual contact in the murk and so I tried to keep my aircraft control as smooth as I could, not easy in manual. With no thrust from my dead engine, I must have presented a very difficult reference on which to fly in close formation. He said later that it was indeed quite a handful because we were 'dropping like a stone' at the higher speed. That was the first and last time that I ever had the strange experience of being a formation leader without an engine!

Now we soon had a big problem looming. At three thousand feet, we were still in cloud with no light from below and, at my higher speed of 300kts, closing rapidly on the airfield at a mile every twelve seconds. I had to think seriously of zooming for ejection because we were getting rapidly short of height for a successful forced landing pattern. Moreover, I couldn't know the precise terrain structure beyond the airfield — only that there were spot heights up to two thousand, five hundred feet at several miles or so to the east. I was also becoming steadily more conscious of a very unwelcome worry as to whether I would make it out of the aircraft in one piece if I had to eject. I had a fear that I might be very close to being too big for a safe ejection. This was a pretty late and stupid time to be thinking about it but I guess it was something to which I had turned a blind eye during the previous years. I should have had myself winched out on the ground, years before, to check the physical clearance but I hadn't wanted to do so in case it brought my Gnat flying to a premature end — very silly, but true. I fought to keep the thought out of my mind but it certainly gave me an increased determination to get the aircraft safely onto the runway.

Very suddenly, we broke cloud at two thousand, eight hundred feet, with a speed of two hundred and eighty knots and with about three nautical miles to go to the airfield, clearly in sight to the north-east of us. I wanted to go for runway 18 the only one with a jet barrier (safety net) at the far end, in case I landed too far in and couldn't stop before the runway end. For the second time that day, Mike chipped in to say, "you'll never make it!" Again, I thought he was probably right, but I decided to stick with my plot a bit longer before finally throwing away the barrier option. But it soon became clear that it was not a certainty that I could reach even the minimum recommended low key of two thousand five hundred feet for runway 18, whereas runway 36 was a certainty, albeit without the barrier. So I manoeuvred hard right into position for 36 whilst reducing speed to one hundred and seventy knots to get the wheels down using the standby air system, the next very important priority. The good book said that this may take up to three thousand feet of descent and I had to fly below that to maintain my view of the airfield. The book wasn't far wrong — but fortunately the error that day was in my favour. I selected wheels down as soon as I could and motored the tail plane by the necessary three degrees nose-up to counter the large forward centre of gravity change. Then there was an agonisingly long wait for the gear to lock down during my final manoeuvring to get lined up with the runway at the right height/range ratio. By now I had begun to notice what felt like a metal band tightening around my chest. The stress was reaching a peak. We finally got the third green light (indicating all three wheels locked down) descending rapidly through five hundred feet, about half a nautical mile before the runway threshold. Only then did I feel that we had got to the point where we would not need to eject. Up to then, I had even been half expecting to hear a bang from the back to indicate that Mike had decided independently that a parachute descent was the better option!

From the good position that I had managed to achieve on finals, it was then fairly easy — starting the level-off for landing at about two hundred and fifty feet — to achieve a nice smooth, flapless touchdown at the recommended one hundred and sixty-five knots, just in from the painted threshold bars. But our troubles were not quite over. Once the speed had reduced below one hundred and sixty knots, the upper speed limit for streaming the braking parachute in the tail, I called Mike to stream it. He pulled the operating lever but no deceleration was felt. I gave my lever a tug too, for good measure, but it made no difference. Meanwhile, Bill had continued to fly beside us at a few hundred feet above the runway and was calling repeatedly for us to, "Stream the 'chute! Stream the 'chute!" I replied rather dryly that we had done so several times. I guess Bill was beginning to let out a bit of his pent-up adrenalin. Mike and I had to wait a little longer for that. The brake 'chute had indeed deployed from its container but it had 'candled' — failed to open — as it often did. I was acutely conscious that we were still hurtling down the runway at a high rate of knots, with no help from the light easterly crosswind, no brake 'chute, no jet barrier and no way even of raising the gear to stop the aircraft.

The ejection option (available down to ninety knots minimum) now began to flicker back into my thoughts but was just as quickly dismissed. Not now! Not after we had got this far, surely! I had to be very careful with the brakes which, in the absence of all hydraulic power, were working off the pressure of the ground-charged accumulator. It was essential not to brake too hard or that pressure might be rapidly lost through the action of the maxaret anti-skid system. As it turned out, the brakes failed totally at about fifty knots. I might possibly have been able to keep the aircraft on the runway by an earlier application of full left rudder but, in the circumstances, I was content to allow it to drift gently just off the right side where it stopped nicely on the grass with about two hundred yards of runway remaining. With the adrenalin still at maximum flow, and to round it all off nicely, I called for "seats safe!" and a quick exit as there was a possible risk of brake fire. After about twenty yards, I turned around to see Mike some way behind — I guess my adrenalin must have been flowing a bit faster than his! Anyway, there was no fire, so I returned to the aircraft to confirm all the switches safe before handing it over to the care of the fire and rescue services. But, before leaving the scene, I noticed that the engine was gently wind-milling in the light breeze. So, it couldn't have been a seizure after all! What had happened, and did we do something wrong?

The first person on the scene after the fire crew was the resident RAF medical officer who whisked Mike and me off to the ATC tower for a cup of tea. I remember feeling that I could have done with something distinctly stronger but, "Doctor knows best," I thought, so I didn't argue. Meanwhile back at the ranch, Pete and others had been busy. Nobody there could have guessed the outcome of our little adventure any more than Mike and I could have done. As a precaution, the Search and Rescue (SAR) Wessex helicopter of C Flight, 22 Squadron, had been scrambled from Valley to head down our way in case we needed lifting out of the water or whatever. We had barely started our cup of tea before the yellow Wessex now hove into view past the window, flaring for a landing immediately outside the tower. As we ran out from the tower to clamber aboard for our unscheduled chopper ride home, there was a familiar wave and grin from the captain in the right-hand seat. The crewman handed me a headset to put on and I was greeted on the intercom by the cheery tones of Flight Lieutenant John Stirling, a very experienced SAR pilot. He was a good friend and a highly accomplished piano player and raconteur in the bar of the officers' mess at Valley.

For the time being, I was entirely content just to enjoy his flying skills to get me home without further incident — the music and the stories could wait till later. However, as he set off and built up a very high speed across the airfield and sand dunes at about ten feet, I closed my eyes and made a little prayer that he wouldn't choose today to get it wrong. I needn't have worried. We were delivered safe and sound less than twenty minutes later outside the line office at Valley where, again for a first and last experience, I was obliged to sign an aircraft back to the engineers having not actually returned it to them. There was also a very large reception committee. Actual forced landings were pretty rare and it seemed that everyone on the station wanted to hear the tale at first hand.

I made my apologies to the station commander, Group Captain David Thornton, for leaving one of his aircraft in reduced circumstances at another airfield. That done and having received his kind congratulations, I turned my attention to Squadron Leader Gerry Woodley, the senior engineering officer with whom I had spent many hours in discussing the minutiae of the new Hawk as well as the outgoing Gnat. Gerry guessed immediately that we had experienced an obscure failure that caused loss of the fuel and hydraulic pumps as well as the RPM indicator and alternator. The first item led to the engine actually flaming out but the total loss of hydraulics and RPM indications suggested a seizure. The possibility of that combined set of symptoms had never surfaced in any discussion throughout my years of flying the Gnat, although I subsequently heard that there had been one other such failure. It was certainly not catered for in any of our publications or procedures, so it was not surprising that Mike and I had been a bit baffled by the combination of some symptoms and the absence of others. Anyway, the happy result was a successful forced landing in difficult circumstances and all that was left now for me was the report writing. But first, my wife needed a brief explanation as to what had happened and an amendment to my pick-up time and location. The pick-up was delayed by a few hours and was switched from the squadron offices to the mess bar.

Epilogue

Within a few days of the incident, I had myself winched out of a Gnat and confirmed that there was indeed room for me to eject without leaving bits of my legs in the aircraft. I continued flying the three types at Valley until the end of 1978. The Gnat passed out of RAF service with the Red Arrows at the end of 1979, but a small number of remaining aircraft are still flown privately in the UK and elsewhere.

In 1988, some four years after retiring from the RAF, I returned to Llanbedr to fly from there as a trials pilot on the Hawk, Canberra and Devon. My wife found a nice cottage with a mature garden for us and some land for our horses and we moved into it a few months later. We liked the area and the house so much that we stayed on there when I left Llanbedr after a year to join the Civil Aircraft Division of British Aerospace.

From my first-floor study, I can look exactly due west towards the airfield, over the sand dunes and the sea beyond it and to the distant

Lleyn Peninsula where we can see the lights of Pwllheli on a clear night. Less than a mile away from me, beyond a couple of fields in which sheep and cattle graze lazily in the low winter sunlight, I can see XP 540's point of touchdown. I feel quite a strong link to this spot and I am very glad to be here.

Gnats in Close line Astern

Spot the Wessex!

Hawk Touchdown

12
ODE TO HUMAN FACTORS

My time at Valley wasn't all as successful as the forced landing, as this short aside will explain...

The following poem is totally unexpurgated and as written by me on the night of 16 January 1978, directly after the event, and read out to my assembled fellow QFIs, students and others at morning briefing the next day at RAF Valley. The circumstances need to be explained a little for the poem to make sense.

As already described, I led a very demanding life during my second tour at Valley. Together with my small team of five QFIs, I was responsible for setting and checking the flying standards of all the instructors and students on the station on the Gnat and the new Hawk. We were an exceptionally busy bunch and somewhat in the limelight. I was one of the first 4FTS pilots to fly the Hawk and had flown about one hundred and fifty hours on type since my conversion to it some nine months previously. You can imagine, then, that the making of such a stupid mistake whilst in my position was going to be a bit tricky to live down. Of course, all we pilots make mistakes and this was a very embarrassing one for me. At the time, I felt that the best way to deal with it was simply to say publicly what happened and why it happened. That hopefully did two things; it let others know that anybody could get quickly into a jam if due vigilance was relaxed and it might restore my tarnished reputation a bit.

In a nutshell, this is how it came about. I had done a routine night check on a QFI who had only recently qualified on the Hawk. It had not gone well for him and I had allowed myself to become impatient and intolerant of the other pilot's shortcomings in flight. The frustration had been building for some time and, during the latter part of the landing rollout, I took control from him as I believed he was about to go past the turn-off onto the taxiway. Anyway, I had misinterpreted the visual cues and turned off onto the grass and got stuck in mid-sermon. The rest is hopefully clear from the poem.

I make no apology for the less than literary style — it was late at night as I wrote and I was just a pilot, not the flipping poet laureate! I can only plead that it comes over best if read out with suitably timed pauses at the appropriate spots. Hopefully it will produce some laughs and maybe give any of those who are pilots something to ponder on their next flight...

DRIVING WITHOUT DUE CARE AND ATTENTION or: DON'T TAKE HEAVY BIRDS ONTO WET GRASS

'Twas on a wet and windy night
From a landing fair and right.
With impatience for the bar,
I thought we'd gone too far!

"I know my way," said I,
"The turn-off's going by!"
No taxi light for me
I know my way you see.

A gentle touch of brake;
This turn-off we'll still make.
Oh dear, this feels quite odd;
Not concrete here, but sod!

A call to tower: "Don't worry.
We'll move it in a hurry."
Wind up the trusty thruster.
(But mind we do not bust 'er)

Now what's this sinking feeling?
We've dug a bloody wheel in!
Once more to tower, "I'm sorry;

You'd better send a lorry!"

Up strides the salvage master
With face of hardened plaster:
"Too tired to taxi in then?
We'll shift it quick with these men"

'Twas lucky it was dark
Where I had chosen to park.
For crimson coloured faces
Don't show in such black places.

But towing arms are not enough
As birds in mud are very tough.
The tractor strains much harder now.
The Hawk makes quite a useless plough.

"Use muscle and spade, heave and grunt,
We'll soon sort out this stupid stunt.
There she goes. We've got 'er out!
Now it's easy; there's no doubt."

Meanwhile thru' Line Hut, cringing low,
OC Standards was seen to go.
"Now my debrief's lost its thunder
After such a stupid blunder."

"Next time I shall use the light
Even though I'm always right.
Yes, of course, I'll surely be.
I know my way you see…"

I know I'll get no glory
From this sordid little story,
But, with God's good grace,
I'll save my face…

13

HARRIER DRIVER

(This chapter is dedicated to Lieutenant Mike Macbeth, United States Navy (USN), course colleague and prospective exchange pilot at No 1 (F) Squadron. Mike was killed on 22 February 1982 during our Harrier conversion course when his aircraft crashed in bad weather in the Berwyn Mountains of North Wales during a low-level navigation exercise <u>and</u> to Squadron Leader John Garnons-Williams, my gentleman helicopter instructor at RAF Shawbury, who died in a mid-air collision of two Squirrels at RAF Ternhill on 10 January 2007).

I completed my second Valley tour in early 1979 and we headed down to the RAF Staff College at Bracknell for me to attend the ten-month advanced staff course. Before leaving Valley, the news came through that I had been awarded the Air Force Cross in the 1979 New Year's Honours List. I was bowled over and very happy. In February, I received a letter requesting me to attend an investiture at Buckingham Palace on 13 March. I duly attended and, in front of my wife and father, had the huge honour of being decorated with the AFC by HM the Queen.

After a most interesting year at Staff College, I was posted into the Plans Department at HQ Strike Command at RAF Naphill near High Wycombe, the tick-in-the-box for my one and only (short!) ground tour. In the spring of 1981, I was enjoying a few days leave with my wife at our home on Anglesey when the telephone rang unexpectedly one morning. On the line was an old friend from my first squadron tour at Tengah in Singapore in the mid '60s. I knew that he was at the RAF Officer Personnel Centre and that he was the postings officer dealing with aircrew wing commanders.

He told me the exciting news that I'd been selected for promotion on 1 July and that he wanted to discuss with me the options that were available for posting in my new rank. To my astonishment, I was actually given three choices: Chief Instructor (CI) on the Hawk at Brawdy, CI on Jet Provosts (JPs) at Church Fenton or OC Operations Wing (OC Ops) on the Harrier at Wittering. I could have been tempted by any one of the three. The first was a logical step. As OC Standards Squadron at 4 FTS, Valley, from 1976 to 1979, I had been in a key role during the introduction of the Hawk to RAF service. The second option was very interesting, partly because I had done my own basic training on JPs in the early 1960s at Church Fenton but also because it would bring new professional perspectives and I thought it would be very satisfying and worthwhile to teach ab initio students. However, either of those posts would have firmly cemented me as a trainer. The third option brought the prospect of returning to operational flying and the chance to fly the coveted and challenging Harrier. That outweighed all other considerations, including the catch that the flying was just part-time with a measly allocation of only eight hours' flying per month, though it was expected that I could top up the allocation a bit by scrounging from the two Harrier units at Wittering, 1 (F) Squadron and 233 Operational Conversion Unit (OCU). I went for the Harrier job. Good choice — I was soon to discover it was one of the most exhilarating ways to aviate.

As a thirty-six-year-old newcomer to the Harrier, I was to follow exactly the same training steps as young pilots newly graduated from the Hawk Tactical Weapons Unit at Brawdy. However, as I had not been in full flying practice since leaving Valley in February 1979, apart from weekends flying cadets in Air Experience Flight Chipmunks, I was first required to complete the renowned senior officers' flying refresher course on the Hunter at Brawdy. Magic! Moreover, by pulling strings with my former senior colleagues at Valley, I first scrounged myself nine trips in the Hawk before going to Brawdy — magic plus! So, throughout the months of July and August, I had a wonderful time, with absolutely no responsibilities other than to get my flying skills up to shape in about twenty-three hours of Hunter flying including low-level navigation, formation and air-to-ground weapons delivery, including strafing, rocketing and bombing on the range at Pembrey on the South Wales coast.

September saw us moving from my ground job as a planner at Strike Command to RAF Wittering near Stamford. We took advantage of a few weeks' leave before I met my four young course colleagues for the first stage of the Harrier conversion process. That commenced with several days of helicopter flying at RAF Shawbury. The aim of the allotted six hours of flying, over three sorties in the Westland Gazelle, was to familiarise ourselves with the concepts and visual cues involved in vertical or near vertical take-offs, manoeuvring and landings. That intensive short course was actually very hard work. Although we had no requirement to attend ground-school lessons nor to learn the intricacies of the aircraft's operation, each of our two-hour sorties was a very demanding session with a helicopter instructor. The flights included hovering, transitions to and from forward flight, spot turns just above the ground and engine-out landings (EOLs) via auto-rotation. Not that the Harrier could emulate EOLs to land following engine failure — in such a case one was obliged to eject — but the Gazelle profile was similar to a rolling vertical landing (RVL — more later) in the jet.

I found the Gazelle an incredibly demanding little beast. It was so 'twitchy' and I found it enormously difficult to avoid over-controlling. Mind you, we were pitched in right at the deep end, doing hovering and transitions to forward flight after only the briefest of introduction to effects of controls, all within the first flight. The mini-course concluded with some tricky spot turns a few feet above the ground between two hangars and in a strong and sharply gusting wind! I have never worked harder, before or since, to stay in control of an aircraft! Vertical flight in the Gazelle was a cheap yet very valuable introduction to vertical flight in the Harrier. It was a very cost-effective way of picking up those relevant visual cues in the hover and in transitions to and from forward (and, occasionally, backward!) flight. I had often wished for the chance to fly helicopters operationally, but you can't have everything.

After Shawbury and a week's sea survival course at RAF Mountbatten near Plymouth, we small band of prospective Harrier pilots returned to Wittering for the ground-school phase of our conversion course at 233 OCU. We each completed three sessions in the Harrier flight simulator before flying. On 5 November I flew the first of my two dual sorties in the twin-seat Harrier T4 with a QFI at the OCU before going solo in the single-seat GR3 the following day.

The heart of the Harrier's capability is of course the Rolls Royce Pegasus engine, a truly marvellous feat of engineering. The chief features that the engine provides are: very rapid, surge-free acceleration; minimum thrust loss during reaction control; pilot-selectable water injection; and, of course, four synchronised exhaust nozzles that allow thrust to be directed from fully rearwards through ninety degrees downward to fifteen degrees forward. Rapid engine acceleration is required so that take-off thrust can be achieved as quickly as possible from idle RPM. The chief reason for that is to minimise the time spent in the crucial ground level to forty or fifty feet height band during a vertical take-off. Within that band there are two problems: first, hot air is re-ingested and therefore reduces thrust available; second, turbulent airflow from the thrust reflected off the ground can interfere with aircraft control and possibly cause minor debris to be ingested by the engine. For these reasons, the minimum hover height for a Harrier is fifty feet. However, since ejection in the event of engine or control failure is very marginal at that height, hovering was usually carried out at eighty feet.

Thrust is bled off the engine for control of the aircraft when in jet-borne flight (rather than wing-borne flight) i.e. to provide 'reaction control' rather than aerodynamic control. The high-speed air is fed to downward-pointing outlets under the nose and tail for pitch control, side outlets on either side of the rear fuselage for yaw and a combined up or down outlet near each wing tip for roll control. Water can be injected into the engine combustion chamber to cool the turbine entry stator and rotor blades. That allows the engine to accept a higher fuel flow, and so produce more thrust, without the higher temperatures that would otherwise damage the turbine. The aircraft can carry fifty gallons of water for up to ninety seconds of injection.

The exhaust nozzles are controlled by a single lever in the cockpit, set just inside of the throttle lever and equipped with an adjustable stop so that particular settings can be selected quickly by the pilot when required. Typical settings, in addition to fully rear for fully wing-borne flight and ninety degrees down for fully jet-borne (vertical) flight, are:

seventy degrees for a rolling vertical take-off (RVTO), seventy-five degrees for a RVL, twenty degrees for a short take-off or landing (STOL) and fifteen degrees forward for power nozzle braking (PNB).

Sensibly, take-offs and landings in the first three sorties of the Harrier conversion course were carried out in the STOL mode as I've mentioned. Only then did we move on to the more tricky, vertical flight manoeuvres and the transitions to and from wing-borne flight. After those initial STOL sorties, I was given a twenty-minute VTOL session in the T4 that consisted of six vertical take-offs and landings (known in the trade as 'press-ups') with an instructor and then went solo VTOL in the GR3 on the same day. Only when all five pilots had completed their VTOL phase, were we shown 'The Film'. This was an anthology of actual accidents and mishaps that had occurred over preceding years in which less fortunate Harrier pilots than us (to that point!) had come a cropper during STOVL manoeuvres. The theory behind showing the film at this delayed point was that we first needed the confidence of having performed VTOL satisfactorily, otherwise it might have put us right off the idea of becoming Harrier pilots! The other delight that came our way after we had all completed our first solo VTOL flight was to drink a 'down-in-one' from a full two-pint (!) tankard kept in the bar of the officers' mess for this ceremonial purpose. The idea was to do it quickly. Of the first two of my colleagues who tried that, the second regurgitated in a desperate attempt to beat his predecessor's time. I went third but my older and slightly wiser head (inspired by a tip from a friend within the audience!) led me to take my time and complete the ritual without an embarrassment that would have been remembered far longer than my slow time!

I could of course write at great length about the nitty-gritty of Harrier flying. Here I will just try to highlight some of the differences from conventional jet fighters to illustrate the voyage of discovery during getting to know the Harrier, or 'bona-jet' as the older hands described it.

Within the cockpit were three particular items of equipment that I met for the first time; a head-up display (HUD), a head-down display (HDD) and an angle-of-attack indicator (AAI) — the latter included within the HUD. The HUD is nowadays much more common and is fitted to most military fast-jets and some civil aircraft. Its purpose is primarily to enable a pilot to see the aircraft's attitude, altitude, heading and speed without having to look into the cockpit. In the GR3, the various parameters were fed into a prismatic sight on top of the cockpit coaming and reflected upwards on to the windscreen in green alpha-numerics and various geometric symbols, all focussed at infinity to match the external view. With such an aid, it becomes much easier to track air and ground targets visually or to carry out manoeuvres in cloud or simply to fly, especially in VSTOL manoeuvres where external visual cues are so vital, all without taking one's eyes away from the outside world. It took quite some time to get used to the HUD or 'the green writing' as it was referred to. The all-in-one display was quite different from the standard layout of analogue instruments with which I had flown for the previous twenty years. (Experience with the HUD display came in very handy some eight years later when I was learning my way around the new Electronic Flight Instrument Displays (EFIS) being fitted to the ATP and BAE 146).

The HDD was essentially a moving-map display fed by an Inertial Navigation system (INAS) but with a host of switches and buttons all around its periphery for selection of various control options. There were two obvious problems with it. Firstly, it was set forward of the stick at not much above knee level, so the business of constantly moving one's eyes and refocusing between HUD and HDD made great demands on concentration and co-ordination, especially at low level and if switch changes were needed around the HDD. The display had been designed for use by the back-seat operator of the TSR2 (we were told) who didn't have the distraction of also having to fly the aircraft! It was little wonder then that the RAF chose to put only the very best of its fast-jet graduates onto the Harrier. The combination of high cockpit workload, especially at low level or in VTOL flight, together with the demands of accurate navigation and weapons delivery (which could include operating a laser-ranging device at very low level) and all with just one set of eyes and hands, could often put even the best pilots right at the limits of co-ordination and capability.

By contrast, the AAI was a very nifty little gadget without which it would have been impossible to fly the Harrier in other than fully wing-borne flight. Once in jet-borne — or partially jet-borne — flight, normal aero-dynamics no longer apply. However, the aircraft can be flown safely at any speed, provided the attitude is at or near optimum angle of attack. For that to be the case, the pilot needs to have information of aircraft attitude with respect to airflow. Today there are of course other fixed-wing aircraft that have AAIs and many pilots would argue with justification that flying to angle of attack as the primary parameter during approach and landing is more accurate and safer than flying to speed.

The concept of the Harrier was to maximise fuel and weapons payload by using as much runway as might be available for take-off but also to be able to operate from short strips or pads when necessary. Of course, very useful loads could still be carried with a take-off from limited distance. A 'conventional' take-off in the Harrier was carried out using ten degrees of nozzle, flying off the ground at around one hundred and forty knots (with thirteen to fourteen degrees on the AAI). Of course, this used a lot of runway so a STO, with fifty degrees of nozzle and typically one hundred knots at lift-off, was the norm. Next shortest was an RVTO, when the take-off run was begun with an initial setting of thirty degrees nozzle, the pre-set lift-off angle of seventy degrees being selected when the engine hit one hundred per cent RPM, giving a lift-off speed of thirty-five to fifty knots. Lastly, a vertical take-off could be used from a concrete pad.

In all cases, the nozzle stop was pre-set at the lift-off angle so that the pilot could select the correct angle quickly and precisely without having to look in to the lever. On a vertical take-off, the engine was slammed from idle to full thrust which gave the quickest lift-off and minimum time through the height range in which hot air recirculation and handling difficulties would occur as already mentioned.

I was always thrilled when doing vertical take-offs from a pad within the wooded area at the west end of the airfield at Wittering. The feeling of shooting vertically upwards out of a relatively confined wooded area and into open sky was quite unique. This was at least matched by getting airborne on a STO from a narrow road in a West German forest during an exercise in which I took part a year or two later. It was most exciting to tear off down the road from a standing start at an astonishingly high rate of acceleration with trees flashing past in a blur at an increasing velocity on either side, then selecting the nozzles quickly down to fifty degrees and just popping up like a cork out of a bottle into the calm of an open sky as the trees fell away below and the visual speed cues dissipated just as fast as they'd built up.

The Harrier did of course have the party trick of being able to use its nozzles across the full range in wing-borne forward flight — known as 'viffing' (from 'vectoring in forward flight'). In order to slow down very rapidly and so shake off a threatening aggressor aircraft from behind by forcing a fly-through, the Harrier pilot needed only to select the nozzles to their limit of fifteen degrees forward to produce a stunningly vicious deceleration. The aggressor would usually be unable to avoid flying past you (unless he was in another Harrier!) and into your forward sight. From here — if speed could be matched again — which was possible as both aircraft would probably have pulled up high into a decelerating yo-yo manoeuvre, the viffing capability could then help the Harrier pilot to nudge up the nose of his aircraft until the gunsight was on the enemy and a kill could be achieved.

Well, that was the theory but of course it needed very fine judgement. In air-to-air combat, energy is all, but viffing of course sacrifices energy and must be used with great caution. During the Falklands War, by which time I had taken command of the Harrier Operations Wing at Wittering, I remember much was made in the press of the Harrier's ability to viff. The newspapers and TV included diagrams suggesting that the Harrier could simply hop upwards and slow down then pop conveniently down again into the aggressor's line-astern position. As I have suggested, it wasn't quite so simple and, to the best of the knowledge that I gleaned from returning Wittering Harrier pilots who had been on our two carriers in the South Atlantic, there was not one known case of anyone viffing to achieve a kill, if at all. Jeffrey Ethell and Alfred Price (an acquaintance during my Wittering tour) in their excellent book 'Air War South Atlantic' say explicitly that viffing was never used by the Sea Harriers in engaging enemy aircraft. So, I'm afraid that myth is debunked should anyone still believe it.

Various landing configurations are available to a Harrier pilot. Surprising to some, that does not include a fully conventional landing with nozzles fully aft — that is done only in emergency. The main reasons for that are the very high touchdown speed that fully wing-borne flight would require and the Harrier's very limited wheel-braking. With limited brakes, on only two main wheels below the fuselage, an awful lot of runway is required to stop after a conventional landing. I did only one or two during the conversion training.

Otherwise, slow landings can be made at various nozzle positions down to seventy-five degrees nozzle for an RVL. For a vertical landing, the nozzles are of course set to ninety degrees down. But before you can do that, it's necessary to make a decelerating transition to arrive beside the landing pad, ideally just as your groundspeed reaches zero. During the deceleration, nozzles are lowered progressively and thrust is increased in unison as the speed decreases, whilst maintaining a constant eight degrees on the AAI. The aerodynamics and stability characteristics in the speed band between ninety knots and thirty knots, when the aircraft becomes fully jet-borne, are complex and that was not a band in which to linger. Later marks of Harrier had various auto-stabilisation aids to reduce the difficulty and workload. Once in the hover at eighty feet, with the nose into wind (a small wind-vane on top of the aircraft's nose is used to confirm that parameter), the lateral and forward markers by the pad could be used to position the aircraft over its centre. The Harrier could then be set into a moderate descent, again to minimise the time below fifty feet, until touchdown when the throttle was smartly closed and the brakes applied to stop any residual fore or aft movement.

Of course, one did have the ability to 'reverse' in flight if the pad was overshot during a decelerating transition. However, there were often times when there was very little fuel and time to spare between maximum hover weight and minimum fuel for flight, so such backing up was usually best avoided. Moreover, if one over-controlled, or especially on a hot day or when close to maximum hover weight (or both!), the extra bleed-off of thrust to power the reaction controls could lead to the automatic fuel control system reducing fuel flow to the engine to prevent infringement of the engine temperature limit. In that case, the aircraft was going down whether you were over the pad or not! VLs were therefore sometimes quite tense affairs! The fascination for all of this and various other Harrier 'party tricks', together with low-level delivery of various weapons and air-to-air refuelling was of course immense and ever-lasting.

The Harrier was used for forty-one years by the RAF for ground attack, air defence and reconnaissance (equipped with a sideways-pointing camera or a full reconnaissance pod) and I felt greatly privileged to be able to dabble in all of that as well as to enjoy the thrills of simply flying the aircraft. It's so sad that our combined Harrier force appeared to be so lightly and so suddenly discarded at the end of 2010 in favour of what was to be the conventional version of the American F35 Lightning, subsequently reverting to the STOVL version that had originally been selected by our government and defence chiefs at the outset. Without Harriers, there would have been no victory over the invaders in the Falklands. A gaping hole existed in our defence capability until STOVL F35 came along recently.

Author (left) with Sqn Ldr John Garnons-Williams

Harrier GR3 in winter

14

THE HUNTING FIRECRACKER — A SHORT INTERLUDE

By 1984, after twenty-two years' service as a Royal Air Force pilot, I had decided to take the giant leap sideways into civil aviation. Since starting pilot training in 1962, I had been lucky to stay flying for all but two and a half years spent in ground jobs — and even then, managed to fly Chipmunks for Air Experience Flights (AEFs) at most weekends. However, the writing was now on the wall and it pointed clearly to a tour in some labyrinthine headquarters or other. I had tasted that life for eighteen months as a planner at HQ Strike Command and was not wild about the idea of going back to it. To me, having to work in an office every day in the same location seemed like a prison sentence — from which I was let out only for the night and at weekends. So, on the crest of a wave, with my last tour spent flying the outstandingly exciting Harrier and with my shiny new air transport pilot's licence in my pocket, the plot was to find myself a slot in an airline somewhere, to learn a new trade and to see some more of the world.

Having given the Royal Air Force its required twelve months' notice of leaving at my agreed option date, there was plenty of time for me to see the plot unravelling rapidly before my eyes, well before the final day's service arrived on 30 June 1984. Airline jobs were drying up and I hadn't got one yet. I had to form a back-up plan swiftly. Plan B saw me enlisting on a one-month business management course at the Polytechnic of Central London during my first weeks as a civilian. In the final weeks as a serviceman, I also started to write a lot of job-seeking letters to companies that might be able to use my management experience, rather than employ me necessarily as a pilot, so long as it involved some travel. I used mainly the Society of British Aerospace Companies (SBAC) and Defence Manufacturers' Association (DMA) lists for the names and addresses. The RAF resettlement service and the Officers' Association also provided some good leads.

Unfortunately, a couple of plum job opportunities in the Middle East (one with Rolls Royce and another with British Aerospace — the latter also a flying job) were vetoed by my equestrian wife who protested that she wasn't going anywhere that had only plastic grass. However, one of my letters fortunately landed on the desk of a former RAF acquaintance, retired Squadron Leader John Davey, former OC the CFS Helicopter Training Flight at RAF Valley when I was there as OC Standards Squadron on the Gnat, Hunter and Hawk. John was Managing Director (MD) of Specialist Flying Training (SFT), a company using three turboprop NDN Firecrackers at Carlisle airport to train pilots for a certain Middle Eastern air force. SFT was also one of the key companies lined up in a consortium to bid for the contract to produce a new basic training aircraft for the RAF.

In September 1984, a new company, Hunting Firecracker Aircraft Ltd (HFAL) was to be formed, comprising SFT, together with Hunting Associated Industries (HAI) and Guinness Mahon, the merchant bank, to offer the Firecracker aircraft as a contender for the new basic trainer requirement. The new trainer was specified as a turboprop but had to provide minimum change at the step up to the Hawk jet. I was brought in to lead on cockpit design and equipment selection from an operational viewpoint. The justification for being entrusted with this weighty responsibility seemed to spring primarily from my experience as one of the RAF's first Hawk pilots. My tour as OC Standards at Valley covered the whole period when we introduced the Hawk into RAF service, from 1976 to early 1979.

I began almost immediately with SFT and Huntings. The first task was to become quickly familiar with Aviation Publication 970 ('Avpee nine-seventy'), the military aircraft designer's 'bible'. I had never previously heard of it! My only association with aircraft design and manufacture was as a boy — building the little pilotless, balsa wood models, e.g. the Hunter, Javelin and Gannet that I remember in particular. Well, they did actually fly successfully — most of the time — the models that is. So my learning curve in this new venture, as so often in my life, was pretty steep.

I worked for much of the time in the design office at Huntings' main plant at Reddings Wood, Ampthill, near Bedford, where coincidentally I had been born and had been educated — at Bedford School. For the remainder, I was mainly at the Hunting Firecracker offices at 1 Duke of York Street, St James's, London. There, a steady stream of bidders for a role in the potential contract knocked on the door to take me out to lunch in the West End, in their quest to persuade me to recommend their flight instruments, ejection system, radio and safety equipment and so on for the cockpit of the new trainer.

In a very intensive five-month period I made many friends and key contacts across the aircraft industry in the UK and overseas. Such contacts even extended (albeit very briefly!) to the Prime Minister, Margaret Thatcher, and the Secretary for Trade and Industry, Norman Tebbit, (and his delightful wife, Margaret, so cruelly paralysed later by the Brighton Bomb), whom I showed separately around the aircraft at the Farnborough Air Show in 1984. I also met a couple of tame members of the two Houses of Parliament, where I was to tag along with our public relations (PR) guru to plead our case one afternoon in Westminster, later in the year. In due course I wrote most of the operational part of the company's proposal that was duly submitted, along with those of the other three contending companies: Pilatus, Shorts/Embraer and the Australian Aircraft Company (AAC), a company that had only a paper design.

The Firecracker was originally designed by Desmond Norman and Andrew Coombes of NDN Aircraft Ltd at Bembridge on the Isle of Wight, who aimed to produce a powerful, light and economical training aircraft. It was hoped the simple design would also be suitable for technology transfer and production abroad. The prototype piston version flew first in May 1977 and gained a limited CAA clearance in May 1979. This was the only piston version to fly. It was equipped with the Lycoming O-540 engine.

In 1982, the design and UK manufacturing rights to the Firecracker were acquired by SFT, the company that had been set up by John Davey and Mike Horton, another retired squadron leader pilot. From the outset, SFT had been alive to Air Staff Target 412, the RAF's requirement for about one hundred and fifty new basic trainers to replace the Jet Provost and had invested in developing a turboprop version of the Firecracker. SFT formed a subsidiary, Firecracker Aircraft Ltd (FAL), and ordered three turboprop aircraft that were to be built by NDN Aircraft Ltd with substantial involvement by Westlands plc. SFT had also bought Slingsby Aviation Ltd, of Kirbymoorside, North Yorkshire, in early 1983 and installed their MD, Jim Tucker, as MD of FAL.

There were, theoretically, twenty-three contending aircraft from seventeen companies to meet AST 412 and questionnaires were issued by the Ministry of Defence (MOD) to the prospective manufacturers in September 1983. By March 1984, the list of likely contenders that had replied had been whittled down from fifteen possibilities to just four: the Firecracker NDN-1T, the Pilatus PC9, the Shorts-Embraer EMR 312 Tucano and the paper design from AAC, the A20 Wamira II. AAC went on to link with Westlands to submit their proposal to the MOD and Pilatus did the same with British Aerospace. Field Aviation Ltd, another Huntings Group company, based at East Midlands Airport, was to undertake the final assembly of the RAF's Firecracker aircraft. In June 1984, each of the four contenders was invited to tender against Specification T301 D&P to meet AST412.

The first of the three turboprop Firecracker NDN-1Ts had flown on 1 September 1983 and had been certified by the CAA in March 1984. They were put into service as soon as possible at Carlisle, where SFT had a contract to train eighty foreign pilots to a syllabus similar to that being used by the RAF on the Jet Provost. My own single familiarisation flight in one of the aircraft, with retired Wing Commander Doug Barden, Chief Flying Instructor (CFI) at SFT, took place on 10 August 1984 from Boscombe Down to Cranfield. Doug was an old friend of mine from some twenty years previously. He had flown Javelins in Singapore and Borneo when I was also there in both countries as a Hunter DFGA pilot on 20 Squadron RAF. He had been on the directing staff of the RAF Staff College at Bracknell when I attended the RAF Advanced Staff Course there throughout 1979 (the first of my two and a half years on the ground and from where I 'moonlighted' on the AEF Chipmunks at RAF Abingdon). I flew the Firecracker throughout the forty minutes sortie, mostly at low level, and thoroughly enjoyed it. It seemed to me like a powerful Chipmunk but with a nose-wheel instead of a tail-wheel.

The required aircraft performance to meet AST 412 was:

➢ Two hundred and ten to two hundred and forty knots sustained speed at sea level with max continuous power.

➢ Optimum range speed at twenty thousand feet: one hundred and seventy knots minimum.

➢ Time from brakes off to fifteen thousand feet: < seven minutes.

➢ Service Ceiling: not less than twenty-five thousand feet.

➢ Endurance: two consecutive one-hour training sorties, plus a one hundred and twenty nautical miles diversion, plus ten per cent fuel reserve.

➢ Manoeuvrability: sustained minimum of 1.5G at twenty thousand feet.

➢ Take-off and landing distance: < two thousand feet.

➢ Fatigue Life: twelve thousand hours.

➢ Flight Envelope: +6.7G to -3.5G

The modified aircraft design being offered by HFAL was to have its turboprop engine, the four-bladed Pratt and Whitney PT6A, uprated from the -25A, 550 shaft horse power (shp) model to the -25D, 750shp, model. It would be fitted with air conditioning and with the zero-speed, zero-altitude Stencel Ranger rocket escape (extraction) system. The cockpit layout and avionics fit would be re-designed to match the Hawk cockpit as far as possible and that was my primary task, along with equipment selection. It was a complex and quite demanding few months. I had a lot of help and learned a huge amount from my other design team colleagues at Ampthill, and my lunch partners in London, as I made the choices on equipment and sketched out the cockpit layout for the professional draughtsmen to turn into technical drawings. There were many meetings to attend and much chewing of pencils as we stared at the complex flow charts that mapped out our steady progress towards submission of the tender. I was thrilled to be involved at the centre of this project. My prospects for the future, had the Firecracker been selected for the RAF, were extremely exciting. I believed I would have had a long-term role with the company, probably including marketing (that I was yet to learn!) as well as flying.

HFAL presented their proposal to meet AST 412 to the MOD on 1 October 1984. Once the proposal was filed, I had little to do until the result was announced. However, totally out of the blue, came two interesting twists, one to the Firecracker project and one to my own, still unplanned, career development. Firstly, was a call from Martin-Baker Aircraft Ltd, the leading ejection seat designers and manufacturers at Denham in Buckinghamshire.

The small, lightweight Firecracker ideally needed a correspondingly small, lightweight ejection seat. I had earlier held detailed discussions with Martin-Baker and they had been adamant that they had nothing available that could be fitted into the Firecracker, nor even on the drawing boards, to offer us. Therefore, we had, somewhat reluctantly, been obliged to select the relatively unknown and very different concept, the Stencel escape system. The call from Martin-Baker was to offer us, after all, a new-design, lightweight seat that had been planned (in a hurry!) for fitment to any of the four final contenders. Martin-Baker, whose senior people I got to know very well over the next three years (but in a quite different role), were also a most astute business outfit and were hedging their bets after all. We submitted the amendment.

The second call came from a well-known UK aerospace company, whose name I cannot reveal to this day (!), and for whom I was to take a short sabbatical of four weeks from the Firecracker project to undertake an aeronautical assignment for them in the People's Republic of China. Yes, you guessed it, thereby hangs another tale!

For less than clear reasons, the Hunting Firecracker — the only all-British contender — did not get the contract but the Shorts/Embraer Tucano did, after a final run-off with the PC9. Although the MOD argued that the decision was made primarily on cost grounds, I was told there were several other, undisclosed reasons. The Conservative government took the opportunity to repay Brazil, who had provided some significant favours to the UK during the Falklands War only three years previously. It also took the opportunity to put much-needed manufacturing work into

Shorts at Belfast Harbour Airport in Northern Ireland (NI), thus currying political kudos from the economic benefit to that troubled province. A third reason lay in a critical report from A&AEE Boscombe Down that had assessed the Firecracker — along with the other two flying contenders — and had described it as unacceptably unstable in the yawing plane at low level. A fourth was the doubts that lay over Huntings' ability to produce the aircraft in the numbers required. They had not built an aircraft since the earlier model Jet Provosts in the mid '60s (the later ones having been built by the British Aircraft Corporation, fore-runner of British Aerospace — BAe) and I guess it was a bit of a leap of faith to propose that Huntings' skills and experience in building their then current product, the JP 233 cluster-bomb dispenser, were sufficient for them to ramp up quickly to building a full-scale aircraft again after twenty years. I reckon the Brazil and NI politics did it. I had flown the Firecracker at low level, as I have mentioned, and, sure, it snaked a bit. However, I'm equally sure it wouldn't have taken much to correct that by providing a bit more fin area.

On 18 December 1984, the news broke that the Firecracker and the A-20 had been ruled out of the competition. The next day I was due to travel down from my home in Nassington, near RAF Wittering, to the London office. I phoned John Davey at the Duke of York Street offices and asked whether he still wanted me there, as I imagined there was little or no chance of salvaging anything from all the work that had been done and he would probably not want me on the payroll for any longer. Magnanimously, he suggested I should come in and tag along with our PR man, Colin Wagstaff, who was to go to the House of Commons to brief one of our 'political advisors', David Ashby, the MP for Leicestershire North-West, in whose constituency lies East Midlands Airport where Fields would have completed final assembly of the Firecrackers. David was to seek an adjournment for an emergency debate about the decision in the House of Commons. HFAL had made much of the fact that the Hunting Firecracker was the only all-British design and so the politicians could have a field day over why it wasn't selected — we thought, incorrectly.

This was to be the first time (and last, so far) that I visited Parliament and I was bemused about how easy it was (at that time!)to breeze into the place, sit down and brief an MP and then go up to the Gallery to watch and listen as he delivered what Colin and I had suggested he should say. I had handled the technical bits and felt awfully important for a short while! Otherwise I simply followed, like a rather large puppy dog, in the shadow of Colin the PR ace, who swept past the policemen and across the floor of the lobby, exuding total confidence and a convincing air of belonging to the place. I was even more impressed when, the motion for an emergency debate having failed, Colin then swept round to the Lords — with me, wide-eyed and closely following in his slipstream once more.

There we sat in a corridor to brief a couple of other 'Friends of HFAL', Lord Fred Mulley and a baroness whose name I have forgotten but was probably Baroness Airey of Abingdon. For this occasion, I can find no record of them actually getting to their feet and making the protest that we wanted. An earlier debate, on 17 October, during the evaluation of the tender bids, had shown much support for the Firecracker in the House of Lords — Hansard runs to eight and a half pages on that and includes speeches by eight noble lords and Baroness Airey. Clearly, once the decision had been announced, there appeared little stomach for a fight from their Lordships and Ladyships.

Sadly, and soon, the Firecracker was doomed to die, but not before John had made me the very kind offer (in fact, it was more of an order as he was still paying me) of taking over almost immediately from Doug as the CFI for SFT at Carlisle Airport. I had to decline firmly; the writing was on the wall for the Firecracker. Moreover, Carlisle was not exactly in my travel plans and I had by then another couple of very interesting offers waiting in the wings.

The end was a little more prolonged than I had expected. At their own expense, HFAL and Westlands joined the two remaining contenders in submitting best and final offers, even though the first two had been warned by the MOD that they were probably wasting their time and money. The decision was finally announced in favour of the Tucano on

21 March 1985. The one hundred and thirty aircraft began to enter service with the RAF in 1988, the last being delivered in 1993.

Working on the Firecracker project was the first of several key experiences in a four-year 'commercial apprenticeship' that eventually helped to land me a cracking, commercial flying job in industry some three and a half years later. That was to be as a training captain, examiner, production test pilot, demonstration pilot and project manager for the Civil Aircraft Division of BAe, based at Woodford near Manchester but operating with many airlines worldwide. In over eleven years with BAe, I was able to apply fully the wide variety of flying experience that I had been lucky to gather in the RAF, SOAF and the RNoAF during several years on operations in each of temperate, tropical, desert and arctic environments. Moreover, before that plum job, I was first to be even luckier to acquire some thoroughly useful aerospace business and marketing savvy, in particular, from the China project and then as the Sales and Marketing Director for another company in the international aerospace and security industry. More on all of this in the next chapter!

Postscript

The Tucano remained in service until 2019, some five years later than its original expected retirement in 2014. It is being replaced by the Beechcraft T-6C Texan Turboprop.

Hunting Turbo Firecracker of Specialist Flying Training

15
JINDIVIK* — A PERSONAL ACQUAINTANCE

[*Australian Aboriginal: 'The Hunted One'... a very old but highly appropriate name for the role of the Australian Government Aircraft Factory (GAF) unmanned target aircraft].

I came to know this little unmanned aircraft whilst working at the Royal Aircraft Establishment at Llanbedr for a year in the late 1980s. After twenty-two years as a fast jet pilot and instructor in the Royal Air Force, I'd left the RAF in 1984 to try my hand as a pilot in civil aviation only to discover that my timing had been unfortunate. Jobs in the airlines in that year were extremely difficult to find. Plan B was quickly devised and, after a one-month business management course in central London, I enjoyed several months in consultancy work, including on the Firecracker Project and on an unusual assignment in the People's Republic of China.

In January 1985 I took up a new post as Export Sales Manager at Helmets Ltd, soon becoming Sales & Marketing Director for the best part of three years. However, a life of perpetual globetrotting, daily commuting when in the UK to an office eighty plus miles from home and an increasing urge to get back to flying, led me to apply for a job as a pilot at Llanbedr. I began work there in May 1988. At that time, Llanbedr had two Hawk aircraft that were used to escort — or 'shepherd' — the Jindivik target drones flown in the Cardigan Bay air-to-air firing range. There were also two Canberra target facilities aircraft that operated to wider locations with towed sea-skimming targets or the air-launched supersonic Stiletto missile target. Two Gloster Meteors and a de Havilland Sea Vixen, each of which could be flown either unmanned or piloted, were used mainly for Jindivik target controller training. Lastly, a single DH Devon C2 communications aircraft was used in the light transport role, primarily to other RAE and RAF sites. I flew the Hawks,

Canberras and the Devon. I wasn't there long enough to take on the Meteor or Sea Vixen. Alongside my airborne roles, I periodically joined the five-man operating team — spread over four separate locations on the airfield — that flew the Jindivik from take-off, out into the range and back to landing.

The Jindivik was developed from two manned Australian Government Aircraft Factories (GAF) Pika (Australian Aboriginal: 'Flier') prototypes that first flew in 1950. From 1952 to 1986, a total of five hundred and two Jindiviks were produced. The aircraft was used by the Australian air force and navy, the RAF and Sweden. In 1997, the production line was re-opened to build another fifteen for Britain.

The Pika had side air intakes and small wheel landing-gear operated from a pneumatic reservoir. On the Jindivik, the Pika undercarriage and the cockpit were replaced respectively with a single skid for landing and a dorsal engine-air intake. The Mk 1 Jindivik was powered by an Armstrong Siddeley Adder (ASa1) turbojet that had been developed as a disposable engine for the project. Only fourteen Mk 1s were made. The Mk 2 and Mk 3 were powered by the Armstrong Siddeley Viper engine. The Viper version used originally had been intended for a short lifespan of about ten hours but a 'long life' version was also produced for later marks of Jindivik and for manned aircraft, e.g. the Jet Provost. The Jindivik's vital statistics were:

Length: twenty-four feet four inches

Wingspan: twenty-six feet six inches

Height: six feet ten inches (eight feet six inches on its trolley)

Empty weight: two thousand nine hundred pounds

Max takeoff weight: three thousand six hundred and

fifty pounds

Maximum speed: four hundred and ninety knots

Range: five hundred and forty nautical miles

Ceiling: sixty thousand feet.

Control of the aircraft in flight was through the aircraft autopilot, directed by radio commands and telemetry from and to the ground respectively, rather than direct flight by a ground controller. Eighteen commands could be issued by radio to the autopilot with six further commands for operation of other onboard equipment.

The operating team comprised five people: a master controller in the ATC visual control room (VCR) adjacent to the ATC local controller, a skipper (pilot) and navigator in a dedicated, darkened radar room within the ATC tower and, lastly, pitch and azimuth controllers in wheeled huts adjacent to the runway. All the controllers were current or former aircrew, mostly former military fast jet pilots. Several also flew some or all of the station's other types.

For take-off, the azimuth controller's hut was positioned at the downwind end of the runway, looking along the take-off path from behind the Jindivik. Launching was from a steerable trolley. The azimuth controller looked through binoculars and steered the trolley, like a model aircraft, via a miniature joystick during the take-off ground run, and transferring automatically to steering the aircraft itself after lift-off. At one hundred and ten knots, the drone automatically applied flap down and elevators up and was released from the trolley.

Soon after take-off, when all parties were ready, control of the aircraft was passed electronically to the skipper and navigator, who 'flew' the aircraft in altitude and azimuth in response to voice-radio commands from the range ATCOs at RAE Aberporth, some forty-five nautical miles to the south south west of Llanbedr.

For landing, the azimuth hut was towed around the taxiways to the opposite, upwind end of the runway, to look beyond the downwind end of the runway, head-on at the approaching Jindivik. The pitch hut was positioned alongside the pre-designated landing area. Landing was at one hundred and fifty to one hundred and twenty-five knots. The azimuth and pitch controllers, operating independently, aligned the Jindivik with the runway centre line and the touchdown area respectively. For both controllers, the most difficult aspect was achieving visual acquisition of the tiny Jindivik in good time to achieve a smooth and safe landing. Often, only the pinpoints of the aircraft's forward facing three lights could be seen until the Jindivik became very close. The Jindivik landed on its extendable skid.

At any stage of the aircraft's flight, were there to be a failure of radio control from any of the four key locations so far mentioned, the master controller was able to take over any one, or all, of the roles from his position in the VCR.

Jindiviks were not cheap, around £1-1.5m in the type's latter years. So, from an early stage, something had to be done to ensure that the aircraft could be recovered, whenever possible, to fly another day rather than be shot down or damaged beyond safe landing capability. The Jindivik was therefore equipped with its own towed targets, either infra-red (flares) or radar enhancers. An onboard winch system could trail one of two infrared flare packs (each containing six flares, used in pairs) on the end of a two hundred-foot wire. The flares, rather than the Jindivik's jet engine exhaust, then became the hot source for an incoming heat-seeking missile. After the 'hostile' aircraft had expended its missile, the spent flare pack (or what was left of it) was wound in and the second could then be trailed for subsequent firings. Both active and passive radar decoys were operated in a similar manner.

For all Jindivik flights, a Hawk shepherd aircraft took off first so that it would be available throughout each target sortie, on constant airborne readiness to join in (very!) close formation with the drone for careful, all-round inspections, especially to check for damage after live-firing exercises. During non-firing exercises, e.g. for team training, the Hawk would usually move into close formation with the Jindivik immediately after take-off. It was a point of skill and pride (and sheer necessity in the event of early cloud penetration!) for the shepherd pilot to be able to fly his Hawk to a position alongside the runway from where he could slot into close formation before the fast-climbing and rapidly accelerating Jindivik reached one thousand five hundred feet or so.

After live-firing exercises, the range controllers vectored the shepherd onto the Jindivik so that it could join up in close formation prior to the target's recovery for inspection as described. As for the azimuth and pitch controllers, the most difficult thing for the shepherd pilot was visually acquiring the tiny Jindivik which, even though painted red, was often very hard to see against certain backgrounds.

If damage to the Jindivik had occurred, and if the aircraft was considered to be unsafe to land, the skipper could send a signal (i.e. down elevator!) to cause the aircraft to destruct by diving safely into the Irish Sea.

A secondary role for the Hawk, when required before live firing, was to carry out range clearance procedures, i.e. to investigate any shipping that might have strayed into the danger area.

Jindivik operations from Llanbedr ceased in 2004. The airfield closed down in February 2005. The Jindivik's role was taken over by the Meteor Mirach system which is operated from Aberporth. Since 2014, a number of low-key flying operations have resumed at Llanbedr, including testing unmanned aerial vehicles (UAVs). There are further plans to turn the airfield into an 'aerospace centre of excellence for trialling remotely piloted vehicles'. Llanbedr is still on the shortlist of five as a potential UK spaceport.

Jindivik with tow

Jindivik showing damaged tail

16
FACTORY PILOT — THE BEGINNINGS

I had joined the RAF to train as a pilot at age seventeen and a half and left at my option point on 1 July 1984 after twenty-two years' wonderfully enjoyable service, spent mainly as a DFGA pilot and fast jet QFI. That time had included two and a half years' loan service with the Sultan of Oman's Air Force during the Dhofar War, two years on exchange to the Royal Norwegian Air Force, a week on a flying inspection of the Royal Jordanian Air Force and two full tours as a QFI at RAF Valley. There had also been a few flights with the Royal New Zealand Air Force, the German Air force and the US Air National Guard. I was very fortunate to finish my service on a high note as a pilot of the iconic Harrier. However, I believed that my future RAF career, had I stayed on, would have entailed being mostly on the ground — an unattractive prospect after all the preceding variety and excitement in the air.

After much heart-searching, I had given the obligatory twelve months' notice to leave the RAF at age thirty-nine, having decided in early 1983 to shift into civil aviation in order to keep flying. However, the subsequent transition from RAF Harrier pilot to airline pilot, didn't go at all as planned. Nevertheless, it did result in some very rich experiences that were to benefit me greatly a few years later, when I became an airline pilot training captain, examiner and test pilot at the British Aerospace civil aircraft factory at Woodford near Manchester. Those roles took me worldwide, training and examining customer pilots of many national and international airlines, helping to set up new operations and routes and carrying out production and development flight testing of BAe's airliner products both at Woodford and overseas. However, before I begin this story, a little more detailed background explanation is needed.

I had flown throughout my career, except for the six months basic officer training at the outset. Even during the year at Staff College in 1979, I had returned to RAF Valley in my summer leave to fly the Hawk for a week. In the following eighteen-month ground tour as a planner at HQ Strike Command, I had kept flying at weekends in Chipmunks with cadets from No.6 Air Experience Flight (AEF) at RAF Abingdon. Later, for the last eighteen months of my final tour as OC Operations Wing (OC Ops) on the Harrier at RAF Wittering, I had been kindly taken on by 7 AEF for occasional weekend flying in Chipmunks at RAF Newton. In fact, and very fortuitously as it turned out, I was able to continue my weekend flying directly after leaving the RAF by enrolling as an RAFVR pilot (in the rank of Flying Officer) with 7 AEF for a further four years until 1988.

Sadly, only six months prior to completing my RAF service, my wife's father died suddenly and airline jobs began to dry up. The former event made us consider restricting our options to a UK basing as my wife felt an understandable need to keep an eye on her newly widowed mother. The latter meant I'd better get to work on Plan B. Regrettably, at that point there was no Plan B, so one had to be devised soonish whilst I pressed ahead anyway with gaining my Air Transport Pilot's Licence. The ATPL process went very well, thanks to some expert ground-school tuition from Trent Air Services at Cranfield and to a similarly excellent Civil Instrument Rating (IR) Course from SFT Ltd at Bournemouth.

The Civil Aviation Authority (CAA) examiner who in April 1984 granted me my first civil IR, in an Aztec, was a former Central Flying School QFI, whom I had known well when I had undergone my QFI training on the Gnat at Kemble, some thirteen years earlier. However, he examined by the book and gave me no favours, quite rightly. I left Bournemouth with a huge sigh of relief at having qualified fully (well, academically at least) as a 'public transport pilot', as the examiner had put it so formally — making me think of bus drivers. I suppose I had indeed just become a bus driver of sorts; it was certainly rather different from rocketing and strafing targets at Holbeach range on the edge of the Wash from my extraordinarily clever and highly exciting jump jet. Nevertheless, I was very proud to have qualified for the ATPL and I looked forward with great pleasure to putting it to use, ideally asap. As it turned out, I had to wait a long five years for that, until just before various parts of the licence would otherwise have expired.

With the ATPL in the bag but the prospect of a decent airline job, or even an indecent one, looking pretty unlikely in the short term, Plan B began to take on a clear shape. Registration with the RAF Resettlement Service and with the Officers' Association had begun to produce some interesting, albeit ground-bound, opportunities. Rolls-Royce and British Aerospace each kindly interviewed me in London for senior and very interesting posts in the Middle East. As mentioned earlier, both were vetoed by my wife before we could go much further for the additional reason that, as a keen horse-rider, she wasn't going anywhere with plastic grass — which at the time was all that appeared available in the slots under offer.

Separately, a kindly CEO at the nearby Peterborough HQ of Thomas Cook — to whom I'd written on spec — called me in, showed me his Senior Executive Succession Plan and, rather testingly, asked me where I thought I could fit into that. He was a former submariner, so I suppose he enjoyed putting people in tight spaces. I'd written in cheekily, describing my wide travel and management experience. That included living and flying for over two years in each of the Far East, Middle East and Norway, my RAF Advanced Staff College Training, my weighty responsibilities in the RAF, culminating as Wing Commander Operations at RAF Wittering blah, blah. I suggested a job in the travel industry would suit me (and him — I thought) rather admirably. I left with no job offer but armed with some very pertinent tips on CV writing.

The RAF granted me a standard, one month's leave for a resettlement course, so I signed up for the one-month Business Management Appreciation course at the Polytechnic of Central London. The course was designed for retiring service officers and was a beacon of light in what I was soon to discover was the dark, hurly-burly, jungle of life in commercial practice. I struggled with the complexities of financial reporting, hostile takeover bids and other unfamiliar and unfathomable stuff but some of it stuck — thank heavens as, unknowingly, I was to become a company director in less than a year.

Meanwhile, I had obtained copies of their registers from the Society of British Aircraft Manufacturers and the Defence Manufacturing Association and began to blitz a large number of their members with my much better-presented CV.

As described in chapter fourteen, one of my letters landed up with a former RAF colleague running Firecracker Aircraft. He offered me an immediate consultancy that involved taking the lead on the cockpit design and the selection of a wide range of equipment for the proposed version of the Firecracker that we were to offer to the RAF as a replacement basic flying trainer, as earlier described. Having led the introduction of the new Hawk advanced trainer at RAF Valley from 1976 to 1979, I brought with me a useful, if not unique, insight into shaping the Firecracker cockpit towards the required seamless transition to the Hawk; it didn't win us the contract though. Nevertheless, I had a great time in our rather prestigious St James Street offices, interviewing prospective vendors of aircraft equipment, listening to their presentations and working on the proposal at the design offices at Huntings near Bedford.

During a break, after the Firecracker proposal had been submitted, I had enjoyed the one-month consultancy assignment with another UK company that involved a two-week stay in Beijing, working on an assessment of a certain Chinese military aircraft. That company subsequently offered me employment in a follow-on capacity on the same project but I declined, nervous of having to work closely with one or two, shall we say, 'politically very difficult' countries.

Around the same time as the Firecracker work ceased, I was offered, and I accepted, the post of Export Sales Manager with Helmets Ltd in Wheathampstead, where I became Sales and Marketing Director within six months or so. Having started with Helmets Ltd in January 1985, with zero knowledge of either sales or export, I spent three fantastically busy years traipsing around the world selling flying, police and fire helmets to major air forces, police and fire services. At least I did know the flying helmet and its environment at first hand and my previous experiences with several other air forces came in very handy too. However, it was still a great challenge in presenting Helmets Ltd's new, 'Alpha' lightweight flying helmet to the world. It was a tremendous commercial apprenticeship in which I made many more great contacts and good friends, learnt much detail about international standards for head protection, export procedures and running a network of international agents and representatives. I made presentations to generals and to sergeants, presented leading-edge papers on new developments in the field at various seminars in the UK and USA, attended all the major air shows including at Farnborough, Paris and Singapore and opened several major new markets for the company, notably in Australia. From my final expedition to Australia, I returned with a hard-won order from the RAAF for the new helmet to the value of about twenty-five per cent of our previous year's total turnover. I could hardly believe my luck. The finance director couldn't stop smiling. The chairman was a very happy man. The production director looked as if he'd been hit by a bus.

Towards the end of 1987, by now nearly three years into my time at Helmets Ltd, I was looking for a further step up in aviation-related marketing. I applied for the job of Product Marketing Manager at Westland Helicopters and was shortlisted down to the last two. The recruitment company told me I was the favourite to win the post. It would have been a great step but would no doubt have grounded me for the rest of my career. Then, unfortunately or fortunately as it turned out for me and my flying, Westlands ran into financial problems and began a restructuring. My prospective job disappeared. However, the recruitment company followed with a generous and flattering offer for me to join them as a recruiter in the defence and aerospace industry and I made the first significant mistake so far in my short civilian career: I accepted. It turned out that I had walked into a can of worms and half-truths and soon left that position.

Up to this point, I had just kept my flying skills going in a small way over most weekends with the AEF Chipmunks at RAF Newton. My salvation came in early 1988 in the form of an advertisement in 'Flight International'. It was for a pilot with Hawk experience to join Airworks' team of pilots at RAE Llanbedr to fly on target facilities duties. I joined, re-qualified on the Hawk that I had last flown full-time five years previously in 1979, converted to the Canberra and the Devon, joined the five-man team that flew the Jindivik (chapter fifteen) and had a quiet, cushy time with zero responsibilities in the beautiful area of south Snowdonia to where had we moved and still live thirty two years later. However, I soon got quite bored and began to look elsewhere for more interest, more challenge and more pay.

By the spring of 1989, my hard-won Air Transport Pilots Licence had not been used for nearly five years — the point at which it would lapse and would incur an expensive and time-consuming re-take of various ground examinations and flight tests to revalidate it. I'd been watching the job adverts in 'Flight International' once more and very closely, when I spotted that the Civil Aircraft Division of British Aerospace at Woodford, near Manchester, were advertising for a pilot to fly their company communications aircraft, the fifty-seat HS 748 twin-turboprop. I had zero civil aviation experience and no qualification on turboprops. Woodford was manufacturing the new seventy-two-seat ATP (advanced turbo-prop), a development of the HS 748, and, along with Hatfield, the four-engine, one hundred-seat, BAe 146 jet. I otherwise had little idea of what went on there although I had visited the place as a Staff College student in 1979 to be briefed on the Nimrod AEW project. The ad stated that there would be opportunities for the right person to progress to training and production test flying in the ATP and 146 and the further possibility of participation in customer demonstrations and delivery flights. I rang the Chief Test Pilot (CTP), Peter Henley, directly.

I explained on the phone to Peter that, despite the apparent lack of suitable or relevant qualifications to meet those of the ad, I thought I had a few things going for me, viz extensive experience as a flying instructor (though in fast jets), quite a lot of engineering test flying in the RAF (again, on fast jet trainers) and a well-proven, if short, commercial and marketing record. Peter was an ex-RAF C-130 pilot and I an ex-fighter pilot and fast-jet instructor; we were of very different species. Oddly, we got on famously straight away. He invited me over for a chat in a few days and, after half an hour or so, offered me the job on the spot. It took another three months for security clearances etc. before I started; they were needed because Woodford was also the production and support base for the RAF's classified Nimrod aircraft as earlier mentioned.

Peter Henley, astutely, had been less interested in my lack of civil flying experience (though I had 'done' passenger and freight flying in Beavers and Dakotas in Oman in the late 1960s, as well as a tiny bit in the Devon at Llanbedr), than he was in my extensive experience as a QFI, the recent global sales and marketing experience and the several flying jobs in which I had been multi-type qualified on widely different aircraft. At the time, BAe Woodford was not long into the production of the ATP (cruelly christened 'Ancient Technology Perpetuated' by its detractors), the replacement for the HS 748. Peter forecast, smoothly (and rather too optimistically as it turned out), that the skies of the world would soon be black with ATPs and that there would very likely in due course be a place for me within the training team on that aircraft and probably on worldwide sales tours and in production test flying. I could not believe my luck. I hadn't even known that such a combination of jobs existed. Had I done so, I would have been after one with all my energy on leaving the RAF though I would not have considered at that stage that I was at all qualified. I was still not, really, but the training, commercial and marketing record had apparently swung the decision in my favour as well as the immediate personal rapport with Peter.

I joined BAe in May 1989. I was about to start nearly twelve years in what turned out to be the most challenging, most enjoyable, most satisfying, most incredibly interesting and, from time to time, utterly exhausting and intensely demanding flying job one could imagine. However, the immediate priority was to re-qualify for my lapsed civil IR. That was very hard work though I'd done some practice on the little Devon before leaving Llanbedr. The re-qualification took place in an Aztec again, this time generously rented (for two flights) by BAe from Northern Air Executive, whose MD kindly gave me the practice run before putting me up with his examiner — I hadn't flown the Aztec for five years since the initial ATPL tests. The practice went well and, as a result, the MD also offered me a job if I should ever need one! The test with the grumpy examiner was a bit of an ordeal but I passed. Heaven knows what BAe would have said or done had I failed.

My subsequent induction arrangements at Woodford looked somewhat chaotic. A meeting on day one with one of the training captains (TCs) there, who had been instructed to make arrangements for me, revealed that they wanted me first to fly the eighteen-seat Jetstream 31 because the arrival of the HS 748 had been delayed. In fact, the HS 748 never did turn up so I didn't actually fly the aircraft for which I was recruited although I did complete the ground-school course on type!

The Woodford TC was a bit dour and suggested that there would be a delay of six weeks before I could get on a Jetstream conversion course. He had little idea of how I was to spend my time in the interim. In the meantime, I was apparently to cadge what flying I could in anything that was going. I was a bit down-hearted and had no patience for any of that. By good fortune, from RAF days I knew Peter Smith, the BAe CTP at Prestwick, where my Jetstream training was to take place, so I rang him and within twenty-four hours was offered a one-to-one ground-school course, starting in a few days, to be followed by Peter training me up in the Jetstream, during and between various production test flights! Prestwick at the time was enjoying great sales success with the Jetstream, especially in the USA, so they were really busy with production and there was plenty of flying going on.

I was thus pitched right into the deep end (for the first of many times in BAe), this time participating in test flying in an unfamiliar aircraft whilst trying to learn how to fly it and to operate it on a few flights with company personnel as passengers! It was intensive, fascinating and thoroughly enjoyable. I owe enormous thanks particularly to Peter Smith, an absolute expert who dazzled me with his multi-tasking skills in the air. After a month, I returned to Woodford and, following six passenger flights in two days under the supervision of a Woodford TC, I was let loose as a civil aircraft captain (!) ferrying company passengers between the three main civil aircraft manufacturing sites, but mostly between Woodford and Hatfield. I had just short-circuited the normal route to captaincy in civil aviation by anything from a few years (in corporate flying) to fifteen years (in some major airlines)! I was amazed at the trust that had been put in me so early but absolutely delighted as I was thoroughly enjoying my new job and responsibilities, whereas I'd had little such to speak of at Llanbedr.

If that were not enough, the next step a week later was jaw-dropping. One of my colleagues who'd been with the company for years, and was therefore very experienced on the Jetstream, was due to go on a course to become a CAA authorised examiner (AE) but decided to opt out as it clashed with his holiday plans. Incredibly, I was offered the chance to take his place. The offer was made by the deputy chief test pilot (CTP being away on holiday) to whom I explained that I thought there was quite a high risk that I would not be successful due to my very, very meagre experience in civil aviation. I had operated as a civil aircraft captain for just one week (!) and had amassed less than sixty hours on type (including my unorthodox training) of which only just over six hours were as captain (!). He accepted the risk and I wasn't going to turn the course down either. I was being fast-tracked at a meteoric rate! The AE course, at Stansted near London, was an eye-opener, unsurprisingly but also because it was carried out over nine days of eight sessions in the flight simulator of yet another aircraft that I'd not met at all before, the HS125 corporate jet. I found it extremely hard to make the grade but did so with some generous plaudits from the CAA chief examiner at the final test — I'd got my ticket as an AE and returned to Woodford as their new examiner. One of my early candidates was the CTP whose type rating and instrument rating both had to be renewed. I'm not sure which of us was the more nervous. We both passed!

After a few months of Jetstream operations from Woodford, the pace quickened again when I began to fly the ATP as well, mostly as co-pilot on test flights. Then, a week before Christmas, I was packed off, along with another new colleague of similar background who'd joined along with me, to fly initially as an ATP first officer with Loganair, where I was to learn public transport flying with an airline (about time too I thought, having put the cart well before the horse up to that point), carrying fare-paying passengers for the first time. Loganair's ATPs were mainly based in Edinburgh but with a second base at Manchester. The MAN-EDI-MAN route comprised the bulk of sectors over which I operated but included excursions to Jersey (JER), Guernsey (CGI) and

Belfast Harbour (now better known as George Best Belfast City). Six weeks later I was duly authorised as a captain for Loganair, in which role I flew with them for a further busy week or so before returning to Woodford. Some of the Loganair flights were on very busy, short sectors, especially for JER—CGI, just twenty-one nautical miles, only twenty minutes chock to chock and barely eight to ten minutes airborne! I revelled in them. I had enjoyed the experience immensely and had learned a lot from some very good and very helpful, friendly people. Most of all, with the refinements provided by the Loganair attachment, I was able to see that I and my colleague had made a pretty satisfactory transition to civil air transport captain.

These early milestones with BAe Prestwick, BAe Woodford and Loganair came after very steep learning curves. There were quite a few more to come — and very soon.

Loganair ATP

Jetstream 31 with crew (air and ground) at BAe Woodford (author at rear)

Last Harrier Flight, 29 May 1984, author (on right) with Wg Cdr John
Feasey, OC 1 (F) Sqn

17
BAPTISM IN BANGLADESH

Over the first nine months of employment as a factory pilot with BAe's Civil Aircraft Division at Woodford, the former Avro airfield near Manchester, I had greatly enjoyed flying the nineteen-seat turboprop Jetstream 31 and the seventy-two-seat ATP. They provided novel and valuable experiences in a wide range of civil flight operations. Firstly, it was a privilege to be flying in these aircraft with top civil aviation test pilots (mostly ex-military) at Prestwick and Woodford during production test schedules and on development test flights. Secondly, flying the Jetstream regularly in BAe company passenger service between Woodford and Hatfield and occasionally to Chester, Warton and a few other airfields, provided experience of corporate operations. Lastly, the concentrated public transport operations in Loganair's ATPs enabled me to exercise my ATPL fully in revenue service as a public transport pilot.

I was very soon to add a third type to the repertoire. On 14 March 1990, within a week of returning to Woodford after two very happy months with Loganair, I flew for the first time in a BAe 146 as co-pilot with one of our senior development test pilots, Peter Sedgwick, later to become CTP. It was a three-hour flight from BAe's Broughton facility near Chester, measuring navigation aerial signal strengths; from the recorded signal data, 'polar diagrams' of the kit's performance were produced. This may sound a touch tedious and basically it was, as it involved flying multiple circular tracks centred on Point of Ayr on the Wirral at a height of two thousand feet. However, I was excited at flying the unfamiliar type for the first time and the overall experience brought two more valuable firsts: a civil jet aircraft and a four-engine aircraft. Two days later I flew on a full production flight test schedule of three hours in a 146 and started to learn a lot more about my friendly and capable new jet.

Meanwhile, Loganair kindly allowed me to continue flying as an ATP captain with them on a part-time basis for a further four months. I was soon appointed as an ATP training captain with BAe and followed that with a full conversion onto the 146 via the ground-school and simulator courses at Hatfield. From then on, my BAe duties were to become spread regularly over the three quite distinctive aircraft types, Jetstream, ATP and 146 for the next three and a half years. After this much delayed and unusual transition from RAF Harrier pilot, I was beginning to feel pleasantly at home in the new roles of airline captain and understudy test pilot. I had also settled fairly well into my other role as a CAA approved examiner, in which I performed the six-monthly and annual check flights on all our pilots for them to maintain the privileges of their aircraft type ratings and instrument flight ratings respectively. As I became steadily more aware of the wider activities undertaken by the BAe Flight Operations Department at Woodford, I had begun to realise there were many more exciting new experiences awaiting me.

In August 1990, BAe delivered the first of three ATPs ordered by Biman Bangladesh Airlines. ATPs were expected to replace the airline's twenty-eight-seat Fokker F27s. The first Biman ATP would be used for base training the initial batch of Bangladeshi pilots at Woodford before being flown out, with the second aircraft, to enter service with Biman from Dhaka, mainly on domestic routes plus two international destinations. Earlier, in April, Biman's Deputy Chief Pilot (Training), Captain Badrul Alam, had visited us to discuss the forthcoming training arrangements and other matters associated with the delivery and entry into service of this new aircraft type in Bangladesh. I heard that the MD of the airline was Group Captain (ret'd) Shaukat Ul Islam. I knew Shaukat fairly well when he and I were fellow students on the RAF Advanced Staff Course at Bracknell in 1979. I mentioned to our chief test pilot, Peter Henley, that I hoped I could look forward to meeting my former colleague, in due course, after nearly eleven years. Little did I know the connection was soon to lead to a surprise.

Come the first day of the visit by Captain Alam, there was a preliminary meeting in the morning during which Peter (in my absence) slipped in the rather unfair bombshell that, on the next day, I would give the brief on our plan for training their pilots! I had made the incorrect assumption that one of the longer-serving training captains would pick up that duty. I'd had no warning that I was to have the key role in the Biman project; good heavens — that was a bit wicked! However, after minimal time for preparation, I managed to fluff my way through the brief without too much difficulty and, a few weeks later, found myself leading the flight training programme at Woodford in the first Biman aircraft, S2-ACX. We had no ATP simulator at that time so all the aircraft flying training had to be in the air. More milestones mounted up rapidly. Of course, I hadn't even taken part in a customer pilot training programme before, let alone heading it up and with the various new cultural considerations that flowed from the process. Nevertheless, the few weeks it took for me and my colleagues to carry out the Biman base training for the first four Bangladeshi flight deck crews passed uneventfully.

After a ten-day leave in the Scottish Highlands with my wife, I returned to work for a few days of Jetstream sectors before boarding a Biman DC-10 at Manchester as a passenger to Dhaka. Meanwhile, the first two ATPs had been ferried out from the UK by colleagues who had made a start on line training Biman's first ATP crews in Bangladesh. This was to be the first of five training assignments that I undertook in Dhaka over the next two years and lasted for five very busy weeks. I was quickly captivated by the perpetual kaleidoscope of colourful, teeming humanity (but less so by the grey, teeming skies — it was the monsoon season!); the cultural vibrancy; the pitiful state of the many beggars at every traffic light stop and elsewhere; the uniquely contrasting landscapes of flooded delta lands and tantalising glimpses of the high mountains of Nepal; the sight of a ship sailing serenely and closely by the runway threshold at Chittagong as I landed there. Not unexpectedly, the experience also brought multiple challenges.

We operated the ATPs from Dhaka to the domestic airports of Jessore in the south-west, Rajshahi in the west, Saidpur in the far north, Sylhet in the far north-east and Chittagong and Cox's Bazaar in the far south, plus the two international destinations of Calcutta and Kathmandu. Many of these airfield surfaces were littered with debris (e.g. stones, bottle tops, and luggage wheels) that was a hazard to our low-slung engine propellers so prop tip erosion soon became apparent. The ATP had no auxiliary power unit (APU) and some airfields had no ground power unit (GPU) either, so engine starts on the batteries were not that unusual. That required some carefully thought out procedures and handling on night turn-arounds, when pre-start electrical power had to be conserved in every possible way.

Some airfields had no jet fuel for uplift so we had to carry extra fuel to cover the return flight. On the ground, we suffered the occasional incursion of inquisitive individuals into unmanned cockpits resulting in haphazard switch operation! Keeping the bottom of the flight-deck 'stable' door shut usually fixed that. There were other minor problems, such as those experienced by some of the very slightly-built cabin crew girls — with such unlikely names as Venus, Cynthia and Lovely — who found it quite difficult to close the heavy passenger doors. It was, of course, always a pleasure for the captain to assist! The high humidity of the monsoon brought a number of issues with electrical equipment and caused excess and slightly alarming condensation into the cabin through the passenger air vents. Nevertheless, it was impressive how the ATP was able to shrug off most of the difficulties, notwithstanding its far greater complexity than the F27 or, indeed, Biman's ancient DC10s.

Some of the engineering and flying staff were particularly slow to adapt to the step increases in avionics and engine technology that the aircraft brought. Thankfully, senior staff recognised the benefits that we training captains and BAe engineers and operations support personnel were able to contribute to the wider operation. We had the potential to raise standards in terms of crew co-operation and procedures, professional co-ordination with engineers and other ground staff as well as in introducing the various new technologies such as the electronic flight instrument system (EFIS). However, there were certain groups who, for brazen self-interest, took every opportunity to make mischief in terms of sullying the aircraft, including spreading false information to the public via the press. All this came dramatically to a head sometime after we left following our initial few months' presence. I will return to that later.

Of course, the dominant feature of the period was the monsoon and its rains, not only for the perpetual drenching we and the aircraft got on the ground, but for the occasional huge difficulties in the air of finding our way around the worst of the weather and turbulence. On such occasions, we needed to switch on the engine continuous ignition system in the pounding rain for very long periods. During approach and landing, we found that our windscreen wipers were inadequate for the task as we struggled to see through the rain. Application of rain repellent helped considerably but that wasn't always done as required before flight.

On one particularly drizzly, grizzly day over southern Bangladesh, a colleague and I, piloting separate flights back from Cox's Bazaar and Chittagong to Dhaka, each had to divert up to forty miles east into Burmese and Indian airspace to avoid a solid wall of cumulonimbus clouds showing up in the ghastly reds and magentas on the weather radar (which served us supremely well). The radar, which indicated the heaviest raindrops and therefore the associated heaviest turbulence, was vital to help us stay out of the worst of the aerial maelstroms. On that day, neither of us could raise Burmese ATC on the radio and so we had to rely on procedural clearances from Dhaka; not at all a satisfactory situation, though we had no option.

The Bangladesh combination of rain, high temperature and high humidity was the worst I have experienced, anywhere! I thought I had seen plenty of monsoon weather during two and a half years in the Far East and two seasons in southern Oman — but it was nothing to match that over Bangladesh at the height of their June to October monsoon. The combination of a ground temperature of thirty to thirty-five degrees C or more and humidity at eighty-five per cent or more (which gave forty-five degrees C and ninety per cent plus on the flight deck) was unique to me. On some occasions, it was even necessary to stop loading or unloading operations when a heavy rain shower could take an hour or two to pass through and would dump two to three inches of rain on the airport apron. Perspiration streamed non-stop from every pore and clothes just stuck to your body. Relief came only when airborne, once the air conditioning had chance to dry you and cool you.

Apart from deviations caused by the awful weather, there were other interesting deviations too. Approaching Sylhet across miles and miles of water-logged land, it was not at all unusual before landing to be requested by the ATC tower to fly a pass or two at low level alongside the usually wet runway to clear stray cattle wandering along it. However, it was a very unusual event for a still quite new airline captain in his airliner. Even though he'd done such things (without the cattle) many times over many years in single-seat fast jets, it seemed a bit naughty with five crew and seventy-two passengers onboard! However, in the circumstances, one had to accept the odd departure from what UK airports were used to. I certainly couldn't imagine being asked to do such a thing at Manchester or Edinburgh!

Elsewhere, Kathmandu (KTM) presented (and still does I guess!) its own special demands, as will be familiar to anyone who has seen the airport from a flight deck. KTM sits in a bowl at four thousand four hundred feet altitude surrounded by much higher ground, so approach, go-around and departure procedures are quite demanding and it was essential to fly them accurately. The approach was particularly remarkable for its multi-stepped, steep angles northbound (to land on runway 02) that required quite high rates of descent. The few flights I made to Kathmandu were mostly in cloud or at night, which sharpened the concentration no end. Unfortunately, it also meant that I got to see very little of the wonderful terrain of Nepal. There was just a fleeting glimpse of Everest at dusk one evening when climbing away from KTM. However, on a good day, the flight to Saidpur could reveal tantalising glimpses of Kanchenjunga and its neighbours in the far distance.

The Biman pilots were mostly quite competent, though we had a few difficulties with a small number of individuals who were not as competent as they themselves thought and became quite excitable when confronted with the truth! However, one significant problem was with some ground personnel where we often encountered a sloppy and inaccurate approach to aircraft loading. The faults were not so much of individuals as of their managers. The locals had obviously regarded the F27 as an airborne truck, so there were multiple issues with loading, both within the cabin and in the cargo compartment. It seemed that many passengers travelled with outsize suitcases with various items of household equipment strapped to them — and that was just the hand baggage! Sometimes, the combinations did not get through the cabin door and were removed from the passenger to be loaded at the last minute into the cargo compartments but then did not show on the aircraft load sheets. In addition to the regular outbound cargo of fruit, vegetables and newspapers, we soon discovered that baulks of timber, beds, furniture and even motorbikes were being loaded! Now, I had once carried sedated donkeys and live, kicking goats in SOAF Beavers but... this time was supposed to be an IATA-approved airline operation! The glaring omission was that the dispatchers did not actually supervise the physical loading of cargo, or did so inadequately. Therefore, the load sheets often did not reflect the true weight and centre of gravity (C of G) of the aircraft, which had a narrow C of G envelope anyway. It took only a few 'incidents' to alert us to that issue and to make us ever-watchful for it. Curing it was another matter. The two events I remember most involved bulk newspapers on one occasion and a huge carpet on another.

One day, I took off from Dhaka at the controls myself (thankfully!) only to find at rotation speed that I needed a very strong rearward force on the control column to raise the nose wheel. So, we lifted off, at a fair few knots more than was the plan and a fair bit further down the runway. As we staggered into the air, I trimmed the aircraft rapidly nose-up to help relieve the pull-force. A quick check showed that the trim had been set properly for take-off. That left only one likely explanation, mis-loading of freight. The ATP has rear and forward freight holds, one at each end of the cabin. Once on the ground at our destination, I was able to confirm my suspicions. Sure enough, the forward hold was packed to the gunnels with hundreds of newspapers in tight, heavy bundles. The load sheet had incorrectly shown the total freight-load spread evenly between the two holds. The dispatcher had simply not fulfilled his responsibility to see that the aircraft was actually loaded in accordance with the load sheet! Moreover, I had been expressly assured otherwise before this particular flight as the issue had cropped up earlier on morning departures out of Dhaka. We thought we'd introduced sufficient safeguards to avoid recurrence and so I was very annoyed. After all, aircraft had been known to crash as a result of being badly mis-loaded. Fortunately, with plenty of runway ahead and a fair bit of muscle, I overcame the problem easily and was able to take the appropriate precaution of approaching and landing at the destination with extra knots, despite the shorter landing distance available.

On the second occasion, whilst getting ready one evening for the return flight by night from my first trip to Kathmandu, I became aware of quite a commotion and many voices all shouting at once in the aircraft cabin behind me. Such sounds were not unusual on the ground in that part of the world, especially for example in and around the busy airport terminals, where scores of beggars would vie for one's attention during exit after a long hard day. However, it was certainly abnormal within the aircraft, so I left my seat on the flight deck to investigate and found a most unusual sight. A very large, rolled-up carpet, probably some thirty to forty feet long and two feet or so in diameter and weighing heaven knows what, had been manhandled into the passenger cabin, prior to boarding our passengers, and set down in the aisle for shipment down to Dhaka. There were a number of good reasons why I did not think this was a good wheeze, however often it had been done before, as I was to be repeatedly and excitedly informed by the local Nepali dispatcher. I quietly and firmly resisted all attempts to persuade me that "it was okay" and insisted that the offending carpet be removed. We left a bit late and carpets no longer travelled in that way, at least not whilst we BAe training captains were around.

One other experience that excited some of the locals more than somewhat and that also had me on my toes for a while, took place at Saidpur. It also became the source of false and derogatory reports in the press about the aircraft. I had landed there uneventfully after the one-hour flight from Dhaka. Some forty-five minutes later, my Biman pilot trainee had started the first engine in preparation for the return flight. As the propeller blade pitch angle was being selected from the stable post-start feather to minimum RPM mode, it over-sped to one hundred per cent RPM. I quickly became aware from aural and visual clues that something was going very wrong and selected fuel off immediately to stop the engine. I had remembered well from days flying Dakotas for a short while in Oman that an over-speeding propeller was a potentially very nasty event. It was expected in the Dak that a prop blade detaching in the event of a serious over-speed would cut into the fuselage somewhere around the flight deck; or so I was advised by my ex-World War II and Berlin Airlift Polish captain. Thankfully we never experienced such an event.

In the ATP, I guessed it might also make it that far forward but, more than likely, it would shred a few passengers in the first rows of the cabin (or any newspapers or suchlike in the forward hold!). Whatever, it was certainly not a good idea to run the risk of randomly cutting up a fuselage on the ground, let alone in mid-air. So, when the prop over-sped, there was of course no choice but to shut both engines down and have our flying engineer investigate. Indeed, it was standard procedure. That was duly done by the BAe engineer, whom we carried on these early flights as there was no technical back-up at the outstations at that point.

After a while, back came Phil the spanner to inform me that we probably needed a part to be flown up from Dhaka. That was not going to happen until later the following day so we were likely in for an unscheduled night-stop (in fact, it became two nights for us and the aircraft was there for four days!). We disembarked the passengers and ourselves and went into the terminal to speak by radio to Biman HQ at Dhaka to fix a few technical and logistical arrangements. That simple task quickly became chaos. Within the local airline office sat three local staff plus me, my local pilot, Phil the spanner, the three cabin crew girls and a dispatcher. A multitude of passengers' heads craned around the part-open door, as one of the local officials shouted loudly and quickly into the radio (perhaps to improve the reception at Dhaka?). He initiated each call with a triple "Dhaka! Dhaka! Dhaka!", sounding like a boy imitating a machine gun. Meanwhile, it seemed that audience participation by the passengers, by now halfway into the room, as well as outside, was the local custom. It was bedlam. It would not do. I had little alternative but to shout, even louder than the radio operator, "STOP!" All went quiet; we got the passengers and the rest of the crew outside the office, closed the door and let Phil get to work efficiently on the radio with his counterpart at Dhaka. With all done and the need for a night-stop confirmed, I agreed with my local co-pilot that Phil and I would join him and the girls to stay overnight at the Saidpur Government Rest House. I had stayed a couple of times at such establishments in the north of Malaya in the mid-1960s and assumed that they would be of similarly acceptable standard here in Bangladesh.

As we passed by our crowd of marooned passengers, a couple of Europeans approached me. "Where are you planning to stay overnight?" one of them asked with a clear Scottish accent. I told him our plan and he drew me to one side.

"I really think you shouldn't," he said. "The Saidpur Rest House is pretty poor standard. If you and your colleague would like to stay with us, you'd be welcome. You can have a shower and a decent dinner with a couple of beers and a glass of wine. You won't get any of that in the Rest House."

I needed no further persuasion, so Phil and I took up the hospitality. It turned out that our new friends were both Scotsmen and were supervising a new fish-farming project in the area. After enjoying all their promised hospitality over a couple of hours, it was suggested that we should take a stroll into Saidpur in the dark evening. Though two hundred and eighty miles inland to the north of the Bay of Bengal coast, Saidpur is nevertheless at only one hundred- and twenty-five-feet above sea level so it was still pretty hot and clammy. Nevertheless, we enjoyed our stroll along the crowded, dusty street, flanked on either side by scores of colourful stalls, selling all kinds of wares, even at nine p.m., to the hundreds of bustling, chattering, colourful, Bengali buyers. I noted that there were many loose and mangy dogs darting about, occasionally coming up to yap at us four passing foreigners. I wondered how many might be rabid, aware of the fact that I had chosen not to be vaccinated — I'd heard that it involved injections in the belly and, as one who flinched at any jabs, that put me right off.

We reached the far end of our foray into the rural Bangladesh town: the railway station on whose platform lay hundreds of local people in their ever-colourful clothing, most apparently sleeping, some chatting, most with their multiple containers in which they were to carry their belongings to wherever the train or trains for which they waited would crawl across the Indian sub-continent through the sticky night. It was, I was told, a perfectly normal tableau, though strange to my eyes, that would be similar at other stations throughout the region each evening. For those many not travelling and with no roofs under which to sleep, it was a safe place to be, amongst the crowd and therefore far from the risk of contact with 'dacoits' as the local paper referred to robbers.

Back in our hosts' house after the evening soiree, we talked more about the rabies risk. It emerged that they had also declined rabies jabs as they explained that was the first thing that would happen anyway on arrival at a hospital.

"Where's the nearest hospital?" I asked.

"Dhaka of course," one answered.

"How long does it take to get there?" I ventured.

"Well, about an hour, as you know," came the reply.

And then the penny dropped. With an unserviceable ATP at Saidpur the only airborne option was dead in the water, so to speak. The alternative was a twelve-hour drive by Land Rover! We were awfully glad none of us had been bitten by a dog. I also got a fresh perspective on rabies vaccination — not to the point of being brave enough to have one though. However, maybe it helped me some fifteen years later when I was obliged to self-inject myself in the belly with clexaine twice a day for a week and, to my great surprise, found it was a non-event!

All in all, the Dhaka experience was a very demanding but highly interesting and (mostly) enjoyable baptism into training foreign airline pilots in their home environment. I flew one hundred and seventeen sectors over ninety-five hours in twenty-nine days with only five days off during the thirty-four-day stay. I must say the most relaxing bits were definitely at the evening meals in the cool elegance of the Vintage Room restaurant in the Dhaka Sheraton, sometimes with a colleague pilot or engineer, where we were served by the delightful, smiling, dusky maidens, gliding effortlessly around the floor of the restaurant, whilst we enjoyed excellent food to the music of the sitars and the slightly strange but enchanting tones of the songs of the region. What pleasant people the individual Bengalis were. I could never understand how even the poorest always had ever-ready, wide smiles. Little was I to know that it would be a full ten months before I would return to Bangladesh and then in rather difficult circumstances. But before then I would be operating in a much cooler climate.

Biman ATP

Author and Bangladeshi Crew

18
TESTING TIMES AND ARCTIC FERRY

In a Christmas letter of December 1990 to family and friends, I'd written that the year had been full of good things for me and my wife and that it would be a hard one to beat. With thirty years' hindsight, I don't think it did get beaten! A short resumé should explain.

At work, the year had begun with several months of flying the line on UK domestic routes in Loganair's BAe ATPs, interspersed with operating our Jetstream 31s on company communications passenger flights and participating in many test flights. In February, I had been appointed as an ATP training captain for BAe. I had also continued with my earlier-appointed role as a CAA-authorised examiner in both types over the period and had converted to the four-jet BAe 146 in July. I had led a civil airline training programme on the ATP at Woodford and in Bangladesh from August to November.

In July 1990, in Washington DC, a colleague and I had attended one of the early and excellent Crew Resource Management (CRM) courses run by Captain 'Pen' Pendarvis of North-West Airlines. During the several days of the course, we'd had the great privilege of getting to know Captain Denny Fitch. He was the off-duty training captain who had played the key role in the harrowing landing of a DC-10 (United Airlines flight 232) at Sioux City, with no flight controls, on 19 July 1989, only twelve months earlier. It was Denny who had 'flown' the aircraft via differential thrust on the remaining two of the three engines, after one had disintegrated and severed all hydraulic power to the aircraft flight controls. One hundred and eighty-five of the two hundred and ninety-six persons on board had survived. It was the first time after the crash that Denny had given a presentation on that dramatic event. We were all transfixed, mesmerised at the skill and airmanship that was displayed after the catastrophic failure and that led to the aircraft being crash-landed with only differential thrust to 'control' its flight path. We studied this and several other iconic accidents of the preceding years and learned permanent, vital lessons from them in terms of pilot handling, airmanship and crew co-ordination.

In amongst all the hurly-burly of work travel, my wife and I had managed to fit in a magical three-and-a-half-week holiday, up the Nile in Egypt, and on safari around Kenya, topped off with four days by the beach at Mombasa. We had also managed to take a week off in our timeshare lodge at Loch Rannoch just before I went to Bangladesh.

Shortly after returning to the UK from Bangladesh, I was surprised and delighted to be appointed by the company and the CAA to command production test flights and certain development test flights in the ATP. Officially becoming a test pilot, especially not having had the usual benefit of completing the Empire Test Pilot School (ETPS) course at Boscombe Down, was a thirty-year ambition realised at last. I had begun my flying career in 1960 as a sixteen-year-old scientific assistant at the Naval Air Department of RAE Bedford, where I had participated — albeit mainly on the ground — in many trials of naval aircraft and associated ship-borne catapult and landing systems. It was there, where I saw top military test pilots flying the fascinating types of the 1960s, rubbed shoulders a little with them on the ground and even flew with some of them very occasionally, that the kerosene got into my blood and I resolved to become a Hunter pilot, having no idea of where it would all lead after that!

I have to admit to being tickled pink at this new responsibility given me by BAe. I had already found at Woodford that there was something especially satisfying about taking into the air an airframe that had never flown before, even though it had been preceded by others of the same type. To be in charge on first flights was therefore both a delight and a privilege. The two production flight test schedules (PFTS 1 and 2) for the ATP were long, typically two and a half to three and a half hours each and, in some parts, very demanding, so there was plenty to learn and plenty of scope for sharpening one's skills. The process always started in long and detailed discussions with the factory floor managers as each aircraft approached the date of PFTS 1. Next was a very thorough and detailed external and internal inspection by the captain of the aircraft. Time constraints often caused that process to be carried out on the day preceding the flight, so that just a shorter external could be made before beginning the pre-flight engine start procedures on the flight deck, then taking the aircraft out to its first take-off.

We always carried a flight test engineer (FTE) who had responsibility for orchestrating the procedures and recording much of the data. The FTE and the two pilots worked together throughout the flight test schedule as a close-knit team and it was a great experience every time. Detailed and thorough tests were carried out to check the full functioning of all systems and controls, e.g. electrical, mechanical, hydraulic and pneumatic. The handling and performance of the aircraft was checked and measured across the full flight envelope with every relevant parameter being recorded by the FTE. Specific system tests included flight instruments and avionics, anti-icing and de-icing, shutdown and relight of each engine, slam accelerations, emergency gear extension, pressurisation and air conditioning, fuel feed, emergency oxygen drop out (producing the 'rubber jungle' hanging throughout the passenger cabin) and various other standby and emergency system modes. As well as full checks of all primary and secondary controls and three-axis trims, flight handling and performance, tests included measurement of range and endurance, stalling to stick push, dives to maximum speed and all auto-flight modes as well as manual approaches and landings.

On PFTS 1, we also carried a couple of assistants whose task it was to carry out the detailed inspections and adjustments of various items of cabin equipment. They focussed particularly on internal doors and overhead bins that usually needed tweaking as the cabin reached its pressure altitude of eight thousand feet and aircraft altitude of twenty-five thousand feet, by which time various bits had shrunk or expanded and required adjustment. In most cases it took additional flights to clear cabin and systems snags that had surfaced on the two primary test sessions. Handling and performance were rarely issues.

The second international work experience with BAe came in January 1991 and was a very different delight. I shared a midwinter ferry flight in a BAe 146 with two pilot colleagues from Woodford to Washington Dulles, via a night-stop in Reykjavik and refuelling stops the next day at Sondrestrom in central Greenland, Goose Bay in the wilderness of Newfoundland and Bangor, Maine. What a total contrast that was to the first overseas adventure in hot, steamy and very crowded Bangladesh.

We arrived in the Arctic darkness even though it was late morning. The instrument approach along the fjord to Sondrestrom was novel as it terminated in a radar ground-controlled approach (GCA) given by a US controller, whose expertise was more than useful; there was little margin for error between the adjacent walls of rock and ice that we couldn't see! GCAs were standard for me as an RAF fast jet pilot in the 1960s to 1980s but rare in civil aviation, so I hadn't flown one in years and I found myself a little on edge until the runway became visible just before the minimum decision height for the landing.

Only three weeks after the Arctic delivery flight, in late February of 1991, I was soon back in the tropics on what was perhaps the best adventure of the whole eleven and a half years with BAe, when the late Kevin Moorhouse and I ferried our ATP demonstrator, registration G-BRLY, from Djibouti to New Zealand via Nairobi, the Seychelles, Colombo, Medan, Djakarta, Bali, Darwin, Cairns and Brisbane to Auckland. The unusual route was dictated by the company insurer's requirements to steer well clear of areas involved in the Gulf War. We needed to stop off to give a few demonstrations in Indonesia and, finally, the biggest objective was to fly demonstrations in New Zealand. As part of that objective, we were also to fly fare-paying routes for a few weeks with potential buyer Mount Cook Airlines, based in Christchurch but flying to a number of domestic airports in both North and South Islands. I was away for a month on that task and it was a splendid experience. It also gave me the opportunity to qualify to give demonstration flights to passengers or pilots in the ATP. That would of course soon lead to more great excursions in other sales demonstration tours.

19
ATP TO INDONESIA AND NEW ZEALAND

(This article is dedicated to my good friend, fellow training captain and test pilot Kevin Moorhouse, with whom I shared the events described below. Tragically, Kevin was killed at the age of fifty in a flying accident on 21 July 1996 whilst carrying out a display in the last flying Mosquito aircraft at Barton airfield near Manchester).

It was a cold, wet and windy day in late January 1991 as I sat in my first-floor office in the Flight Test Centre on the south side of Woodford airfield near Manchester. Despite the rain I could still see quite clearly across the few hundred yards of wet tarmac to where the tiny, round-topped hangar from 1925 and the adjacent clubhouse stood as silent sentinels over the historic airfield. Those sentinels had watched over so many first flights, for a while from Woodford's grass strips then later from the single east/west runway. They had witnessed, too, a few aircraft falling cruelly to the ground. This place in the soft Cheshire countryside, still bordered on three sides by quiet farms, was once the home of the Avro dynasty of aircraft, the 504, Manchester, Tutor, Lancaster, Tudor, Lincoln and the later Shackleton and Vulcan. More recently, Nimrods and HS 748s had taken to the air for the first time from here.

Much further away, through the rain blowing in vertical swathes across the runway to drench the north side of the airfield, I could just make out the large 'New Assembly' buildings of the British Aerospace Regional Aircraft factory. Inside the tall, brightly lit, dry, warm and modern buildings, brand new aircraft were still being built here by men and women with great skill — ATPs on one production line and BAe 146s on the other. In 1991 the ATP was still in its early years of production. The seventy-two-seat aircraft was a stretched development of the HS 748, with state-of-the-art six-bladed composite propellers driven by new Pratt and Whitney 126 engines, a totally new EFIS-based flight deck along with other modern avionics and a completely revamped, modern and quiet cabin. What a contrast to those early, flimsy Avro biplanes.

On that wet winter's day at Woodford, I was happy to be contemplating my coming tour with the ATP demonstration aircraft to Far Eastern lands with climates much warmer and considerably more exotic than quiet Cheshire. With charts and open manuals spread all around, I was finalising my plans to fly the demonstrator from Woodford on its sales tour to Indonesia and New Zealand. The tour would reach its climax with the aircraft spending two weeks at Christchurch in South Island to fly public transport services on behalf of Mount Cook Airlines, an HS 748 operator looking for new equipment. But first of all, we had to sort out a significant problem with the routeing. Our favoured flight plan to the Far East would have taken us on the well-trodden path of refuelling stops at Brindisi, Luxor, one or other Arabian Gulf airports, another in southern India and then on to Djakarta via Sumatra. However, the BAe insurers didn't want us anywhere near the Gulf. Saddam Hussein had invaded Kuwait in August 1990 and the ground war to remove Iraqi forces from the Gulf state would be starting very soon. The air war had already been going on since 16 January.

Working under Captain Kevin Moorhouse, the production test and training manager, I had been tasked to come up with a suitable route to get the aircraft, along with its sales and support team, to Indonesia in time for the first customer demonstration flights that were due to start on 26 February in Djakarta. Kevin and I were both production test pilots and training captains on the ATP. Kevin was an old hand at sales tours and demonstration flights on the 748 and the ATP, as well as having been with the new aircraft since its early development testing. By contrast, I had only been with BAe for less than two years and so I was very glad to be in his expert and friendly company for my first exposure to a major sales tour. At least I had become very familiar with the aircraft, not just from flight-testing it, but also by having cut my teeth in airline service with it over several delightful months with Loganair. I had next worked as the project pilot for Biman Bangladesh Airlines, base training their pilots at Woodford before staying for over a month in Dhaka to help set up their ATP services to Calcutta and to various airports in Bangladesh. I had already accumulated about five hundred hours on the aircraft during flight-testing, training and airline service.

Kevin and I had looked at three routes to Indonesia. Two were a bit too exotic and were soon rejected. The first to be binned was that through Eastern Europe, Russia, Central Asia and Western China. Though it had the distinct advantage of being the most direct of our three options, our multiple doubts at that time over the availability of fuel supplies, the likely poor quality of ATC facilities, language difficulties, diplomatic clearances and, perhaps most of all, the continental midwinter weather soon caused us to discount that option. Next to go into the bin was a west-about route through the northerly Arctic latitudes. That would have had us flying out at first on our familiar North Atlantic ferry route through Iceland, Greenland and eastern Canada but then continuing on through Canada to Alaska, the Aleutians and down to Indonesia via a North Pacific island or two. However, this was by far the longest option and one or two of the final legs were really rather too long. Also, again, the freezing winter weather across Canada for an aircraft with a service ceiling of twenty-five thousand feet and not the most fantastic de-icing systems was likely to prove problematic. So we turned our attention to the third and final option, which was initially as per the standard route to Luxor but continuing south to Djibouti and Nairobi, so avoiding both the Gulf and Somalia within which there was no effective ATC and over which we thought we could possibly be met by unfriendly local air activity. From Nairobi it was left-hand down and across the Indian Ocean to the Seychelles and Colombo, then finally on south-eastwards to Medan in Sumatra and Djakarta in Java. I had taken on the detailed planning for this third option and continued with the final route from Indonesia through Australia to Auckland, our first of many destinations in New Zealand.

In between the planning tasks for the long journey to New Zealand, I got on with my other work flying company passengers around the UK, training flights for two new co-pilots in the Jetstream 31, delivering a BAe 146 across the North Atlantic via Reykjavik, Sondestrøm, Goose Bay and Bangor Maine to Washington DC, several test flights and a type and (a second) instrument rating renewal for our chief test pilot in the ATP demonstrator that was scheduled for the New Zealand trip, G-BRLY. Such was the variety of the very interesting and thoroughly satisfying work for our busy team of pilots at Woodford in the early 1990s. However, as the scheduled day of departure for our odyssey to the Far East rapidly approached, it became clear that G-BRLY was not going to be fully ready on time. That was worrying news because we were to carry out a number of VIP demonstration flights in Indonesia and we did not want the embarrassment of a delay to the published programme for our three-day stay there. We had planned for several night stops on the long route to Djakarta as well as a contingency day or two to take care of any unforeseen problems on the way. That was necessary because we expected little opportunity for rest between arriving in Indonesia and completing the first phase of demonstrations in New Zealand some two weeks later. The tremendously busy schedule at Woodford meant that there were no other company pilots who could be released to accompany us to Indonesia in order to reduce the need for stopovers and ultimately to ensure that Kevin and I were sufficiently rested on arrival in Indonesia to complete the full programme and press on to New Zealand to do the same in North Island.

A compromise plot was hatched to enable G-BRLY to be flown out by another crew as far as Djibouti. They could then return immediately to the hectic tasks at Woodford, whilst Kevin and I took her onward to Indonesia. It was the best we could do. We took a flight as passengers via Paris to Djibouti, checked into our hotel and settled down to rest up for two days in the pleasant warmth and wait for the arrival of our aircraft. The air campaign in the Gulf was about to reach a crescendo. We spent a fair bit of our time watching CNN as the events unfolded in Kuwait and eastern Iraq. There was not a lot else to do in Djibouti, the former colony of French Somaliland, apart from lazing around the hotel swimming pool. G-BRLY finally arrived at Djibouti from Luxor at eleven thirty p.m. on 22 February, late even on the revised schedule, so Kevin and I had no option but to fly her straight down overnight on the four-hour, forty-minute flight to Nairobi.

We took off about an hour and a half later, with our newly arrived band of sales and support staff who had come in with our aircraft, and headed south for Kenya in the dark African night over the Ethiopian mountains. Kevin had suggested generously that we share the captaincy, flight by flight, and kindly gave me this first sector. It was a quiet, clear and uneventful night. The contrast of flying over that part of East Africa, with little to see below but the faint lights of a very few campfires and tiny settlements, was stark compared with night-flying over Europe with its voluminous bright lights that were left on all night. The unknown but potentially dangerous country of Somalia lay not far east of our track. We speculated only briefly on whether we could have got away with flying direct to the Seychelles across Somalia instead of taking this huge dog-leg to the south to avoid that desperate, war-torn land. We guessed there was always the risk of meeting one of the ragged Somali Air Force's few serviceable MIGs, not to mention the problem of where would we have gone in the event of needing a diversion. We agreed that Somali airspace was best left well alone. Apart from a few brief exchanges on the radios with Addis Ababa, initially on HF then on VHF, there was nobody else to talk to until we approached Kenya and made contact with Nairobi. Arriving just before dawn to land at Eastleigh, five thousand, three hundred and eighty feet above sea level, we emerged from our aircraft tired and ready for some sleep. Within an hour or so we were at a hotel, had a quick breakfast and went straight to bed, enjoying only a fitful few hours' sleep — as usual after an overnight flight — before having to return to the airport to set off again. We left Nairobi on a direct track to our destination, passing well north of Malindi to coast out on the long sea leg to the Seychelles and arriving after four hours to be transported to a particularly nice holiday hotel for our second night-stop after leaving Djibouti. The schedule had been regained and we were able to enjoy a pleasant evening and dinner, followed by a much-needed proper night's sleep.

The next day was something of a unique adventure in that we had a very long sector, all over the Indian Ocean, for the one thousand six hundred and forty nautical miles to Colombo in Sri Lanka. For much of the middle part of this flight we were flying a very long way indeed from a diversion airfield. At the point where we crossed the equator northeast-bound, just before midway to Colombo, the runway at Gan in the Maldive Islands still lay a greater distance ahead on our track than the only other option, Diego Garcia, some four hundred and ninety nautical miles to the southeast — nearly two and a half hours away on one engine should we have had an engine failure. It was 24 February, the day that coalition land forces invaded Iraq. We had learned from CNN that Diego was still very busy sending B52s and other aircraft off to bomb Iraqi forces in and near Kuwait. I recalled the earlier brush with a B52 at Clark Field in the Philippines, twenty-five years earlier at the height of the Vietnam War, when I was told rudely to get my 'ass' (or, rather, the 'ass' of my Hunter FGA9) out of the way of the eight engine giant in a hurry on the taxiway behind me. I didn't mind that as much as I did mind being referred to as an 'Australian fighter'! I guessed that our insignificant ATP would more than likely not have been welcome at Diego. We became more relaxed as the distance to the Maldives eventually shrank down to a few hundred nautical miles. The planned fuel calculations for the whole route showed a margin of only three hundred and eighty kilograms over the minimum required over Colombo Bandaranaike airport to allow a diversion and hold at Ratmalana airport twenty nautical miles away. We arrived after a very long seven hours, forty minutes flight from the Seychelles, forty minutes longer than planned and one hour after dark, leaving us with an actual margin of about twenty minutes over the minimum fuel load to reach Ratmalana, if needed— not a lot to play with, but enough. Colombo was just another airport and another hotel then we were off the following day to Medan, the capital city of North Sumatra (five hours, forty minutes), then Djakarta Halim in Java (three hours, fifty minutes), arriving on the evening of 25 February, again by night.

The journey from Colombo to Djakarta was uneventful except for the usual ritual that we encountered in some countries where we had to pay for fuel by cash in used, unmarked, US dollar notes. As the agent at Medan painstakingly examined each of the $50 and $10 notes for any markings, I remembered the trouble I'd had before leaving Woodford in persuading a new young member of the cashiers' office that I really did need $25,000 in used, unmarked $50 and $10 notes with which to pay for fuel and other expenses en route. I watched the agent in Medan counting and scrutinising the money as we sat together in the aircraft cabin and I wondered wildly where all those dollar notes would end up.

In Djakarta, we stayed in the very comfortable Hilton in the centre of the city. We had arrived at Halim airport, which was a little closer to the city centre than the busier main Djakarta Soekarno international airport some way outside. That reduced the chances of wasting time holding for departures or arrivals whilst we conducted our demonstration flights over the next three days. We flew ten demonstration flights, two for pilots only and eight for passengers. For fairly obvious reasons, it was not a good idea to mix the two though sometimes it became unavoidable, and then necessarily limiting for the guest pilots involved. Pilots from potential customer airlines or local aviation regulating authorities are usually interested in seeing the corners of the flight envelope and, even in a passenger aircraft, that often means exploring high roll rates, aileron reversals, stalling characteristics and so on. By contrast, the aim always in passenger demonstrations is to give your guests a smooth, quiet and very comfortable in-flight service with fine food and wines and a little bit of gentle sightseeing. Even in a fairly benign aircraft such as the ATP, it does not help to convince the buyers and other decision makers to place orders for your aircraft if they are subjected unexpectedly to a sudden roll or pitch manoeuvre at the instant of popping a delicate canapé of smoked salmon and caviar into their mouth or whilst sipping ecstatically on a glass of premium champagne. Moreover, such bad behaviour from the pilots upfront would certainly not endear them to the ladies of the cabin crew at the rear. On this occasion, as on subsequent similar tours, we were blessed with the presence of two attractive and delightful part-time British Airways stewardesses, Marilyn and Ann, whose skills in passenger service had been well-tested with British Aerospace on numerous prior occasions and found to be beyond fault. As well as being highly professional cabin crew, they were also good friends and they deserved as strong support from us as they gave to us.

Our demonstrations seemed to go smoothly and very well. We usually flew out to the quiet area around the island of Anak Krakatoa, the 'Child' of Krakatoa, that former volcano well to the west of Djakarta and off the southern tip of Sumatra, that had erupted with such devastating effect on 27 August 1833. The 'Anak' remained inactive and quiet during our visits and that allowed me — at least with the passengers — to practise my dulcet tones on the PA system whilst airing my little knowledge of the geography and the geological history of the area, though on reflection I would imagine most of my captive audience knew far more than I did of Krakatoa. We went to the same area to do our pilot demos, partly out of habit and partly to make the navigation easy so that we could keep a closer eye on the handling by our guest drivers. As well as the flights from Halim to Krakatoa and back we also flew on three occasions into Bandung airfield, the Indonesian aircraft manufacturing centre in the middle of the city of Bandung, two thousand, four hundred feet up in the mountains and one hundred nautical miles south of Djakarta. Two of those flights were to drop off Dr B.J. Habibie and his entourage, on one occasion at Soekarno International and on the other at Halim. At that time, Dr Habibie was chief of Indonesia's burgeoning aircraft industry and later became the country's president — albeit for a very brief period. We must have been reasonably successful with Dr Habibie because the local domestic airline, Merpati Nusantara, subsequently ordered five ATPs. Within eighteen months I found myself returning to Djakarta for the first of two most enjoyable stays to train their pilots in service on their new aircraft. The Indonesian part of our sales tour came to an end after nearly eleven hours of demonstration flying spread over three days and we set off for New Zealand in G-BRLY on the final day, March 1, via night-stops in Bali and Cairns with an intermediate short stop for refuelling in Darwin.

Bali seemed an idyllic place, especially from our perspective in a beachside luxury hotel, and I regret that I have still not found an opportunity to return there. Darwin looked much more civilised than when I'd seen it for the first time as a young RAF pilot, twenty-four years previously in 1967. It had been largely rebuilt after Christmas 1974 when tropical cyclone Tracy had laid much of it to waste, killing seventy-one people. I have always associated Darwin with the legendary Reg Meisner, an F86 Sabre pilot of the Royal Australian Air Force Wing at Butterworth near Penang, whom I knew well in the days of Confrontation by Indonesia against Malaysia from 1963 to 1966. I had met up with him again at Darwin in 1967. Reg had the perfect line in dry Australian humour. Over a few beers in a bar at Darwin, he had regaled me with tales of the new single-engine Mirages that he was flying. I wondered what had become of him. I recalled with some sadness that Indonesia, the lovely country in which Kevin and I and our team had just spent three busy and enjoyable days, was the same country that we Air Force pilots had known from our target study of its airfields and other installations. We would have been sent to attack those targets had Confrontation escalated to something more serious, as it had once looked like doing.

I had planned our route to fly from Darwin to Cairns, which seemed the most appropriate place to make a refuelling stop en route to Brisbane, our exit from Australia to New Zealand. However, Darwin — Cairns — Brisbane turned out to be an unexpectedly unnecessary dog-leg. Whilst flying across the Gulf of Carpentaria and about halfway between Darwin and Cairns, with Kevin flying and me doing the radio bits, I found myself having quite a chat with a very friendly Aussie air traffic controller with the apparent callsign of 'Mownoiza'. I asked him where exactly he was. He repeated, "Mownoiza — abowd a hun'ed an fifdy moiles roid uv yer currand trekk." I looked across the fold of my chart and saw an airfield marked with the name: Mount Isa, and the penny dropped. We could easily have stopped off there instead of Cairns and saved quite a bit of time and fuel on a more direct route to Brisbane. However, 'Mownoiza' was on the edge of the Simpson Desert and probably not as attractive a place for a night-stop as Cairns, on the coast by the Great Barrier Reef. The short stop there was again enough to learn of the delights of the area and to vow to return one day, another as yet unfulfilled wish.

After refuelling at Brisbane, the next day, we set off across the Tasman Sea for the one thousand two hundred and fifty nautical miles flight to Auckland, where our first demonstrations in New Zealand were to take place for the Royal New Zealand Air Force. After four hundred nautical miles we passed over Lord Howe Island, the crucial landmark on Francis Chichester's epic first east-west flight across the Tasman on 3 April 1931. Chichester had landed his tiny Gypsy Moth floatplane on the lagoon at Lord Howe, having navigated there successfully with only a sextant and a notepad strapped to his leg! And there we were, overhead only sixty years later at twenty-five thousand feet, with our twin turboprops, electronic navigator, EFIS, air conditioning and many other mod cons. We spent two busy days at Auckland, on the first day flying to the RNZAF transport aircraft base at Whenuapai, around the city to the north west, where we gave a demonstration flight to Air Force pilots. On the second, we flew to Rotorua where we and the operations staff wanted to evaluate the special take-off and landing procedures that were in force there to cater for the constraints of the local terrain, as was common for many other airfields in New Zealand. On the same day we landed also at Palmerston to pick up our first group of invited passenger guests. Once again, Marilyn and Ann did the airborne cocktail party hostess bits so expertly for the benefit of the invited civil and military VIPs in the cabin.

With most of our North Island demonstration programme complete, we took off for the last time from Auckland early on the third day for two more stops en route to Christchurch in South Island where we were to be based for several weeks flying the line with Mount Cook Airline. First stop out of Auckland on the final day was Taupo, another airfield that needed to be evaluated for ATP operations. Next was Wellington, windy Wellington, living up to its name and where Kevin flew us through a very turbulent approach to land smoothly in a strong and gusty cross-wind. After an hour's passenger demonstration, out and back again to Wellington with yet more guests grazing away on champagne and caviar, we took off for the fourth time that day to arrive finally at Christchurch in South Island to meet our hosts at Mount Cook Airline. We had completed twelve sectors and twelve hours flying in the three days since arriving in New Zealand. We had even begun to get used to the sun tracking around the sky past the opposite end of the compass needle, together with that other unique oddity of flying in New Zealand, a Flight Level (FL) system divided by an east/west line rather than the conventional north/south used elsewhere in the world. Since most routes in New Zealand were oriented roughly north/south, the revised FL system made adequately good sense but I didn't ever get fully accustomed to the sun being in the north at midday.

There was no rest to be had just yet. The following morning, we were airborne early on a demonstration flight for several Mount Cook Airline pilots, a flight which I conducted having 'solo'd' at Auckland with the RNZAF pilots and having by then learnt thoroughly from Kevin the principles of demonstrating the ATP to potential customer pilots. I operated out over the Banks Peninsula to the East of Christchurch and over the surrounding sea area then back into the circuit at the airport for the locals to try their hands at landing the ATP. There were no difficulties. As seasoned 748 pilots, the Mount Cook drivers were very quickly at home in the aircraft despite the considerable differences with the Pratt & Whitney 126 engines and the totally different, EFIS-based, flight instrument panel. I took the chance to have a closer look at the Banks Peninsula by car a week or two later. This area, an attractive miniature version of Wales, was in 1840 the site of a very short-lived French settlement in New Zealand before Britain quickly asserted sovereignty over the whole country. There were some very attractive properties for sale when I visited, including a ranch house with an adjoining thirty-acre deer farm for half the price of my Welsh home and its few fields. So I could have bought two. Tempting, but by then my wife and I had already decided that we had found our forever home in the coastal area of south Snowdonia.

The next flight of that day, 7 March, was to be the most memorable of the whole tour. We were to fly a large group of airline, government and industry VIPs and representatives of the press, from Christchurch southwards down to Mount Cook airport at the foot of the long Tasman glacier and then on, after a short stop at Mount Cook, to Queenstown. Both of these airports, but particularly Mount Cook, had fairly demanding features. But first of all, I must mention the thrilling experience of the flight at relatively low level down the length of the Tasman Glacier to Mount Cook at its foot. Kevin quite rightly chose to do the first landings from the left-hand seat at Mount Cook and Queenstown. He was, after all and by a large margin, the more experienced of the two of us on the ATP and as the boss it was his right to choose. However, as we started the left turn to fly down the glacier from its highest point, it became quickly obvious to me that from my right-hand seat perch I was to have the advantage of being hands-free to take some very nice photographs of the scenery, where numerous side glaciers flowed past jagged peaks into the main glacier. Luckily, the only tasks I had on the flight deck were to handle the radio calls to Mount Cook and to achieve visual separation from one of the locally based Turbo Porter aircraft flying up with a group of tourists to land on the glacier itself — an experience I was to enjoy for myself a week or so later. We drank in the scenery in the crystal-clear air of South Island as we followed the glacier down its valley. Then, as the ice petered out beneath us and the narrow airstrip at Mount Cook came into view, it was time to put the camera away and help Kevin with guidance for the right turn onto finals as he kept a close eye on the mountain wall to our left!

The landing itself needed to be very accurate. Although the landing distance was adequate, the width of the sealed landing strip was only forty-seven feet, a 'low-cost' width perhaps! That left less than ten feet each side of the twenty seven feet, nine inch main-wheel span on the ATP. The width of the strip had been designed at an earlier time to be sufficient to cater for the narrower track 748. Part of the day's demonstration was to show that the ATP could be safely operated to and from Mount Cook without the need for changes to the strip. Kevin made his usual copybook landing and we turned off onto the small parking area for a break that allowed us and our passengers to stroll around and admire the stunning scenery of the Southern Alps, including Mount Cook itself with the valley of the glacier to its north-east. Kevin and I then turned our attention to the special take-off procedure for runway 31 that included a prompt right turn once abeam a checkpoint marker three thousand feet beyond the end of the TODA (Take-Off Distance Available) on the left side of the extended centre-line. The initial take-off on 31 was towards the steeply rising Wakefield Spur but, provided the turn was begun accurately at the checkpoint, there was just enough room to complete it at thirty degrees bank (even twenty degrees bank in the event of one engine failing on take-off), leaving the Spur just off to the left. The turn had to be continued through more than one hundred and eighty degrees onto the departure heading and just inside the Liebig Range of hills to the north-east of the strip, whilst maintaining minimum speed in the climb. Halfway round the turn the aircraft had to be flown directly over a second marker, on the west bank of the Hooker River, and then the rest was easy. Yes, having done it on the day, there was just enough room. The local procedures stated clearly that there must be a minimum headwind of ten knots for take-off on runway 31 — i.e. blowing away from the Spur — I wouldn't question that for one moment!

With the stunning scenery during the initial approach down the glacier, and the demanding landing and take-off procedures, Mount Cook became one of those particular airfields that will always stay etched sharply in my memory along with the likes of Kai Tak, Kathmandu, Dominica, Bogota and a handful of others. With the day's first great experience behind us we headed on down to Queenstown which, had we not already just visited Mount Cook, would alone have been the landmark experience of the New Zealand tour. Queenstown too is a slightly tricky little airfield but it was already being used by Mount Cook Airline's 748s and also by the BAe 146s of Ansett New Zealand. So Kevin and I were looking at this airfield primarily from the point of view of ATP operations but also as 146 pilots.

Queenstown is a bustling and very popular tourist destination, endowed again with beautiful mountain scenery and the lovely Lake Wakatipu, and is home to the extreme experiences of bungee jumping and the Shotover Jet — more later! There was a gondola lift up the side of a hillside on the edge of the town to a fine restaurant with panoramic views over the town, the lake and to the 'Remarkables', the mountains to the south. Egged on by a senior Mount Cook Airline executive, Kevin swooped down gracefully out of the north in a lazy left turn to pass at an impressive — but legal (!) — distance, directly in front of the wide windows of the restaurant on the hillside, to announce simultaneously to our passengers, and the restaurant diners alike, the arrival of the first ATP flight at Queenstown. We turned to pass by the waters of the Frankton Arm then onward to downwind and finals for runway 23, noting the downdrafts over the cliff just before the runway. This was also a fairly short strip so we thought it would be easier to operate the ATP from here, with its excellent reverse pitch propeller system, than the 146 that had to rely on anti-skid brakes alone to stop.

After refuelling and settling the aircraft down, Kevin and I followed all the cabin occupants in taxis and then for gondola trips up to the restaurant to enjoy a fine lunch and the congratulations of the restaurant staff for livening up their daily routine with the pass in front of the windows an hour earlier. We flew back to Christchurch that afternoon, having enjoyed a successful day in and over one of the most attractive areas of New Zealand. On the next and ninth continuous day of flying, I conducted another demonstration for pilots before we set off again to fly further south to Dunedin, where we picked up yet another group of guests to fly around, before returning for a civic lunch at the airport with a most friendly bunch of locals, each of whom seemed so anxious to ask us what we thought of New Zealand. Since this was my third, extended and most enjoyable stay in their country since first visiting it in 1967, I was pleased and honest to be able to tell them that I loved it!

At long last, on the next day, we were able to have a day off as several additional colleagues began to arrive from the winter in far-off UK, raising our numbers to those required to put the ATP into full service for a couple of weeks with the airline. However, the process of official clearance from the New Zealand CAA for us to carry out public transport service with the new aircraft took a little longer to complete than had been planned. The delay allowed us a few unexpected further days off in the following week during which several of us were generously given free tickets on one of Mount Cook Airline's 748 flights back and forth to Queenstown and Mount Cook to enjoy a bit of sightseeing. Kevin and I and the two girls, Ann and Marilyn, enjoyed a super day out on and around Lake Wakatipu, where we were dropped off by boat well up along the shoreline and took a long walk back in the woodland by the lake's edge, listening to the many strange calls and sights of New Zealand's unfamiliar birds and animals. We also had time to experience the 'Shotover Jet', a (literally) hair-raising trip in a fast jet-boat down a very narrow, rocky, shallow water gorge where the boat driver dashed to within a hair's breadth of the rocks every twenty seconds, convincing the four of us every twenty seconds that we would be smashed to death against the rock face. There had previously been some nervous bravado in discussion between us about doing a bungee jump as well. By the time we'd done the Shotover Jet, there wasn't an ounce of courage left between us, so we binned the bungee jump immediately, unanimously and permanently.

Another fine experience that I enjoyed on one of these bonus days off was to take one of the Turbo Porter flights from Mount Cook airfield up onto the glacier. This gave me an even better opportunity for photography than I had enjoyed in G-BRLY with Kevin. Fortunately, I sat at the front in the right seat next to the single pilot and, once again in crystal-clear air, got some of the best shots of the whole tour since leaving Djibouti three weeks earlier.

The sightseeing was soon over and we went to work in earnest, flying passengers for the airline between Christchurch, Queenstown, Rotorua, Nelson and Wellington. I also managed on my last day in New Zealand to 'borrow' G-BRLY for an hour to renew the instrument rating of one of our own captains who had joined us for the revenue flying. It was now time for me to return to the UK, leaving my colleagues to complete the final week with the airline before they flew the aircraft back to Woodford. In those days, we globetrotting BAe factory pilots were privileged to choose our own travel arrangements and so I toyed seriously with the idea of completing my first ever global circumnavigation by returning home via Tahiti, Hawaii and LA, perhaps taking another day or two off in one or both of the first two places. I had no wish to stop long in LA, where I'd been twice before and didn't think much of it. Whichever way I flew home, it was going to be a long way from Christchurch, New Zealand to Snowdonia.

I had by now been away from home for four weeks and in that period had spent ninety-seven hours and thirty minutes in the ATP demonstrator, doing some fairly demanding work, all in initially unfamiliar places and striving hard constantly to miss no opportunity to help 'sell' the aircraft in every way that I could. I was tired and began to think that I didn't really need yet another new place and another new hotel, however attractive both might be. So, I took the option to fly back by the quickest route possible via a few hours' stopover at Changi Airport in Singapore, where I could get a shower then sleep on the night flight back to Manchester. That was to be my last time in beautiful, friendly

New Zealand and the only opportunity to visit the Pacific Islands to the north of it or to make a global circumnavigation. I have come to regret my decision not to explore Tahiti or Hawaii whilst I had the chance. Never mind, I did get home on the Friday afternoon in time to make the Porthmadog Dining Club monthly dinner that same evening and to win the prize for travelling the furthest for the occasion. Most of my fellow diners were simply happy to accept 'Christchurch' as my winning entry but few would really believe that it was the one twelve thousand miles away rather than three hundred miles away on the south coast of England!

BAe were not successful in selling ATPs to Mount Cook Airline but five were sold to Merpati as I mentioned earlier. I subsequently spent two most enjoyable periods in Djakarta during the following year, training Merpati's pilots on routes in Indonesia, as well as much further time with Biman Bangladesh and in Ankara and Istanbul training ATP pilots on routes all over Turkey for THT, a domestic subsidiary of THY, the Turkish National airline. After the Far Eastern tour, I was let loose in subsequent years in G-BRLY on demonstrations in the Caribbean and along the Atlantic Coast of the USA, in China, South Korea and the Philippines, and with Kevin in Iran and the Gulf. ATP production was moved up to Prestwick at great expense in 1993 in preparation for a commercial tie-up between BAe Regional Aircraft and Taiwan Aerospace Corporation when it was agreed that production of jet aircraft only would be carried out at Woodford. Having joined the Jetstream series of aircraft already under production at Prestwick, the ATP was renamed — somewhat bizarrely and rather confusingly — as the Jetstream 61. However, the joint venture at Woodford never happened and, sadly, the ATP/Jetstream 61 did not catch on enough to continue in production. It was terminated in 1994 after only sixty-two aircraft had been built. The other Jetstream types eventually suffered the same fate. Fortunately, I was able to spend the rest of my time at Woodford on the more successful BAe 146 and Avro RJ aircraft that took me to yet more interesting parts of the globe.

Merpati ATP - Author on left (during the airline's later introduction into service in 1992)

ATP Over South Island. Author (left) and Captain Kevin Banks of Mount Cook Airline

Flying Down the Tasman Glacier in the ATP

Take-off from RW 31 - Wakefield Spur at One O'Clock!

Two at Once on the Tasman Glacier

20

GOOD TIMES AND TRICKY CHALLENGES

After returning to the UK and a welcome week off, I picked up my routine duties on the company Jetstream shuttle flights to Hatfield and elsewhere. I also found myself in yet another new role — captaining two customer acceptance flights on the ATP, for Air Wisconsin (AW), our US customer who had ordered fourteen of the aircraft in April 1989. These flights were, essentially, proving sessions for the airline and we used many of the PFTS procedures. That was followed a few days later when a colleague and I flew out to AW's Appleton base to test an ATP there, before returning it to Woodford via night-stops in Goose Bay and Reykjavik. Sadly, AW was to be the only US operator of the ATP as no further sales were made there. Nevertheless, I was able to maintain an occasional association with them, including later when I flew with them in the USA.

For a few weeks, I had a temporary and pleasant change of direction in training three new company pilots and providing conversions to type for two other test pilots, all in the Jetstream. As always, providing instruction to other pilots enables the instructor to improve his own skill and knowledge so it was very useful to add the Jetstream to the ATP in terms of becoming a trainer on both. The 146 and Avro RJ were to follow later. I remembered how, when a QFI at RAF Valley during my second tour there as OC Standards Squadron from 1976 to 1979, I had the privilege of leading the introduction of the Hawk to RAF service at 4FTS whilst concurrently training student pilots on the Gnat and Hunter.

Earlier, I had enjoyed concurrency on operations in Arabia with Piston Provost, Beaver, Dakota and Strikemaster. From a personal point of view, I think the three situations, though in vastly different aircraft and roles, were very similar in their demands and certainly in the excitement and satisfaction they provided. I counted myself as extremely fortunate to be able to enjoy such variety — though I had barely started yet with BAe! Another new type soon surfaced with the BAe 125-1000, in which I was to enjoy a small number of test flights with our 125 expert, George Ellis, though I never had chance actually to qualify on the aircraft. No worries, I had more than enough on my plate.

In June and July 1991, I was given the opportunity to return to my good friends at Loganair, who had kindly agreed to provide me with some line flying experience within their BAe 146 fleet. I spent another five very enjoyable weeks with Loganair, this time in their jets, having first been checked out as captain by the fleet chief pilot, Owen Walters. Many of the routes were the same as those flown in the company's ATPs though this time, of course, everything happened rather more quickly. It took me a little while to adjust to the increased pace on the short sectors. For example, MAN — BHD (Belfast City) was about forty-five minutes flight time in the ATP but barely thirty minutes in the 146. Moreover, it was standard procedure to try to eat breakfast on the outbound leg! Checks when passing ten thousand feet in the climb included: headsets — OFF, breakfast — SERVED! It was a very quick breakfast, as there was very little time between top of climb and top of descent, by which latter point it was, of course, necessary to have completed the approach brief and set up everything for the landing at BHD.

As with everything, practice makes perfect and I was soon able to make the grade without incurring indigestion, almost keeping up with Owen! I also gained an insight into charter operations during this session, since Loganair flew night charters to Spain and the Balearics in the 146 as well as on its UK domestic routes. I must say I hated flying in the middle of the night and would not have wanted to do that for long on a regular basis. However, it was, of course, good background experience and very relevant to widening my understanding of our customers' operations. It also notched up a few more unfamiliar airports to add to the already wide list since joining BAe. The charter destinations were Alicante, Ibiza, Palma and Murcia.

By the end of July 1991, I'd been flying with the Civil Aircraft Division of BAe for twenty-six months and had packed in one thousand, one hundred and fifty hours, mostly in three different types, across the globe from the USA and Canada to Indonesia and New Zealand. The next twelve months were to see me devoted almost exclusively to ATP tasks, spanning most of the same area but with a few more countries thrown in, including Turkey, Indonesia, the Caribbean and even Iran. But, first, came the tricky assignment of the return to service of Biman's ATPs.

When we had completed our initial training contract with Biman towards the end of 1990, we had expressed our disquiet, amongst other things, over the low experience levels amongst their ATP pilots and the planned further dilution of that experience as the more senior pilots were to be promoted out of the ATP fleet and onto the DC10. At the end of December 1990, very soon after we'd left, an incident occurred in which an ATP had 'made an emergency landing' at Rajshahi 'with technical problems'. The runway there (and at Saidpur) was only one hundred feet wide; the ATP wheel-track is just over thirty feet and I remember deep, parallel monsoon drains, only just off the runway edge so I guess these various features may have played a role in the outcome. Whatever it was, the airline and the CAA Bangladesh (CAAB) seem to have panicked somewhat in the face of the frenzy of adverse criticism of the ATP by the press that followed this incident. The CAAB grounded the two aircraft — the third ordered aircraft had not been delivered.

However, to be fair, I doubt that it was just the Rajshahi incident. In my report to my boss on 9 November 1990, I had mentioned that a rash of niggling electrical faults had sometimes caused serious delays and therefore highly adverse passenger reaction. For example, the faults had included half a dozen spurious take-off configuration warnings that had resulted in aborted take-offs. I understood that various electrical connectors around the engines and in the nose wheel bay had not been 'tropicalised', i.e. had not been protected adequately against moisture ingress and high temperatures. If that were true, then BAe had scored some notable, unwanted, own goals. In contrast, my colleagues and I had also identified a number of flaws in the (previous to ATP conversion) training and experience of some Biman pilots. The re-introduction into service at least gave us the eventual opportunity to correct that last issue, partly by having cadet pilots sent to Prestwick for twin engine training instead of coming direct to the ATP from the local flying club (!), so it wasn't all bad news.

Nevertheless, it took some seven months of discussions and negotiations between BAe, Biman and the CAAB for a decision and a plan to be agreed to re-introduce the ATPs into service, including certain aircraft modifications. I inherited the somewhat unenviable task of flying the re-inaugural service from Dhaka to Rajshahi and return, on 31 August 1991, two hundred and forty-five days after the grounding — as the press duly and accurately recorded. With a Biman Bangladesh captain as my number two, plus forty fare-paying passengers, representatives of press and TV and nineteen various dignitaries including the Minister for Civil Aviation and Tourism, the Chairman of the CAAB, the MD of the airline and the British High Commissioner, the flight went well. I was interviewed at Rajshahi by Bangladesh TV — fame at last!

'The New Nation' (one of *forty* newspapers that reported the event — mostly in advance!) recorded the occasion on the front page, quoting the minister as saying that he: "appreciated the courage and determination demonstrated by the passengers by taking the flight so easily" (*author: what about the captain then?*). Another passenger, a local lady doctor returning from abroad, expressed the view that she, "knew nothing about the grounding and re-introducing ATP planes in Biman fleet" (sic). "I do not care about the type of aircraft and its safety measure (sic); I believe in destiny," she ventured. Quel courage, Madame!

Thankfully, simultaneously with the re-introduction, BAe were able to announce orders in the preceding weeks for twenty-four ATPs by three airlines. That news helped considerably to set a more positive backdrop for the task ahead. It included orders for a further five aircraft for British Airways to add to the eight already bought. The other two airlines were THT, the domestic subsidiary of THY, the Turkish national flag carrier, and Merpati in Indonesia to whom I had demonstrated the aircraft with Kevin. No prizes for guessing where I was to find myself in the very near future!

Meanwhile, it was my job to lead the initial refresher training for the other Biman pilots over the next few days in Bangladesh. A colleague had earlier visited Dhaka within the BAe team that had been sent to discuss the re-entry into service and to agree a training plan. It was clear from his report that we were not going to get full co-operation from some individuals, especially a small number of pilots who had already completed DC10 conversion courses and were looking forward to the easier life and higher pay that came with the transfer. They had been held back by the airline, at our suggestion (if not our insistence), to capitalise on their ATP experience and their supervisory capabilities for the re-introduction.

I was personally taken aback by the surly attitude of one senior individual with whom I had enjoyed a very good professional and personal rapport in the previous year's operations from Dhaka and whose DC10 slot was on hold. Although others were very positive and recognised there was a job to be done, it exercised all my efforts at diplomacy to get things running again with as few confrontations as possible — but it was not easy. Happily, the airline had accepted fully our further recommendations on retaining experienced ATP pilots during the first twelve months after the re-introduction. We were also greatly helped by our new ATP simulator coming on line so that more effective and more efficient training could be given before new pilots set foot in the aircraft for the first time.

After the initial few days, I left the operation in the hands of two very capable colleagues before flying back to the UK for a short break before resuming the lead in Dhaka for another month. Apart from the specific aspects related to restarting the operation, I found on my return to flying ATPs in Bangladesh that many of the problems first seen at the outset a year earlier were continuing. These included mis-loading of freight, propeller erosion and new problems related to unorthodox procedures and infringing duty or rest period limits. The ATP had replaced the Fokker F27 but it was a struggle to get the airline and some other staff to ramp up its safety standards to exploit the ATP's increased capabilities, fully and safely. However, I was fortunate to enjoy a good rapport with Biman's director of flight operations. He welcomed my recommendations for improvement, in a number of areas of the ATP operation, that I left them with him on my departure on 10 October.

I was to return to Dhaka next at the end of January 1992 but first, I had some Turkish Delight to sample by courtesy of Turk Hava Tasimaciligi (THT), the domestic subsidiary of Turk Hava Yollari (THY) the national flag carrier, followed by an unusual little adventure in the Islamic Republic of Iran just before Christmas.

United Express (Air Wisconsin) ATP

Loganair 146 at London City

Biman ATP - Reintroduction Into Service

21

TURKISH DELIGHT, CARIBBEAN CAPERS AND FROZEN SEALS

At the end of October 1991, a couple of weeks after returning from the re-introduction of the ATP into service with Biman Bangladesh Airlines, I flew to Turkey to help start up ATP operations with the new customer, THT, the domestic subsidiary of THY the national flag carrier. I and my two training captain colleagues were based mostly in Ankara but with occasional night-stops in Istanbul. It was winter already and I was very surprised at that fact and to see so much snow over Turkey, which I had to that point regarded as having a Mediterranean climate. I was to learn very soon that the Turkish winter can be quite harsh and that many airports in the hinterland have snow for much of the season. Indeed, my first few base-training flights with THT pilots at Ankara revealed a snow-clad landscape each day, all around the airport as far as one could see.

We seemed to get on well with the Turks right away. They were all very friendly. Most of the THT pilots were ex-military so, for those two of us who were ex-RAF, that clearly provided us with an easy understanding of them. With the commonality of our backgrounds and working within a largely Muslim culture — albeit in a secular country — the scene fitted well with my recent experiences in Bangladesh and the much earlier ones in Oman. There was nevertheless plenty to keep us on our toes in other new aspects of the Turkish background.

For starters, the airports and routes were of course largely unfamiliar to us visitors. Therefore, as in Bangladesh and later elsewhere, we had to bring ourselves up to speed rapidly in the local environment whilst simultaneously training our Turkish colleagues in their new aircraft. Naturally, the THT pilots were keen to impress us with their local knowledge and customs. However, there were a few 'customs' that we weren't really able to go along with. There was, for example, a clear tendency in some individuals to press on in hope, rather than to evaluate realities effectively. This manifested itself in particular at one or two airports where there were only non-precision approach aids available but where, in the interests of getting the job done, local ATC would, quite often, greatly understate the weather conditions to us. There were several occasions where we had made approaches with a reported cloud ceiling comfortably above minima only to find that we were still firmly in the murk when we got to the decision point for landing or going around. On one such occasion, as I went around from minima to hold or to divert elsewhere, ATC urged us to have a further shot, but 'come lower!' since they had sighted us and so we "would easily get in as another aircraft had done just ten minutes earlier". A very useful mantra that I had been advised to adopt earlier by a seasoned BAe trainer was: "beware the local expert!" That tenet was to serve me well in pretty much all the countries where I trained local airline pilots on their familiar routes and, for sure, in Turkey. It was usually applied to pilot trainees but in Turkey we had to beware the local ATC 'expert' too.

During this opening session with THT, we flew to the domestic airports of Elazig, Batman, Adana, Izmir, Samsun, Kayseri and Denizli. Another eight or nine airports would be added to the list of destinations during later stays in the country. The first session was relatively uneventful and I much enjoyed a couple of short opportunities on days off to have a good look around Ankara and Istanbul, the latter holding a particular fascination for all its fabulous, ancient sights. I soon began to make a few good friends amongst my Turkish colleagues, one of whom kindly invited me to his home.

Back in the UK after a month in Turkey, there was a brief interlude of Jetstream flying and test flights in a 146 and an ATP before heading out East again, on another sales tour. I was both surprised and intrigued when I learned that BAe had arranged a full-scale demonstration tour in the Islamic Republic of Iran for several days with all three airliner products, Jetstream 31, ATP and BAe 146. At that time, very few westerners were visiting Iran. I was delighted to learn that I was to share the ATP demonstrations with my very good friend and immediate boss, Kevin Moorhouse, who was tragically to die later as I mentioned earlier.

Kevin and I set off early on 12 December, first to Hatfield to pick up most of our sales team and operations support personnel and then onward to Istanbul. The ATP cruised at much less than jet speeds so Hatfield to Istanbul took us all of seven and a half hours. Not surprisingly, we took a night-stop there before flying the last leg to Teheran, a further five and a half hours to the east. Snow-clad Turkey had by then become quite familiar after flying with THT but it was fascinating to gaze down eventually upon the unfamiliar and somewhat mysterious terrain of Iran, especially the tall snow-capped mountains immediately north of the city of Teheran as we made our arrival.

We spent the first full day in Teheran in preparation and briefings to Iranian personnel, with all three aircraft on static display at Aseman Airlines' hangar. After our second night in the Azadi Grand Hotel, Kevin and I began our in-flight demonstrations in the ATP by flying over to Sanandaj, west of Teheran in the province of Kurdistan, some forty nautical miles from the Iraqi border. For the outward and return flights, we carried a small number of Iranian airline officials and pilots. The pilots all spoke good English, were friendly if a little reserved, and seemed of much the same attitude and outlook as ourselves. They wore similar uniforms but were distinguished by not wearing ties, which were regarded (we were told) as a mark of western custom and therefore not allowed. We, by the way, had been briefed not to carry a camera, nor to wear short-sleeve shirts at any time, nor jeans when off duty. We were also advised to take our own soap, shampoo and toilet rolls — I'm therefore uncertain as to what the local arrangements were in those respects!

Between the two transit flights, Kevin and I flew an airborne display over the airport at Sanandaj which was followed by a similar display at Teheran the next day. We then departed with our team for Abu Dhabi. All had gone to plan and we had enjoyed the experience. It had been fairly unremarkable for us other than to have actually been to what was, and still is, regarded as a country set apart from the rest of the world. We sold no aircraft in Iran, as it turned out, though I guess it would have been surprising had we actually done so. Whether it was worth the effort to send three aircraft and a team of twenty-eight personnel seems questionable — especially with hindsight!

In passing, there had been one or two noticeable oddities in the hotel to reflect upon. One such oddity was the large, coloured mosaic of George Bush's face which covered the reception area floor, across which all incoming and outgoing guests had to walk, thus, by Islamic custom, contributing to a strong insult to the US President.

Once in Abu Dhabi we enjoyed a couple of night-stops and two more demonstration flights for local airline pilots and officials, then flew on to Dubai for another pilot demo and passenger demo for Emirates Airlines and senior staff from the local CAA. In both countries, we enjoyed a more relaxed atmosphere and the chance to have a beer or two! Our return to the UK was via Luxor and Corfu, two airports that I was subsequently to use when ferrying 146s to the Far East.

A fortnight after arriving back at Woodford, having had a good, uninterrupted break at home over Christmas and New Year, I flew again to Ankara for another couple of weeks with THT. Once more, there was a mixture of base training and domestic line training to all the previous destinations plus to Urfa, the very ancient town (recorded from the fourth century BC but possibly going back to 9000 BC) some twenty-five nautical miles north of the border with Syria. On two flights into Urfa during my several stays in Turkey, I carried the Turkish Minister of Agriculture (whose nephew, a THT First Officer, I was to train during a later visit).

The Minister was very much a VIP and so the aircraft was met each time at Urfa by a most impressive, welcoming throng. The crowd included a large group of girl dancers, brightly dressed in traditional costume, musicians with various strange instruments and very many onlookers. I had a ringside view from my left seat on the ATP flight deck. With the window open, I was utterly charmed by the unfamiliar music and the exotic dancing. However, on the first occasion especially, I was rather less charmed by what happened next. I spotted a couple of men bringing several goats on leads into the crowd from my side. I guessed correctly what they were up to as the crowd closed around them, thereby blocking my direct view of the goats' throats being slit.

After a few minutes, the music, the dancers, the Minister, the dead goats and the crowd all melted away after the high point of the welcoming ceremony. All that was left was a very large pool of blood on the concrete surface some fifty yards from my aircraft — but not for long. Along came a couple of fire trucks; the pool of blood was thoroughly hosed down; we loaded our passengers and off we went back to Ankara. Thus ended — for me — a sobering, mixed experience of joyful celebration and the harsh, ceremonial dispatch of the innocent animals. At the time, we kept goats at home on my smallholding, so I guess it disturbed me a little more than it should have done. The only knife my goats ever saw was when I was trimming their hooves— oh well, all in the life of a factory pilot I suppose?

At the end of only a fortnight in this second session in Turkey, I was required to fly over to Dhaka and pick up the reins once more with Biman Bangladesh for ten days. That was to get two of their experienced captains qualified as trainers on the ATP and in itself was fairly straightforward. However, it was still quite demanding as it had to include what we would mainly have confined to a flight simulator, i.e. simulated engine failures on take-off and approaches, go-arounds and landings on one engine. Training captains needed to qualify in the left-hand and right-hand seats of the aircraft in all those exercises. The ATP had some tricky little characteristics on one engine; that made it imperative that training captains should be fully skilled and fully confident at handling them. I was able to get one of the individuals checked out as a trainer but, unfortunately, the other fell very well short of the required standard and so was unsuccessful.

Meanwhile, the ATP sales effort elsewhere in the world was gathering considerable momentum. Shortly after I returned from Bangladesh, our primary demonstration aircraft, G-BRLY, decked out in full British Airways colours, headed off for South America via the other Dakar (with the other spelling) in Senegal, bound for Recife in Brazil. The aircraft had a really busy schedule ahead of her until I was eventually to bring her back into Woodford from Greenland on the 29th February, appropriately marking the leap year as well as the aircraft's several 'leaps' over the preceding month.

First however, Chief Test Pilot Peter Henley took her down to Dakar and Recife. Peter's leg across the mid-Atlantic was quite an epic. Until that day, I believed Kevin and I had held the record for the longest distance and time on a single ATP flight. That had been a year earlier, with our one thousand six hundred and forty nautical miles, seven hours, forty minute-leg from the Seychelles to Colombo in the same aircraft, en route to Indonesia and New Zealand. Peter's odyssey was another one hundred nautical miles, i.e. about twenty-five minutes more than Kevin and I had flown. From what I recalled, I thought we'd had only about twenty minutes of fuel over the minimum required on arrival at Colombo — heaven knows how little Peter had landed with!

Peter and his team 'did' Brazil, a couple of other South American countries and the SW Caribbean. It was then my huge privilege to pick up the aircraft and her team of twelve men and three ladies in Barbados for a wonderful series of demonstration and transit flights throughout the Leeward Islands, Jamaica, Cuba, then on to some pretty important stuff along the Eastern Seaboard of the USA and, finally, some brief cold-weather trials in Greenland. I have to say that I was rather daunted at the responsibility of being let loose in charge of the aircraft and the team during such crucial events. This was to be my first time leading a sales tour, let alone in the Caribbean, where it would be my first ever visit to those wonderful islands and then in the busy USA, where I had almost no flying experience at all, and finally Greenland with its mystic and magnificent (and very, very cold!) full winter scenery.

It all started with a very good omen. I flew out from Heathrow to Barbados as a passenger aboard a BA747. I was booked into business class but managed to wheedle myself an upgrade to first class and then, via a brief chat with the captain over my lunch in first class luxury, wangled a post-prandial invitation to the flight deck of the big jet, where I remained for the approach and landing. That in itself was a further, double treat, on top of the upgrade, as I got both a good airborne preview of the southern end of the island and the airport, plus I was able to realise a long-held ambition to see at first-hand how the 747 behaved during landing.

I'd bought and read the book 'Handling the Big Jets' over twenty years earlier and remembered particularly the implication of the pilot's eyes in the 747 being some thirty feet above the main landing gear and over ninety feet ahead of it. So, in the landing flare, as I understood it, there would be a distinct impression from the pilot's eyes of the flight deck climbing just before the gear touches down — or something like that! Anyway, my hospitable captain did it pretty much as I had imagined but with no sweat. I really thought I'd be able to handle that okay but, unfortunately, never got the chance. Handling a big jet was one of the few gaps in my very varied aviation career — but at least I'd watched it at first hand.

Just to complete the good first impression of Barbados, some half an hour later as I was exiting the terminal building, in taxied the BA Concorde to the sound and sight of a steel drum band set up outdoors to welcome its rich passengers. All this was on a typically warm day with a light breeze under a beautiful, cloudless sky. I felt quite excited about it all, as if I were on an exotic holiday (which I suppose it was in a way but with some super, paid flying around the islands thrown in as a bonus!)

That night I had dinner with the team, including Kevin who had taken over from Peter a short while earlier and who, in turn, was handing over to me. Next day, I took G-BRLY up to Antigua where we were to be based for the next five days of the tour. Day one proper of my contribution kicked off on 17 February with two return flights to nearby St Kitts, with a couple of loads of invited passengers representing potential customers and local tourist, government and other aviation-related organisations. On return to Antigua I flew again, this time with several local airline pilots, to give them a demonstration of the ATP's handling characteristics. Over the next few days, a similar pattern was repeated with visits to Dominica, Tortola, Barbados and finally on to Kingston, Jamaica.

Dominica, with rapidly rising terrain to the north, south and west of the runway was fun and merits a short mention. To see why, here's an excerpt from the Jeppesen approach instructions of the time for Melville Hall airport (now Douglas-Charles airport), on the north east coast of the island:

*"Take-off runway 27 prohibited. Turbulence may occur on approach to runway 09. While circling north of the runway on left downwind runway 09, visual contact with the runway will be obscured by a ridge-line, from the point of passing abeam the threshold of runway 09 until completing the turn from base to final, which is **normally made over a recognizable field of coconut trees.**"*

For an aircraft such as the ATP, the terrain and the relatively short runway compelled both landing and take-off only on runway 09. Take-off over the sea was dead straightforward. However, landing did require one to fly quite close to the aforementioned field in order to be able to distinguish one's coconuts from one's bananas (which latter completely surrounded the quite small coconut plantation); then, putting all one's faith in the procedure, a descent was made in a sharpish left turn into what initially looked like a blind, wooded valley. The runway appeared when further along the valley and being able to see round a slight kink to the right, when a minor correction to heading could be made: 'jink at the kink'. It needed some guesswork and good luck to arrive at that point at the correct angle for the final bit to touchdown. For an experienced forester like me (!), spotting the coconuts was of course a piece of doddle! I managed the rest okay for three approaches and came back a few years later to do it all over again several times in a 146 four-jet. Great sport!

Our purpose in taking G-BRLY to Kingston, apart from one short demonstration flight to Montego Bay and back, was for us to use Kingston as our base for a one-day sales visit to Cuba. Up to that moment, I had been flying throughout the tour with a US captain from Bae's Washington Division as my first officer; one of our cabin crew was a US citizen too. The US people weren't allowed to visit Cuba so we had to have UK replacements for them flown out to Kingston.

At the time, Cuba — with its then population of ten million and having attracted three hundred and forty thousand visitors to the island in the previous year — was poised for its subsequent rapid opening up as a holiday destination. State-owned local carrier Cubana and charter airline Aerocaribbean were operating predominantly uneconomic and unreliable Soviet-built equipment, though the latter airline also had three

US Douglas DC3s, manufactured in the early 1940s and featuring first-class cabins with real leather seats! However, it was still early days so our marketing people regarded the major aim of our visit as fact-finding and the establishment of contacts to see if there was a real determination to develop the Cuban airline and tourist infrastructure.

Along with other team members, I was uncertain of what to expect in what, at the time and along with Iran, was regarded as something of a pariah country. In the event, and largely as in Iran, there weren't so many differences as I had anticipated. The people we met were all well-dressed and friendly and a sense of normality soon pervaded, within our sheltered group at least. The demonstrations involved flying a group of dignitaries east to Varadero and back to Havana. Varadero, on the coast, was already becoming established as a holiday destination. There, we were to collect General Rogello Acevedo, the President of the Cuban CAA and therefore the man directly responsible for Cubana. He would join us on the flight-deck jump seat to observe the ATP in operation at close quarters. An interpreter would hang over the stable door as neither I nor my young BAe first officer, Mike Skelhorn, spoke Spanish.

The general arrived, slightly late, in full green military uniform and (I quickly spotted) sporting a side-arm. Well, he was the boss of the CAA so I wasn't going to start an argument over that, however much it was mostly not allowed — outside Cuba at any rate. We soon got airborne off runway 06 and, as I began my turn onto a westerly heading for Havana at five hundred feet, the general said something in rapid Spanish to the interpreter. That was immediately translated to me:

"The general wants you to stop climbing and fly at low level along the beach for him", he said, accompanied by a hand gesture clearly suggesting a swooping descent.

Tricky moment. The armed head of the local CAA and national airline flag-carrier wanted me to do a beat-up of the beach in a passenger aircraft with thirty to forty dignitaries in the back, including two ambassadors. Hmm! I was helped by the fact that it was a very inopportune moment to make such a demand. Mike and I were busy with the usual post take-off actions. I continued climbing and mumbled something to the effect that I would be unable to comply: the cloud, the turbulence, ATC, other traffic etc. After translation of that, the general made a distinctively dismissive gesture and went all sullen. He hadn't been that friendly anyway and said hardly a word from then on. Cuba did not buy any ATPs. I hope it wasn't my refusal to comply with the general that stopped them. Oh well, at least I didn't get shot nor lose my licence.

From Kingston, we headed off to Fort Lauderdale in Florida and then on to Washington Dulles, where we had a day off before beginning what was to be the most demanding section of our tour. There were demonstrations to do at Philadelphia and Portland New England, JFK New York, Bangor Maine and Manchester New Hampshire, before returning to Dulles — all crammed into just two days. Apart from the two ferry flights to and from the USA a year earlier, I'd had no experience of flying in the USA, certainly not from such a busy airport as JFK. Wow, was it busy! The US air traffic controllers mostly seemed to speak at twice the speed of anyone elsewhere and gave no quarter should one dare to offer "say again" as a response. This two-day apprenticeship through the north-east USA served me well and was extremely timely. On the final day of the US tour, I was to fly a pilot demo from Dulles with none other than Mac Tippins, a very well-known aviation journalist and fully qualified commercial pilot on the Boeing 737 and Learjet series.

I put Mac in the captain's seat and let him have as much of the flying as I could on a flight which lasted just under two hours and in which we explored every corner of the envelope. That ranked as one of the most demanding flights I have ever undertaken in my whole career. Mercifully, I was well supported from the jump seat by my BAe Washington pilot colleague who took care of all ATC communications. I was far too busy in the right-hand seat, demonstrating to Mac then keeping a very watchful eye as he carried out the various manoeuvres including an engine shutdown and restart, emergency gear selection, stalling and a crosswind landing. With a bit of timely advice from me, Mac pulled off two superb landings at two different airfields — the first in a twenty knots gusting crosswind — so he was a very happy bunny at the end.

Mac was very skilful, a natural pilot, and wrote a superbly positive article in praise of the ATP that was published in the June 1992 issue of 'Professional Pilot' magazine. I thought I had made up in spades for refusing the beach beat-up at Varadero but I regret that didn't lead us to sell more ATPs in the USA than the eight already ordered by Air Wisconsin.

Directly after the demo flight with Mac, I and my team left in G-BRLY for a night-stop in Goose Bay, Labrador. We flew onward the next day to Sondrestrom in Greenland, where we had a series of trials to do in the very deep-freeze temperatures. The weather was clear on the flight into Sondrestrom and we had plenty of fuel so I took the opportunity to drop down early to one thousand five hundred feet to allow all of us onboard to admire the magnificent snow-clad scenery. I'd seen it a few times as a passenger from high altitude but it was a treat to get up close for twenty minutes or so. There was a long queue of my BAe passengers to see the view from the flight deck. It was spectacular.

The master plan was to do some local cold-weather test flying for a day or two. However, when the aircraft was due to start the tests on the following morning after an intentional overnight cold-soak, a number of small hydraulic leaks were found around the undercarriage and brake systems. This, of course, was what we had come to discover or, preferably, not to discover! It is one of the potential weak points with hydraulic seals that they harden and shrink in very cold temperatures. The aircraft had been left outside all night to cold-soak and, sure enough, the weaknesses were revealed. All we could do was to get G-BRLY into the warmth of a hangar for the following night so that we had a chance to fly her out to the UK, without hydraulic leaks, and come back another day to carry out the tests with more robust replacement seals.

When I came to do my external walk-around checks prior to leaving on 29 February, I had quite a shock. I had served two winters during an exchange tour with the Royal Norwegian Air Force in the mid-1970s, in which I'd spent a number of weeks in the Arctic North of Norway, flying F5s where ground temperatures were down to about minus thirty degrees C or so. I reckoned I was well-seasoned to low temperatures. However, the temperature that morning at Sondrestrom was minus forty-three degrees C! It actually hurt to breathe; I did one of the fastest externals ever!

The eight-hour return flight to Woodford necessitated a refuelling stop at our Prestwick facility. We all arrived happily home, tired and tanned (as Mac Tippins had observed in his article), slightly disappointed at losing the cold-weather trials but all content that we'd done a pretty good job of showing off our aircraft and that it was now down to the marketeers to sell it.

For my part, I was indeed very pleased with the way everything had gone for me and for the team. I was relieved that there had been no hiccups and that I'd survived a very busy, varied and often very demanding experience in so many different environments. Unfortunately, fate was very soon to interrupt my satisfaction and deal me a temporary medical grounding for four and a half months before I could resume serious globetrotting again!

Author (2nd from top) with THT Crew

In the Deep Freezer at Sondrestrom

22

WESTERN EXCURSIONS, INDONESIAN INDULGENCE AND FORAYS TO CHINA

At the end of March 1992, a few weeks after returning from the very hectic ATP sales tour in the Caribbean and along the Eastern Seaboard of the USA, the brakes came on for me rather hard and rather swiftly.

Over the preceding year or so, I'd had a few very minor and short-lived episodes of a quite small and stereotyped visual disturbance that each lasted about twenty minutes. When one happened in flight, I decided I ought to get the matter checked out with the medics. I saw my GP, a former RAF doctor with good connections, who quickly arranged for an examination at the RAF Central Medical Establishment in London. From there I went to the CAA medics at Gatwick who decided I'd been experiencing 'abortive migraine', in other words the visual aura associated with migraine but without the headaches. Although I thought the issue relatively trivial, the medics were full of the story of a then recent BA747 captain who had been obliged to turn back from mid-Atlantic with migraine, so they weren't going to take any chances. The upshot was that I was grounded as a pilot for three months, as a precaution, whilst I attempted to identify triggers and take steps to avoid the visual problems. Meanwhile my employer, British Aerospace, was very understanding and kept me on the books whilst I devised a few ways to continue doing something productive in return for my generous salary as a training captain and production test pilot.

There was actually nothing to stop me flying per se, provided I was not acting as first or second pilot. In response to a prod from our CTP, the CAA had replied specifically that I could operate from the jump seat in a training or test-flying situation as long as two qualified pilots were at the controls. Acting as a third pilot was definitely not an option during test flying, where the jump seat was invariably occupied by a flight test engineer. So, I decided it might be useful to set up some liaison visits to an ATP customer or two and see if I could help them in any way through offering my experience as a manufacturer's training captain and test pilot on the aircraft. That could also, of course, be a potentially good PR move for BAe. The initiative was welcomed by the CTP and the first airline that we approached, the Portuguese operator SATA, flying ATPs in the Azores, were pleased to accept me. That gave me a great opportunity to see somewhere well off the beaten track.

Although I flew for only the planned two days with SATA, starting initially each day from their base at Ponta Delgada, it included five hours of flying on the jump seat to and from the four further local airports and islands of the Azores; Lajes on Terceira, Horta on Faial, Pico and Sao Jorge. These short, island-hopping sectors provided me with a new perspective into ATP operations. I remember them particularly for the preponderance of strong surface winds which, I was told, was a regular feature of the local environment. On one occasion I was a bit surprised that a local captain decided to land in a very gusty crosswind considerably beyond the demonstrated limit. The ATP was not an easy aircraft to land in such conditions, as I had learned well for myself by that time. However, I was amazed at how well he pulled off the landing, which he told me was by no means the first time. He was certainly better at it than I would have been, though I guess he'd had years of practice in similar conditions on other types. Otherwise, I managed to have a free day when another kindly SATA captain took me on a guided tour to a local extinct volcano, where I saw at first hand a wonderfully abundant display of huge azaleas growing wild in the crater.

After returning to the UK from the short mid-Atlantic excursion, I set off as a passenger some ten days later from Manchester to Chicago to join Air Wisconsin for a longer version of the jaunt in the Azores but all in a vastly different environment. Chicago O'Hare, as anyone who has been there as a passenger or a pilot will know, is one of the world's busiest airports. The Air Wisconsin network, in the heart of the USA, was operated in very dense airspace, a great contrast from the quiet Azores. I flew on the jump seat again from O'Hare and from the Air Wisconsin company base at Appleton and enjoyed eleven sectors and ten hours over three days flying. The trips were to the provincial airports of South Bend, Lansing, Green Bay and Fort Wayne. As expected of a US airline, the operation was smooth and professional and I suspect the greater benefit of the visit accrued to me rather than to my hosts.

The temporary medical grounding brought one bonus and that was the chance to get in a three-week leave just before the CAA released me back to partially restricted flying (as or with a qualified co-pilot) in early July. I was soon able to fly a recurrency check within test flights in an ATP and in a 146, so by the middle of the month I was on my way to Djakarta for a three-week line training assignment with Merpati, the Indonesian domestic airline, who had signed up for ATPs following our sales demo there early in 1991. Since all the Merpati co-pilots and captains had qualified on type during their base training, there were no restrictions upon me for training them on line operations. I had a marvellous time. I'd had a long-standing great love of the Far East as a result of my two and a half years spent as a young Hunter FGA9 pilot, based in Singapore and flying all over Malaysian Borneo and the Malay Peninsula. I had also explored the Malay Peninsula extensively by car. I liked the climate; I liked the food; I liked the cultural vibrancy and colours and, this time, I also liked staying at company expense in the Djakarta Hilton.

The Indonesians I came across were utterly charming and friendly. Just over twenty-five years earlier, my new Indonesian colleagues and I had been on opposite sides during the conflict between Malaysia and Indonesia. Along with my fellow RAF pilots and navigators at Tengah, I had spent quite a few hours in the study of various targets in Indonesia in preparation for launching attacks on them, should the conflict have escalated to such a stage. In the event, I had fired not one shot in anger though I had flown many fighter patrols, up and down the border with Indonesian Borneo.

I flew with Merpati in their ATPs to their airports of Semarang, Kidjang, Pekanbaru, Sembawang and Surabaya. Whilst the ground milieu was fine for my stay in Indonesia, the flying was not without its special challenges in the face of the occasional tropical storms that caused a few detours and delays. However, by and large, it was a most enjoyable experience, much less stressful than Bangladesh and I relished it. I also packed in the flying hours and made up a little for what I'd missed in the preceding few months. After August leave with my wife, cruising up the Rhine from Holland to Basle and walking in the Swiss Alps, I enjoyed some welcome continuity with Merpati when I returned to them for a further couple of weeks.

There followed a break from travel whilst I returned temporarily to a mixture of Company Jetstream flights around the UK to BAe airfields and other sites. There were also a number of exciting new experiences. These included: a couple of test flights in the Jetstream 41, the stretched version of the 31/32; steep approach trials at London City airport in the new Avro RJ70 as part of its certification process and an autoland test flight in each of the RJ85 and RJ100. (The suffix numbers of the jets marked the nominal number of seats in each version). These first three trips in the new aircraft gave me an early look at the Avro RJ variants that were later to become the primary aircraft that I was to fly with BAe and its customer airlines. The principal new feature of the RJ was its Category 3A autoland capability, enabling it to land in visibility down to two hundred metres with a decision height of fifty feet.

Steep approach operations may be worth a special mention. The short runway and the various surrounding obstacles and restrictions on approach to London City airport gave an opportunity for BAe to exploit the short take-off and landing capability of the 146 series in the RJ 70 and 85 versions. However, certain procedures and restrictions were required. Principally, the operation required the capability to adopt an approach angle of up to six degrees instead of the usual three degrees. In fact, in certification, we demonstrated an angle of seven and a half degrees.

I still remember, clearly, setting off from Hatfield on my first test flight to London City. It seemed most peculiar to be heading for the obvious landmarks of central London at a couple of thousand feet and even more peculiar to be carrying out visual circuits in close proximity to Big Ben and Tower Bridge! Only multi-engine, fixed-wing aircraft with special aircraft and aircrew certification to fly five and a half degrees approaches were allowed to conduct operations at London City.

The Avro RJs were the first jet aircraft to achieve that certification and it was quite some time before others were able to follow in our footsteps (or tyre-prints I suppose I should say).

The year could not end without another visit to help Biman in Bangladesh, so off I went to Dhaka at the end of October for ten days. The visit had been deferred from a few months earlier. The aims were to discuss future pilot training requirements, to fly with a selection of their pilots to pass on new ATP operational information and to assist with any difficulties — a fairly wide-ranging, yet familiar, cocktail of tasks!

In the event, the plot was changed by mutual agreement for me to fly with all fifteen available pilots over thirty sectors and to carry out an ad hoc test flight on the first of the two aircraft as it completed its upgrade modification programme. Happily, it was good to discover that on most sectors the aircraft flew with all sixty-two passenger seats full. Regrettably, it was very disappointing to discover that the one aircraft that I flew on the line was in several respects in a poor state and that many long-term defects were not being reported. In particular, the aircraft was in a filthy condition both inside and outside with cabin carpets so grotty that the cabin smelt badly. All but one of the overhead bins were not functioning correctly.

On a more positive note, I was able to see that the airline had achieved a very high level of pilot standardisation in flight deck procedures and aircraft handling. There seemed little doubt that all the new first officers had been very well trained. In that respect, I was impressed and delighted that our earlier recommendations for improving the training of new pilots had been implemented. That said, there was still much to be done in terms of supervision, as the more experienced captains were still being siphoned off to the DC10 at an alarming rate and I was unable to recommend any of the candidates with whom I flew, for appointment as training captains. Worryingly, pilot fatigue limits were being regularly exceeded by large margins — a clear recipe for danger. I reported all this to the Biman director of flight operations with whom I agreed that we in BAe would do our best to provide further direct engineering and operational support.

The remainder of that year, 1992, was overshadowed to a large degree by BAe's plans to transfer turboprop production from Woodford to Prestwick, as part of its intention to form a joint venture with TAC (Taiwan Aircraft Corporation) to manufacture the Avro RJ and support the family of 146/RJ aircraft from Woodford. Little were we to know at the time that this was to be the first of two ill-fated liaisons for regional aircraft production, the second being with Aerospatiale in forming AIR (Avions International Regionale) neither of which liaison could prevent the eventual closure of the factory sites at both Hatfield and Woodford and the ultimate cessation of commercial airliner production in the UK.

For the time being, it seemed that I and many of my pilot and ground colleagues would have to transfer to Prestwick or lose our jobs, as it appeared that the Hatfield jet operation would come north to Woodford with most of its personnel; indeed, I was advised that there would not be a slot for me at Woodford. Thankfully, as I'll recount later, that forecast was wrong. Meanwhile, BAe was very mature and kind to its personnel in providing company BAe146 flights from Woodford up to Prestwick for employees and partners to have a look at the area, do a bit of provisional house-hunting and so forth and return the following day. I flew several of those trips both as a pilot and, as an interested party, along with my wife on one occasion. We began to think of trying to move up there whilst still hanging onto our house here in Snowdonia.

Apart from the shadow of possible redundancy or relocation, life continued at Woodford with the usual great variety, mostly flying Jetstream 31s on communications flights and pilot recurrency checks, but with a sprinkling of test flying in 146, ATP, Avro RJ and 125-1000 aircraft. Then came what was to be my big, very lucky break.

One cold December day, between flights, I was queuing up for my lunch in the excellent Woodford canteen with a 146 pilot colleague, from Hatfield. He was miffed about having to do a delivery flight in a couple of weeks to China, over Christmas, as well as about having to face the prospect of relocation to Woodford, as I was similarly threatened with Prestwick. I spotted the opportunity immediately. Apart from the attraction of a ferry trip all the way to Xian, there was the chance, with my generous (!) offer to fly over Christmas in his place, to raise my profile a bit in the jet with the movers and shakers at Hatfield. My wife, as always, sprang to my support for what would be our first Christmas separation ever, recognising the importance of the gesture and promising to give me a Christmas as soon as I got back — that way she and her mother got two Christmases of course!

I and another pilot colleague from Hatfield left Woodford in the 146 on its delivery to the airline, China North West, on 23 December, flying first to Bari on Italy's south Adriatic coast and then on to Luxor for the first of two night-stops. Christmas Eve saw us set off for Sharjah and then on to our second night-stop, at Karachi, not at all a convivial place in which to celebrate the occasion. We had to go to great lengths just to get a couple of beers served in our rooms, after signing disclaimers of some kind. Never mind — I knew my substitute Christmas was yet to come at home. Meanwhile, on the real Christmas Day, we left Karachi to refuel at Calcutta and then to make the longer flight 'over the hump' to Kunming and finally to Xian, where we landed by night in what appeared to be a yellow-shaded fog.

Once out of the aircraft it was clear that the yellow-shaded fog was indeed exactly that; we drove in it by taxi to the hotel. When I got up to my room, I found said fog being sucked in through the gridded ventilation (!) system inlet in the ceiling. Well, I knew this was China and it wasn't my first time here; nevertheless, I felt I had to do something about it. I spent the first half hour painstakingly blocking each hole in the vent with tissue paper then went for a Christmas beer or two with my colleague and our two resident BAe engineers. After a good night's sleep and breakfast on a very cold Boxing Day, we treated ourselves to a tour of the fascinating Terracotta Warriors. On returning to my room, I found that the cleaner had removed all my fog-blockers.

Back in the UK and after my delayed Christmas, the priorities for me had changed. The good news was that the restriction on my aviation medical clearance was lifted fully on 4 January, so I was able to resume base training for pilots converting to the ATP. On the other hand, the likelihood of a transfer to Prestwick for several colleagues and me had increased and I was therefore to become more involved in Jetstream training. As a result, I spent some of the next few months up at Prestwick, base training customer pilots from Regionair (France), Air Botnia (Finland), Slovak Aviation and Loganair. There were nevertheless sufficient ATP, 146 and Avro RJ flights at Woodford to keep my hand in with those types as well. That was useful as, in May of 1993, I set off on a new adventure to demonstrate the ATP in Beijing, Seoul and Manila.

A ferry crew took the aircraft out to Hong Kong, where I duly joined the team led by our CTP Peter Henley and Kevin Moorhouse. As part of the coming transfer of BAe turboprop manufacture and operations to Prestwick, the ATP was rebranded, rather incongruously, to the 'Jetstream ATP'. So, our demonstrator had been re-christened to G-JATP and, just in case that wasn't obvious enough, the new title was emblazoned along the top of the front fuselage on both sides of the aircraft. Peter and I set off to fly the aircraft first to Gangzhou (Canton), just forty-five minutes away, where we carried out an uneventful passenger demo the same day. With that completed, we left the airport for our hotel. On arrival there, we were very pleasantly surprised to find a full orchestra of Chinese players performing western classical music expertly in the large reception area. I and another pilot colleague were so taken aback and entranced at their expertise that we watched them for ages before checking in.

The following day I flew the Jetstream ATP on the longer, one thousand two hundred nautical miles flight up north to Beijing, where I carried out the next passenger demo a day later, before we set off to Seoul for a further few days of demos. I had never visited Korea before and so it was an uncanny experience to undergo one of those thousand-to-one coincidences that nevertheless do crop up in life from time to time. I was at the desk of the Seoul Hilton, checking in, when I heard a familiar voice from the past say, "Hello Gamblin; what are you doing here?" It was my near namesake, John Gamble, whom I hadn't seen for nearly ten years, though his name had cropped up, significantly, early in that period as I shall explain.

I had known John in the RAF. At the time of our first meeting in 1965, he was a young ATC officer visiting Labuan from Tawau in North Borneo during the Indonesian Confrontation. At that time, as an equally young Hunter pilot on 20 Squadron, I was taking part in low-level fighter patrols of the border with Indonesia to deter incursions by their aircraft that had led to a couple of Malaysian villages being shot up. ATC officers and their Hunter pilot customers were always on good terms. We relied implicitly on their GCA radar expertise to allow us to land from low cloud or in low visibility as our aircraft had no Instrument Landing System (ILS) equipment. John was no exception and quickly struck up a friendship with us Hunter jockeys. In due course he had followed us to be based alongside us at Tengah. It was in the officers' mess there that he and I were forever having our mail mixed up due to the similarity in surnames. In time, he was able to switch to becoming a pilot, in which role, as by then he had become an instructor on Harriers, I met up with him some fifteen years later when I arrived at Wittering in 1981 to convert to the aircraft. The connection didn't end there.

After a further few years, in 1984, I had left the RAF to pursue a career in civil aviation. One of my first assignments had been the rather exciting and somewhat cloak-and-dagger trip to Beijing to carry out a ground analysis of the Chinese F-7M, their copy of the Mig 21, for a well-known UK company. That company had hoped, amongst their other plans, to help the Chinese to market their aircraft to third world air forces. Following the assignment, I had been offered a permanent job to follow up from the initial activity. Having declined to do so for various reasons, I had then been contacted privately by the same company a couple of months later who asked me to help in vetting an alternative candidate for the role, no less than John Gamble, whom I was very happy to endorse, though he and I had no direct contact over the matter. After a further nine years, he had by then become the Far East marketing manager for the company and was in Seoul on business totally unrelated to our ATP demo tour. The coincidence that brought us together briefly on this last occasion, in Korea, was really quite remarkable. By the way, he went on to fly the F-7M at its manufacturing site, Chengdu, to which I also later flew several times as a BAe 146 training captain whilst training Chinese pilots.

From Seoul, we flew next to Taiwan and, to complete the tour, finally to Manila from where I flew two more demos, landing at Cebu between them. One final treat in store for us at Manila was that the then brand-new Airbus A340 demonstrator was in town at the same time. Kevin and I managed to get a conducted ground tour of her by the demo crew. We drooled over it, in envy of this mighty ship and her many clever aspects.

Our long route home to Woodford was flown over five days via Brunei, Bangkok, Bombay, Dubai, Luxor and Corfu. We took the opportunity for me as an instrument rating examiner to renew Kevin's IR on the sector from Bombay to Dubai. Thus ended, a kaleidoscopic tour of the Far East, where my professional career as a pilot had begun and to which I was to return, yet again and quite unexpectedly, before the year was out and in our 146 four-jets.

SATA Air Azores ATP

Author (left) with Merpati ATP & Crew

Jetstream ATP

23
TRANSITION

After the odyssey of the three-week sales demonstration of the ATP in May and June of 1993 to China, Korea and the Philippines, my role as a factory pilot with BAe at Woodford was soon to switch onto a different and more secure track. Lady Luck was to smile widely upon me. Initially though, uncertainty loomed.

For various reasons, I had declined the offer of a transfer to Prestwick under BAe's plan to manufacture ATPs there alongside the Jetstreams that were Prestwick's staple product. Apart from the ongoing military Nimrod project at Woodford, the Company wanted to use the Cheshire factory exclusively for production of Avro RJs under a joint venture with Taiwan Aerospace and to close the Hatfield 146 production line. So, for a while, I faced redundancy and would need to look elsewhere for a flying job. In the meantime, BAe wanted to extract as much as it could from me and from my ATP training experience.

I was duly packed off to the USA for a couple of weeks to obtain a US type rating on my US licence. The type rating was needed to train pilots for United Feeder Service (UFS) in the Woodford ATP simulator. They had taken over the ATP aircraft from Air Wisconsin and were flying in United Express colours, for whom UFS operated them. My training included four sectors over a few days from St Louis to Springfield, Peoria and Dupage followed by a two-sector check-ride with an FAA examiner from Dupage to Rockford and return. All went well and so I found myself 'sentenced' to eighty-seven hours in the simulator over the next two months! Simulator training was never my favourite occupation though, on this occasion, at least my students had English as their first language and, by and large, their capabilities were good.

Happily, I was able to gain some particular satisfaction in helping a couple of struggling first officers to make the grade.

Scattered amongst the simulator sojourns at all hours of day and night — ugh! — was the familiar mix of Jetstream, ATP, 146 and Avro RJ flights spread over company shuttles, test flights, the annual Woodford Air Display and licence rating checks for colleagues. However, the most significant event was the arrival of a letter in August 1993, offering me an appointment as a 146/RJ training captain in the new set-up at Woodford, stingily (I thought) at the same salary but even that was to improve markedly in the coming years. I was of course both relieved and delighted. I seemed to have made a satisfactory mark in the jets with the right people and, more importantly, only two of the Hatfield pilots had elected to come north and so that meant there were jet slots available for some of my pilot colleagues and me. Unluckily, a few other flying and non-flying colleagues who accepted the transfer to Prestwick were soon to be made redundant in the new location, stranded away from family, friends, children's education, wife's job and so on; but such were the circumstances of the time — I counted myself most fortunate indeed. The new company at Woodford was to be known as Avro International Aerospace.

As the months flashed by, I found myself flying the ATP more rarely and instead flew quite a few company shuttle flights on a new WFD-HAT-WFD schedule in a 146; there was much to-ing and fro-ing of personnel from Hatfield as the latter approached closure. My very last ATP flight was in October 1993 and the last Jetstream flight in the following March. Very soon, I was sent to China to carry out the most demanding training assignment of my life, during seven weeks in 146 aircraft with China North West Airlines, based at Lanzhou.

24
ASSIGNMENT LANZHOU

By the autumn of 1993, I had been working as a training captain and production test pilot for British Aerospace's Civil Aircraft Division, based at Woodford near Manchester, for some four and a half years. For most of that time, I had flown the Jetstream, ATP and BAe 146 concurrently. With the coming move of ATP production to Prestwick and consolidation of all 146 production at Woodford as the Hatfield production line closed, I was in the process of separating from the turboprops to concentrate for the future on the 146 and its derivative, the Avro RJ.

I had just under three hundred hours total on the 146 and RJ variants but, until then, no experience of training others on them, except when acting as a TRE/IRE (Type Rating/Instrument Rating Examiner) for licence checks on my pilot colleagues. Moreover, the few hundred hours on the 146/RJ had been thinly spread over several years. This was not the ideal background for pitching into a difficult airline training assignment on an aircraft that I felt I was still getting to know. On the other hand, sales demonstration tours, test flights and aircraft deliveries spread over the three types had taken me to a wide variety of countries. I had also completed quite a few overseas training assignments on the ATP, usually with customer airlines in fairly demanding environments. I had become well accustomed to being thrown in at the deep end in all sorts of 'interesting' situations by my masters at BAe. So, I was duly despatched to Lanzhou in North West China in the November to cut my teeth as a line trainer on the 146 with China North West Airlines (CNWA).

Luckily for me, I was to be teamed up with Vic Nightingale, probably the most experienced and highly competent 146 training captain in the industry. I also took the opportunity before departing to talk extensively to my recent boss and close colleague, Kevin

Moorhouse, who not long before had also spent some time on a similar assignment at Lanzhou. When I eventually got there, I found things had simplified a little since Kevin's experience. The Chinese domestic operation had at least moved on from using inches of water for altimeter pressure settings to millibars — so one less conversion chart was needed — but there were still plenty of surprises to come to make up for that little leap forward.

I set off with Vic to fly with SAS via Copenhagen to Beijing. In Beijing we transferred to a local TU-154, equipped with what must have been the smallest passenger seat pitch and width in the world, to fly down to Lanzhou. True to the tales I had been told by Kevin and Vic, as the TU-154 'lead-sled' slowed at the end of its landing run in the late afternoon at Lanzhou, many of the passengers got to their feet before the aircraft had turned off the runway and gathered their belongings to queue for the door whilst the aircraft taxied to the stand. My six foot three inch frame was still wedged into my window seat with my head stuck at an odd angle against the curve of the cabin ceiling, with my legs jammed into the seat frame in front, so this luckily saved me from being trampled in the rush. It also gave me the opportunity to see how domestic passengers of the time treated the aircraft cabin, little better than a rubbish tip since discarded food cartons and other detritus littered the floor throughout.

In the baggage hall at Lanzhou, we were met by our colleagues, training captain John Cresswell who was due to return to UK in a day or two and resident BAe engineer, Barry Horton. As we chatted cheerfully to our two friends, who seemed very glad to see us, the baggage conveyor gradually became empty and then eventually stopped. Vic had retrieved his luggage by then but mine had not appeared. Oh no, what a start to my stay in China! Baggage delivery was complete but my precious suitcase with all my notes, training materials, personal 'bible' of BAe 146 snippets, personal headset, uniform, shirts, underwear (all in six foot three inches, sixteen and a half stone, very non-Chinese sizes), and so on, was nowhere to be seen. For a few moments, I was gripped with a mixture of despair and panic. What on earth was I to do? In the UK it often took a couple of days or so for missing baggage to turn up, but out here on the edge of the Gobi Desert — who knew if I would ever see it again? I even began to think of flying down to Hong Kong to get some clothes and uniform but how on earth would I manage without all my vital written information?

As I wrestled mentally with the consequences, I saw Barry climb up onto the conveyor and disappear behind the rubber curtain to the area behind. Within a few moments he reappeared, clutching a large red suitcase. "This must be yours then," he said in a matter of fact way. "They often stop the conveyor before all the baggage has finished coming through," he continued. A great wave of relief swept over me as we set off for our rooms in the 'hostel', a converted former military barrack block.

I was not a complete stranger to China nor to the Far East in general. I had lived in Singapore and flown around South East Asia with the Royal Air Force for a few years in the 1960s, when I had also spent several weeks in Hong Kong. In 1984 I had spent two weeks in Beijing on a special consultancy task and had since taken part in an ATP sales tour from Hong Kong to Canton, Beijing and Shanghai and had flown a 146 delivery to Xian over the previous Christmas, so I was reasonably streetwise in the region. I wasn't expecting too many cultural shocks on this trip — but there were certainly a few to come. I knew there would be a lot of differences in the flying though, for this time I was to be using the domestic network, quite different from the 'special' network and procedures which were at that time provided separately for foreign airlines.

Before going out to 'dinner', John wanted to get cracking with an initial handover briefing, mainly for my benefit as the newcomer. We should bear in mind that BAe and other manufacturers, including Airbus, had been doing line training in China for quite a few years, so what I was about to learn had become a fairly well-established method, and John was an experienced practitioner. One of the first things he did was to hand me a set of route maps and approach and departure charts, written almost entirely in Chinese with only the numerals and a very few abbreviations in 'roman'.

Now, as I've said, I was reasonably streetwise and had used Jeppesen charts on my previous short flying visits to China. Moreover, I thought I was old enough to recognise a good 'spoof' when I saw one and indeed had myself been a practised 'spoofer' of new pilot arrivals to my first RAF squadron where it was a strong tradition. So I thought I saw this one coming before the charts touched down on my side of the table. Yet there was an oddly authentic ring to John's protestations of 'Honest!' in response to my disbelief, which eventually convinced me that this was no spoof. The only charts that existed — or were available to us at that time anyway — for most of the domestic destinations and the routes that we were to use, were in Chinese! For the second time that day, I felt very uncertain. How could I possibly learn to use these charts safely and effectively? Well, to my great surprise, I learned that it wasn't that difficult really and I was soon to recognise quite quickly what I needed from the charts once I was armed with the knowledge of a few basic characters of the language.

The second surprise of the briefing was to learn just how many persons would be on the flight deck during our line training trips. In common with most modern jet airliners, the 146 cockpit is equipped with only three seats, two for the pilots and an 'occasional' fold-down 'jump seat' for an observer or third crew member when required. I was to learn that every pilot in the airline appeared to be a captain, but only certain 'captains' were allowed to fly in the left-hand seat, a minor adjustment on safety grounds to the egalitarianism of the political system. None of the pilots under training spoke any English whatsoever. Moreover, all the ATC communications on the domestic network were in Chinese, so an interpreter gentleman (or lady) was essential. He or she was a very important person in the aircraft and had overwhelming claim to the jump seat. But there were to be rather more than just these three people.

None of the interpreters were trained aircrew — though I was to find that some of them seemed to think they had seen enough of this stuff over the years certainly to know better than most of the trainees and, occasionally, though almost always wrongly, better than the foreign training captain. So, there was a need for a further qualified local aviator to handle communications with ATC. He was the 'radio operator', an experienced Chinese pilot from CNWA, who also usually spoke no English and whose job it was to relay all ATC instructions through the interpreter to me and vice versa in respect of my responses. I was to find that this was a fairly time-consuming process and fraught with the chances of misunderstanding, particularly in time-critical radio exchanges, and more of that later too. I was also to find that most of these radio operators also regarded it as their right to step into the training process whenever they thought things were getting difficult. You would think it was quite enough, wouldn't you, to have four people, plus ATC, carrying on a bilingual conversation? But there were yet more people to come. First though, I need to continue to describe the seating (and standing) facilities for this burgeoning team.

The radio operator sat behind the right-hand seat on a wooden stool, known in the trade as 'the 6G stool', a light-hearted reference to the complete absence of any form of attachment to the aircraft structure. So, we have four persons up to now. On most occasions, it was thought very useful to have another trainee pilot along to observe the process, much as we did in the west where the individual would occupy the jump seat. In China, on this operation, he would stand, throughout, behind the left-hand seat. Five enough? Not quite. Although it was unusual, on my very first line training flight I was to have two others, a trainee interpreter(!), standing (wedged in between the primary interpreter and the observing trainee pilot) and yet another observing pilot stood in the aisle behind the jump seat — a total of seven in a cockpit designed for three! Was this sensible? Absolutely not! Did I have any choice? Absolutely none, if I was to get the job done and avoid upsetting the customer by challenging what was a well-accepted custom and practice with us and other manufacturers' training teams. I'm afraid that this was by no means the only highly unorthodox practice that had to be accepted in this very unique environment. By accepting a few such practices in the short term, we gained a start on the longer-term aim of introducing safer and more effective practices to the immature safety environment that then existed.

The third important component of John's brief to me was to explain a list of key phonetic phrases in Chinese for use when time didn't allow the normal courtesy of passing instructions through the interpreter. These included such commands as: *Fu Fe!* *(Go around!)*, *Pay Ping!* (Trim!), *Sudu!* (Speed!), *Boo How!* (No good! — sounds rather better in Chinese I think) and *Ting Drou!* (Stop!), together with numbers from one to ten and for a hundred and a thousand. I reckoned that it would be quite a while before I could move on to the higher linguistic levels such as *San Sh' Sandu!* (Flap 33!) since I could always make a grab for the flap lever if necessary! I already had a handful of cultural ones such as *Nee How* (Hello) and *Shay Shay* (Thank you) left over from previous visits. The one that has stayed in my memory over the years is, through repetitive usage during my stay, *'Way Ee, Tie Toe'* '(V1, Rotate!).

So, initial briefing over and it was time to step out to the rather unkindly nicknamed 'Salmonella Boulevard', about a twenty-minute walk outside the airport perimeter, where we would find the BAe favoured eating establishment, run by 'Jo', a cheerful, former resident of Shanghai who had apparently been exiled from there during the red-guard era of the '60s for being a bit non-conformist. Jo spoke a tiny bit of English, not much and certainly not enough to avoid some interesting culinary misunderstandings as I shall describe later. Suffice to say for the moment that I ate here on almost every evening in the following seven weeks of my stay (except once a week or so when Barry prepared one of his excellent curries in the hostel) without a single tummy upset, despite ostensibly very grotty conditions in the front of the house and in the kitchen, that would certainly have caused a heart attack to any passing western public health inspector and which led to the unkind nickname of Salmonella Boulevard. Some weeks after I got to know him, Jo gave me the high honour of a kitchen tour from which I have some interesting photos for those who are not too squeamish. However, I can say with no exaggeration that this was, and still is, amongst the very best Chinese food I have ever tasted, in or out of China including anywhere else in the Far East.

Before leaving our restaurant in Salmonella Boulevard, I ought to mention the heating arrangements. Lanzhou is at six thousand, three hundred and sixty feet altitude. The temperature outside in the early evening in November was usually several or more degrees below zero degrees C. In common with other basic parts of China and Eastern

Europe at that time, central heating was a community affair with hot water piped in, sometimes over hundreds of yards, from a remotely sited heating plant via outdoors, wide-bore, overhead pipes that were not always well lagged. Our particular 'restaurant', towards the end of the row of buildings, was equipped with bog-standard iron radiators that only managed to struggle up to about ten degrees or so above ambient, leaving us to bask indoors normally in only a few degrees above zero. I quickly learned to try and grab the seat nearest the radiator whenever I could and I always wore several layers beneath my insulated anorak so that I could take the anorak off to cover my frozen legs whilst I ate.

I suspect the airline or the Chinese authorities were paying a lot of scarce dollars to have us expensive Western training captains aboard for the month or so that we were expected to stay, so it came as quite a surprise to us to discover that we had to await 'authorisation to fly' for quite a while. The delay actually went on for about two weeks and we never did discover its cause. There were two theories. The Chinese had experienced a spate of fatal accidents in that year, including a recent one (rare, even on a global scale) to a CNWA 146 in which the crew had inadvertently attempted a flapless take-off and finished up in a lake beyond the end of the runway at Yinchuan, killing many passengers and seriously injuring the captain. So, the first theory was that some prolonged debate was going on about the presence and role of foreign pilots at this sensitive time. The second, quite plausible theory, was related to several airports to which we would be scheduled to fly. Some of our routes took us well out to the far North West of China, uncomfortably close to the Chinese nuclear and missile testing area at Lop Nor. We surmised that maybe some tests were scheduled.

Anyway, we filled the waiting time with various activities. Vic gave some excellent line training briefs to the locals, with me in attendance taking copious notes for my own future benefit. We paid a visit to Xian as passengers on a Chinese-crewed 146 to meet our senior resident engineer in China and several of the airline management team. On this visit, I cadged the jump seat and, although I didn't understand one single word of what was being said, I was at least able to get some practice in using my Chinese approach charts. Crucially, as it turned out for my subsequent first trip at the helm, I was able to store a mental picture of the somewhat featureless last few kilometres leading to runway 23 at Xian. Another similar opportunity arose ten days later, just before we were let loose to train, when I also got a brief look at Chung Qing. I was to learn that brief looks were usually all one got anyway because, although the weather at Lanzhou and to the west, north and east was usually very dry and clear of cloud, there was a perpetual thick haze both from dust in the winds from the big dry areas of the Ghobi and the Takla Makan and from severe pollution from the industrial areas, including Lanzhou City some fifty kilometres to the south. Further south to Chung Qing, Kunming and other airports, there was often rain and low cloud with poor visibility below.

Vic and I, sometimes accompanied by Barry, also got into the routine of going for long walks during the days of waiting. We had a couple of favourite circuits which took us well into the open country surrounding the airport and through several very rural, very basic villages. We found to our surprise that a very few habitations were actually built directly into the dry, dusty hillsides, effectively modern 'cave-dwellings'. However, when we mentioned these to our hosts, we were met with very firm denials that any people were living in caves anywhere in China. By contrast, most of the other small villages of sandy-bricked houses had an apparent headman's house that was set behind walls and often very smartly painted. Agricultural techniques looked pretty basic. On one of our walks, I took the opportunity to do some local 'bonding' by helping to stack loose hay in the 'village square' and on another we were invited to take tea and food in a 'headman's house'. Everywhere we went we were met with great friendliness and particularly huge smiles whenever I produced my camera.

Eventually, on returning from one of these walks, we were given our clearance to start flying and I made my final preparations for the first sector from Lanzhou to Xian, home of the Terracotta Army and scene of my forthcoming baptism into line training in China.

It was Monday 22 November 1993. The morning of my first line training flight for China North West Airlines had arrived. I was to have two trainee pilots, Gao Li Gang and Song Shui Qing, for a flight from

Lanzhou to Xian, then on to Kunming for a short stop before returning via Xian again to Lanzhou. The four sectors would take about six and a half hours block time with the final return leg to Lanzhou at night.

I set my alarm clock for seven a.m. but I needn't have done so. My room in the former barrack block at Lanzhou airport was on the first floor of the building, on the side which bordered the main alleyway leading to the airport buildings and along which the airport workforce began to walk in to their various jobs from about six thirty a.m. By seven a.m., I had been awakened as usual by the sound of scores of Chinese workers chatting noisily, hawking and spitting just as noisily, through the alleyway on their way to work.

I met my crew, two smartly uniformed pilots, the 'radio operator' in a leather jacket, the chief interpreter (the very experienced Mr Li Fung Gung, whom I had by now got to know quite well during our two weeks of waiting to start flying), a young lady trainee interpreter and a third pilot observing — seven in a cockpit designed for three, as previously described.

The four sectors went ahead fairly smoothly and gave me my first encounter with some of the unusual features that typified the next thirty days of line training. By the end of the day I was pretty tired from operating the four scheduled passenger flights into unfamiliar airports, whilst trying to coordinate the actions of my core crew of four and with all ground/air communication taking place in a totally unintelligible language. Thankfully, the weather was fairly good and Mr Li had seen it all before hundreds of times. On this and subsequent flights he was to prove a first-rate goalkeeper in preventing the majority of linguistic or cultural misunderstandings from slipping through the net. But the flight deck was occasionally a tower of Babel. The following description of day one illustrates some of the problems we faced each subsequent day.

There was a short departure delay whilst someone fetched a set of smoke goggles to replace one of the mandatory sets missing from the flight deck — the goggles were ideally suited for motorcycling and were always being pilfered. We started up, took off from Lanzhou and established smoothly in the climb after the rather lengthy process of winding the altimeter subscale up from the QFE (airfield ambient pressure level) of eight hundred millibars to the standard flight level setting of one thousand and thirteen millibars when passing transition altitude. The Chinese were still using QFE for airfield operations, even for field elevations up to and beyond the six thousand, three hundred and sixty feet of Lanzhou. Their aircraft had specially modified altimeters to allow the very low airfield pressure levels to be set. The time taken to change the altimeter setting through two hundred plus millibars was a prolonged and unwelcome intrusion, especially during the busy descent and approach phase back to Lanzhou that evening. On this first occasion in the climb, the trainee pilot in the left-hand seat was flying, so I was busily winding away and watching as much as I could of what he was doing whilst also responding to Mr Li's translations both from ATC (through the radio man), and from the pilot flying.

Meanwhile the radio man, on the '6G stool', lit up a rather evil-smelling local cigarette and began immediately to produce choking smoke in which we were all quickly enveloped. I found time, between altimeter winding, watching the trainee and communicating through Mr Li, for a rapid request for the radio man to put out his fag — I doubt that I'd have survived halfway to Xian without donning my oxygen mask and smoke goggles if the gentleman had disagreed.

As soon as sensible in the cruise, we briefed for the descent and approach at Xian. We had to cover both runway directions as the runway-in-use had not been specified by Xian control and Mr Li became deaf to my attempts to wring this important item of information out of the system. The wind was slack so I couldn't even make a guess as to which runway we'd use and, of course, I was totally unable to monitor communications between other aircraft and ATC — a usual source of much vital 'situational awareness' when operating in the generally global English language environment. It transpired that neither area nor approach control were allowed normally to announce the landing runway. That was the responsibility of local control — their rice bowl. The arrival chart at Xian showed that all traffic was routed via a common point serving each runway, so it was only as we reached that point and were transferred to local control that we were told the runway for landing. At that point, my interpreter nonchalantly added that we were to join visually downwind for runway 23.

The visibility was only a few kilometres, barely meeting the legal visual meteorological conditions (VMC), and therefore not really suitable for a visual join from ninety degrees to the runway at an unfamiliar airfield. Not only that, but I didn't want my trainee to have the additional demands of a visual circuit in these conditions on his first flight. I declined the offer and asked Mr Li to tell ATC local that I wanted to join for an ILS (Instrument Landing System) approach. "No!" said Mr Li. "You must join downwind visually."

"No!" I said. "I'm unfamiliar with the area and need to join the ILS." There then ensued a four-way debate in Chinese between Mr Li, my trainee (by now confused), the radio man and ATC local. Eventually, after I had confirmed again that it was to be an ILS, agreement was reached and we were cleared for ILS 23 as the multiple chatter thankfully died away.

After a fair flurry of activity — pity the poor trainee — we turned finals for the ILS at about twelve nautical miles, on autopilot and in reasonably good order. The runway lay ahead, hidden by a haze of dust and pollution but I could just about make out ground features for about a kilometre or two ahead of the aircraft. I wanted my trainee to take over manually in good time to stabilise his control for the landing rather than to continue using the autopilot down to its limits, with a last moment manual reversion. As we reached about three miles from landing, I still could not see the runway and so I asked Mr Li to confirm that the runway lights were on. "No!" said Mr Li, for at least the second time that day. "Lights not available in daytime. Lights only for night-time." There was no time to argue about it. Anyway, at two miles I had just picked up a distinctive parallel trench that I had spotted from the jump seat on my earlier observing flights and which led straight in to the approach light system — so I felt safe in asking Mr Li to tell the trainee to disengage the autopilot. Later that evening a discussion with Vic revealed that it was useless to ask for any form of airfield or approach lighting to be on during daylight — it just wasn't done. The remainder of the day passed off fairly successfully though there were certainly more strange aviation practices to come — but first a culinary tale or two.

I much enjoyed my evening meals at Jo's on 'Salmonella Boulevard', despite the risk of hypothermia and the need to turn a blind eye to the standards of hygiene. One evening, I took the opportunity to ask Jo if he could do toffee apples for dessert. I remembered from my earlier times in the Far East how much I had enjoyed freshly prepared toffee apples that were dunked into cold water at the table to harden the hot toffee. "No," said Jo. "No can get apples." I tried this request several more times over a week or so and always got the same answer. One day during an afternoon off, Vic and I walked in to the small market near the airport. I spotted some apples for sale and we bought four. That evening in Jo's I made my usual request and got the usual answer but, in response to Jo's expected 'No!', Vic and I whipped out an apple in each hand from our pockets. Jo grinned broadly, disappeared off to the kitchen and reappeared later with four superb toffee apples and a bowl of cold water.

We were subsequently able to get toffee apples occasionally without having to buy the apples ourselves, but we came unstuck the weekend Jo was away downtown visiting his family. Since none of his staff could speak any English, he had thoughtfully provided a little list of our various favourite dishes, with the Chinese translation alongside each one, so that we could then indicate what we wanted to the waitresses. This we did carefully on night one of Jo's absence, but something went terribly wrong in the translation somewhere. Instead of getting toffee apple, the waitress proudly brought us toffee *potato*! We didn't have the heart to show displeasure, and they actually tasted quite good, and certainly quite unique.

About halfway through the thirty-day period, I was allocated a flight to Urumqi, (pronounced 'Ooroomoochi' by the locals). This was an exciting prospect from several points of view. Urumqi ('Fine Pasture') is a very remote place still rarely visited by foreigners when I flew there. It is the capital of the Sinkiang Uighur autonomous region in the far North West of China, one thousand nautical miles to the north of Everest, beyond the vast Tibetan Plateau and at the northern end of the gap leading from the Tarim Basin into the Dzungarian Basin. It lies at an altitude of nearly two thousand, eight hundred and fifty feet, with mountains to the east up to eighteen thousand feet, past which we would fly from Lanzhou. It was nearly three and a half hours flying time from Lanzhou, into the prevailing strong westerly wind, and therefore towards the very limit of range for a BAe 146. There was clearly a need for some very careful fuel planning and assessment of the very limited diversion options. Alternate airports in the final part of the route were limited to Ha Mi, a military airfield two hundred and sixty one nautical miles before Urumqi, at which clearance to land would no doubt be very difficult to obtain with a foreign captain, and Kuer Li, a civil airfield one hundred and fifty-one nautical miles to the SSW of Urumqi, but necessitating a climb to seventeen thousand feet or more, minimum en route altitude, over the Tian mountains. Each of the two alternates had only non-precision aids (Non-Directional Beacons — NDBs) for approach.

I did most of my planning on the day before the flight, so that I was as well prepared as I could be when I reported for the trip. The most vital weather information was obtained for Urumqi, less some detail, and for the route. Frustratingly, but as usual, there was little up-to-date information on weather at the alternates. The local practice normally was for ATC to take the decision to divert flights and, at that point, you would be given 'all relevant information', quite different to the practice in the Western world where it is usually the aircraft captain's decision. Nevertheless, the weather looked reasonable, quite good en route with some cloud and precipitation at Urumqi. We took on a full load of fuel and set off. Ha Mi eventually slipped by and, as we passed over the Bogda mountain range, I briefed my trainee for the descent and approach at Urumqi. In common with many of the airports to which we operated, both departure and arrival traffic followed the same ground track in opposing directions. This often meant that there was much levelling off in the descent or climb until opposing traffic had passed by. That day was no exception, so as we neared Urumqi, with fine views of the high mountains immediately to our left, it was obvious that we had a significant excess of altitude and would have to descend in the holding pattern before starting the approach.

My trainee, a right-hand seat 'captain' (i.e. a co-pilot), had about five hundred hours total flying experience, but that was almost entirely on the twelve-passenger Y5N (Antonov 2), single-engined biplane (!), which he had operated almost exclusively at low-level in VMC. His only real instrument flying experience was gained during his 146 conversion course, in the simulator at Woodford and on some of the few line training flights that he had by now completed with me in his home country. So, I was monitoring him quite carefully and adding a few helpful tips through the interpreter, this time a young lady — Miss Soon, as he entered his first hold in the descent. At the same time, I was urging Miss Soon to get me the latest weather (via the radio man as usual) asap as there had been an earlier report of 'rain on the runway from yesterday' that was puzzling me a bit.

As we levelled off at the correct altitude for the intermediate approach, Miss Soon announced: 'Oh sorry — rain on runway from yesterday is snow!' Well, that cleared up the puzzle, though I doubt if Mr Li would have made that mistake. Perhaps I might have twigged it from the temperature if that hadn't got lost in translation somewhere. Not to worry, I'd landed on snow plenty of times before (albeit not in a 146!) and the runway was long enough, even for the 146 — unequipped with reverse thrust — provided it wasn't *too* slippery. However, there was certainly no time for further discussion on the finer points of runway state or friction coefficients as my trainee had his hands full getting rid of the excess speed off the descent and getting configured for the ILS. I was also beginning to get a bit worried as the ILS localiser signal was a bit jittery during the turn on to finals. As we established on finals at two thousand feet above the airfield, I calculated as expected that we had insufficient fuel to return to distant Ha Mi. The only alternate, should we be unable to complete our approach for any reason, was Kuer Le, one hundred and fifty miles away over the Tian mountains immediately to the south, probably with similar weather but with a long climb and only an NDB approach available.

At this point, I was not overly concerned about missing the approach since the reported weather was only light snow in almost no wind with a cloud base of eight hundred feet and visibility of four kilometres.

Moreover, the light wind had got me thinking more about stopping problems in the landing run itself. I must admit that, lurking also in the back of my mind, was the fact that a China Northern Airlines MD 82 had crashed at Urumqi only nine days previously, on this same approach in poor weather, but in otherwise unexplained circumstances, causing twelve fatalities. But the next event put my brain into overdrive. At about three miles, just as I was beginning to see glimpses of the snow-covered terrain directly in front of my aircraft, the ILS localiser signal failed totally. The correct action in response would have been to make a go-around, then prepare for a NDB approach at Urumqi. In the circumstances, I could possibly have reverted to the NDB approach there and then, though this was not recommended practice for several reasons, not least that it would have been unbriefed. Moreover, I was rapidly approaching the minimum altitude for the NDB approach and could assess that I would probably not be able to see well enough to complete a landing from it anyway. As well as the concern to resist pressing on — usually the worst kind of action — the other thoughts that flashed through my mind had been mostly anticipated, but not all at once! There would be the time and fuel spent in briefing the other pilot and ATC, each through the interpreter, about the new plot and getting clearance for a prompt second approach or diversion. There was an unwieldy and inefficient missed approach and diversion procedure (involving a long climb in the hold), a one hundred and fifty mile-transit to an NDB approach at Kuer Le with only just enough fuel (or maybe not enough if significant interruptions in climbing occurred) and probably no better guarantee of landing there. And there was the unpleasant thought that I had probably stumbled upon the cause, or a contributory factor, of the MD 82 crash, and I didn't want to follow that into history.

But I had to make a very rapid decision. I was entirely happy with the glide-slope signal. The on-track NDB signal from the airfield was also strong and steady and had tallied closely with the ILS localiser so far. So, reining back the instinct to do the professional thing and go-around, I instructed the trainee to disengage the autopilot, maintain his heading and continue on the ILS glide-slope, whilst I strained into the distance to locate the (unlit!) snow-covered runway against the surrounding snow-covered terrain! With one or two minor heading changes that I issued to the trainee and with the help of a strobe light from a previously landed aircraft, which identified the parallel taxiway and so, in turn, the runway, we made it from my first and last NDB/glide-path approach! This was totally unorthodox but then so too were the circumstances and, especially, the unique operating environment. Needs must and I judged it was the safest of the two undesirable options.

I took control of the aircraft from the trainee at about two hundred feet, because he was starting to 'hold off' for a long landing, and so we landed a little longer than ideal. I popped the nose wheel on quickly, slammed the spoilers out and immediately started braking. It felt like the brakes had failed — the runway was very slippery in the inch or two of snow that was at or just above freezing point. The brakes eventually began to bite, but only in small amounts — as the anti-skid worked overtime — and we were rapidly using up runway. In the circumstances, I used the rare option of closing down the two outboard engines, thus removing half the idle thrust, which helped a bit. I had to do all of this myself whilst controlling the aircraft as there simply wasn't time to get all the information to the trainee through Miss Soon, however 'soon' she might have been, so my hands were flashing around the flight deck selecting generators and engines off and so forth whilst keeping straight and braking carefully. There was not much runway left by the time I brought the speed under control and turned off at the end, greatly relieved but with my brain somewhat over-boosted by now. But the little adventure was not quite over yet.

After taxiing in and disembarking my passengers, Miss Soon came back to the flight deck, after talking to the ramp staff, to give me the unwelcome news that there was a three-and-a-half-hour delay for routine aircraft de-icing due to lack of ground equipment. Oh well, I thought, at least that will give me time to get the books out to work through the relatively complex data for taking off from a contaminated runway with a heavy aircraft, not least to see whether I might have to limit fuel upload or passengers to meet the take-off weight limit in these conditions, and so perhaps have to land somewhere else for a fuel uplift en route back to Lanzhou. Also, I thought, I should be able to relax a bit and eat my lunch.

I was sitting alone on the flight deck, with the heavy operations manuals spread all around and the rest of my crew resting in the passenger cabin, when lunch arrived in the usual lidded mess tin in the hands of Miss Soon. "Great!" I thought. "I'll take a break and enjoy my lunch." I lifted the lid for the last surprise of the day. There, 'perched' on a bed of rice were four, large, whole, boiled, yellow chickens'… feet! I resisted the urge to slam the lid back on — these were, after all, a perfectly normal culinary item in China. Once again that day, my brain went into overdrive. "Very, very sorry," I lied wickedly, "but my religion doesn't allow me to eat chickens' feet. Is there anything else?" Miss Soon found me some insipid sandwiches and we all returned uneventfully, but very late, to Lanzhou without the en route stop.

I had not known that the Chinese were so greatly respectful of foreigners' cultural and religious quirks, so I was rather lucky to pull that one out of the hat at short notice. Especially so, since my ever-polite hosts asked me almost daily afterwards if I was now happy with my on-board meals and to confirm that I had not been given chickens' feet again, in contravention of my religious beliefs.

There were quite a few other events to illustrate the stark differences in operating methods between China and the West. It seemed to me, unsurprisingly, that most flowed directly from the cultural and political differences between our two societies. However, perhaps I should conclude for the moment. Vic and I were greatly honoured at the end of our stay to be invited to Beijing to give a presentation on our experiences to several very senior members of the Civil Aviation Administration of China, and our suggestions for change were positively received. We had quite a moving send-off from Lanzhou when every one of our trainees, and many others, turned up to see us on our way. The assignment had been a very difficult one for me and had made a deep and lasting impression. It was a unique and very often strange experience and it will be forever remembered against the background of the exceptionally friendly and hospitable people who were our hosts for our seven weeks stay in the Middle Kingdom. Well, at least I got home for Christmas this time, having spent the previous Christmas in Xian. Exhausted on return, I was very happy to enjoy taking some delayed leave. I had a whole month off!

Welcome to Lanzhou

Author, Vic, Interpreter & Trainees

Author and Full Crew (5 men on the 3-man Flight Deck!)

Author and Cabin Crew

Jo in His kitchen

25
SOUTH AMERICA, THE CARIBBEAN, SOUTH AFRICA AND THE FAR EAST

We had sold ten Avro RJ100 aircraft — the largest version — to THY, the Turkish national airline, so I was sent off with a couple of colleagues at the end of January 1994 to train many of the same pilots (amongst other new ones) whom I had trained on the ATP in Turkey just two years previously with THT, the domestic subsidiary. We were based once more in Istanbul and Ankara and, though it was again a winter task, I enjoyed myself tremendously for three weeks flying all over Turkey, often with old friends. A number of new destinations, including Erzurum, Gaziantep, Trabzon on the Black Sea coast and distant Van in the east were added to the seven airports previously visited in the ATPs of THT. I returned for yet another three happy weeks in March and April when the international destinations of Rome, Milan and Athens were added. During this period, there were usually two or three BAe training captains at a time in Turkey so we were able to meet up frequently in the evenings to compare notes on progress, evaluate many gastronomic establishments and, on the occasional day off, to explore the many fascinating historical sites in Istanbul particularly. The introduction of the Avro RJ in Turkey went really well in more ways than one!

Back on the ranch at Woodford after the second stay in Turkey, I was appointed as the project pilot for SAM Colombia, a new customer who had ordered nine Avro RJ 100s. I gave base training to SAM's first six pilots in one of our RJ 70s before their own aircraft were ready for delivery a few weeks later. Unusually, I was to spend the summer almost entirely in the UK with not so much flying as in previous years. However, I was also appointed to write the all-weather procedures manual for the Avro RJ, the first BAe airliner to be equipped with autoland, so there was plenty to keep me occupied.

We were fortunate to have on our staff, Dan Gurney, a test pilot who had been involved in the very early days of autoland development at BLEU, the Blind Landing Experimental Unit at RAE Bedford (where my own aviation career had started in 1960 as a sixteen-year-old scientific assistant with the Naval Air Department). Dan had led the RJ autoland development flying at Woodford, in which I had also participated. The new aircraft and its new capability meant that appropriate operational procedures for airline use had to be devised and written from scratch by us at Woodford. With a lot of help from Dan and his colleague Alan Foster, plus a most informative visit to observe a British Airways crew in a 737 simulator at Cranebank, I managed to put the RJ all-weather procedures manual together. It wasn't long before I would be using those procedures for real, for the first time, on a passenger flight into Lyons in thick fog with Delta Air Transport, the Sabena subsidiary, and frequently thereafter.

The absence of overseas trips for a few months enabled my wife and me to enjoy a week off in May at Loch Rannoch, another in September at Aviemore, and me to do a one-week summer school at Stirling University as part of my Open University degree studies. The reduced amount of flying still brought the great variety that was part of the role of being a factory pilot, often accompanied by new experiences and challenges. As well as production and development test flying in 146s and RJs, there were nine test flights in the development programme for the new BAe U125A (a search and rescue aircraft for Japan, based on the 125-800 series aircraft), a proving flight from Paris to London City in a steep-approach RJ70 and a two-day trip to Johannesburg to carry out a re-acceptance test flight in a 146 with SAFAIR, prior to the aircraft changing leaseholder. There were also customer acceptance flights at Woodford in 146s for Air Jet of France and in SAM's first three RJs, a couple of RJ70 demos for British Airways, plus flying as display co-pilot in an RJ70 at the Woodford Air Show and then, in October, a delivery flight all the way to Bogota with one of SAM's RJs.

I always got immense enjoyment from long-range delivery flights. The one to Bogota was unique in getting me to South America for the first time and for the experience of landing at Bogota itself. We staged in the RJ 100 via Keflavik, Goose Bay and Bangor, Maine for the first night-stop, on to Washington Dulles for the second, then Miami and Montego Bay for the third before arriving at Bogota El Dorado International airport on day four. The airport sits at eight thousand, three hundred and sixty feet, within a bowl of higher mountains. It was by far the highest airport at which I was ever to land an aircraft, after Lanzhou (six thousand three hundred and sixty feet), Nairobi (five thousand three hundred and thirty feet) and Kathmandu (a mere four thousand three hundred and ninety feet!).

The single-engine-out performance for the RJ 70 in the event of an engine failure on take-off from runway 13 at Bogota met certification requirements, of course, but with not a lot of room to spare in which to get the necessary right turn completed inside the close and rising terrain. That factor had been the subject of much concern and discussion with our SAM customer and, as project pilot, I had been required to demonstrate the procedure fully to their pilots in the RJ simulator, so it was particularly interesting to see the area 'in the flesh' for myself. Sure enough, I landed on runway 13 and, when I saw the adjacent terrain rising beyond and to the right of the runway, I rather hoped that I would not have to fly the procedure for real, especially in cloud!

I had fully expected to spend some interesting time, along with my two other colleagues who were already there, in training SAM pilots from Bogota and their other base, Medellin, to their various destinations in and around Colombia. However, we had each been a bit disturbed on reading BAe's travel security brief for the country — all sixteen pages of it! The brief stated quite clearly that the only safe way to travel between the airport at Medellin and the town was by helicopter! In the event, after just one night in Bogota, I had to fly back with American Airlines via Washington to the UK. I had been re-tasked with participating in yet another new service introduction, of RJ85s with Lufthansa, based at Munich for a couple of weeks in the early November and again in December.

Apart from renewing an old acquaintance with the Hofbrauhaus on a day off in Munich, the Lufthansa experience brought me to the new destinations of Amsterdam, Brussels, Cologne, Copenhagen, Florence,

Milan, Sofia and Vienna. The operation in and out of Munich was certainly slick. I remember being particularly impressed with the airport's ground movement radar that quickly spotted a wrong turn I had made — after landing in fog and during the early taxi in to the stand — and the superb de-icing facilities installed near the take-off holding point. German efficiency was around in bundles and the training I carried out was straightforward with very competent individuals.

After a Christmas break in the UK and time-off at home again, the New Year of 1995 started in great style with another most enjoyable long-range ferry flight, shared with colleague pilot Alistair McDicken, this time in a 146 to Kaohsiung on Taiwan for Makung Airlines. It was to be the first of three long-range ferries for me in that year. We staged over three night-stops via Corfu, Luxor, Dubai, Bombay, Colombo, Phuket and Brunei. It was on this flight that I had a tantalising high-level view of the greatly modernised area around Bait al Falaj, near the city of Muscat in Oman. It had changed vastly from when I had been there with the Sultan of Oman's Air Force, twenty-five years earlier during the Dhofar War (as mentioned in earlier chapters). Another highlight of the four-day ferry was passing Mount Pinatubo in the Philippines on the final leg up to Kaohsiung. The eruption of Pinatubo, on 15 June 1991, had been the second largest volcanic eruption of the twentieth century, ten times larger than the 1980 eruption of Mount St Helens. It was the largest eruption to affect a densely populated area; eight hundred and forty-seven people had been killed. The eruption had produced high-speed avalanches of hot lava and ash, giant mudflows, gas, and a cloud of pyroclastic ash hundreds of miles across. Three and a half years later, as we passed it on our starboard side, we had a ringside view of the rivers of ash and the mudflows that had continued to be spread from the volcano by heavy rains for years afterwards. We arrived in Kaohsiung just in time for the airline's Chinese New Year party, a happy coincidence but probably rigged by our (Chinese) BAe operations support rep who accompanied us on the trip from the UK.

Before I went to Kaohsiung, plans had been laid for BAe to support the start-up of a new airline in the Caribbean, Carib Express, with three second-hand, expensively refurbished Bae 146s. The venture was part-funded by a twenty per cent share from British Airways, who supplied some of the cabin crew and operations staff. The new airline was set up in competition to LIAT (Leeward Islands Air Transport — known jocularly at local level as 'Lost In-between Antigua and Trinidad' — and other unkind variations) with its all-turboprop fleet. BAe were to provide line training to local pilots, some of whom came over from LIAT, and to support the early months of the new jet operation, similar to that which we'd done recently in various countries but whereas those had been with existing airlines. This was to be the first of three completely new airline start-ups in which I was to participate.

Within a month of returning to the UK, I was again on my way in a second long-range ferry, delivering a 146 for Carib Express across the familiar North Atlantic route and down the Eastern Seaboard of the USA to Fort Lauderdale, then onward to Barbados. There followed what was probably the most enjoyable and satisfying training assignment of all times, four weeks on Barbados, flying all over the Leeward Islands, in and out of one or two quite demanding airstrips and enjoying the climate at the best possible time of year. The pilots were all up to the task. The cabin crews were the best I ever came across. I finished most days with a couple of hours on the beach in the mid-afternoon and the seafood was outstanding in the evening. Well, somebody had to put up with all that I suppose — I absolutely relished all of it.

We began the operation with just two of the three aircraft ordered. There were three of us BAe training captains there to run the daily schedules to St Lucia, Dominica, St Vincent, Grenada, Trinidad and Tobago. On St Lucia, we used Vigie (later George F.L. Charles) the smaller of the two airports and in the northern part of the island beside the bay and harbour at Castries. I remember the airfield firstly for its very limited parking areas that often required holding overhead until a space was available on the open apron. Secondly, the usual approach was for landing on runway 09 but large yachts or cruise ships entering or leaving the harbour could pass just under the aircraft on short finals, sometimes causing further delays. Thirdly, I had a notable experience after parking one day, with such limited space that the top of a palm tree was just ahead of, and slightly higher than, my port wing tip as I came to a halt.

I had little option but to park in that position as I had been urged forward by ATC to allow other aircraft to pass through a narrow gap to my right and rear quarter. There were no towing facilities but I had reasoned that the slight up-slope that I faced would allow me to roll back a little with brakes off, before boarding passengers or starting engines for the return flight, and then to turn sharp right to avoid the palm. Wrong! — the aircraft refused to budge, despite a dozen helpers trying to push it! I had to start my engines, taxi forward very gently with the port wing tip brushing through the upper fronds of the palm and wait for a chap whom I'd pre-briefed to check from the top of a stepladder for the very unlikely chance of damage to the aircraft. All was well, though I guess it was not the cleverest of things to have done. By the way, attempts at bending the tree had failed miserably!

Dominica was fun, as before in the ATP, for the final turn over the coconut plantation and the dive into the wooded valley before the runway could be seen round the bend to the right. St Vincent too had its challenges. It was a short runway, only one thousand, five hundred yards. Even in the 146, every yard was needed at times. Take-off was always towards the sea on runway 25, take off on runway 07 being prohibited due to high ground in that direction. However, there was no turning pad at the eastern end of the runway for a runway 25 take-off. We had a copy of the LIAT Operations Manual which warned of the need for special care, when turning, to avoid wing tip damage from a high (open mesh) fence in close proximity to the runway 25 threshold. (I don't know if their manual wrote of my palm tree at St Lucia but at least I was onto this St Vincent problem before I went there). Not only that but there was a high earth bank just beyond the fence. Because of the short runway, we needed to power up the 146's four engines against the brakes, contrary to the normal airliner practice of a rolling take-off. The result of the jet blast from four engines pointed back at the bank could cause severe re-circulation of the blast (let alone soil) and buffeting of the tail, so we had to avoid that by taxing forward for a few precious yards to stop before opening the throttles. I much enjoyed the month's flying in the Caribbean, especially for all the experience of visual flying on short sectors into interesting island airfields and the bright and friendly crew members with whom I flew. Very sadly and despite its very professional operation, the airline was not a commercial success and closed down only fifteen months later.

Having returned to the UK with a good tan at the end of winter and in a very happy frame of mind, I was on my way westward again within a matter of weeks, this time on a very different and potentially quite exciting task. Late April found me flying out to Miami with a colleague pilot to join two US pilots from BAe Washington and a commercial team assembling to plan the repossession of two of our leased aircraft, whose operators in Bolivia had not paid their bills for a very long time. After several days in Miami, which included a rather long drive down to Key West for lunch one day (it's about one hundred and thirty miles each way!), we set off on the overnight American Airlines flight to Santa Cruz, via La Paz (altitude thirteen thousand, three hundred and twenty feet — phew!), prepared if necessary for a 'hostile extraction' and all that was entailed in such a venture. In the end, after quite a few days around the pool of our hotel, our US colleagues took just one of the aircraft out on friendly terms. Successful negotiations had allowed the second aircraft to remain with the customer.

We two Brits returned to Miami for another task. The consolation prize was that this task, to ferry another 146 back from Nashville, Tennessee to Marshalls at Cambridge, was not due for a few days, so my colleague and I travelled part of the way from Miami to Nashville by car. That allowed us to visit the Kennedy Space Centre and the Jack Daniels distillery on the way (well, some twenty-five miles or something off our route), on two separate days! We then ferried the aircraft back to Marshalls of Cambridge on the usual route, thus completing my third long range ferry within the first half of the year. That actually was to be the last ferry ever (more later as to why!) but for one to Athens which probably doesn't count as long range.

The summer came and, after a trip to Luxembourg with my friend and boss (as newly appointed training manager), John Davies ('Jed')*, to carry out demos in a RJ85 for a potential customer, I prepared to return once more to Turkey where I was to spend the next three months with THY.

*Captain John Eldon Davies was tragically killed on 5 June 1998 in a private Hunter F4 following an engine failure in the circuit at Dunsfold. He had been promoted to chief test pilot at Woodford only one day before the accident.

Lufthansa RJ 85

Carib Express BAe 146 with Happy Captain & Crew

26
TURKISH FAREWELL, BRUSSELS BONANZA, AEGEAN EXCURSION AND LAST LANDING AT PALERMO

From July to September 1995, I enjoyed a further three months of line training THY's Avro RJ pilots during scheduled passenger flights to most of the domestic airports in Turkey. New routes were opened to Diyerbakir, Antalya, Gaziantep, Malatya, Mus and Sivas plus Kiev across the Black Sea in Ukraine. Though unknown to me at the time, those were to be the final weeks of my association with THY and indeed in Turkey. Thankfully, it was summer for a change and I was to make the very best of the time in several respects.

The THY operation was going mostly quite well as far as flight operations and training were concerned. However, there was a worrying number of continuing issues with aircraft maintenance. Though they were not my province, I reckoned I should flag them up with the engineering, operations support and general management departments at BAe Woodford (by then renamed as Avro International Aerospace), which I did in a detailed report. The next couple of paragraphs illustrate the kinds of issues that my colleagues and I came across frequently during our various overseas pilot training and support contracts.

During the three separate stays in Turkey between 2 July and 23 September, I flew one hundred and twenty-three hours over one hundred and three sectors in all ten of the THY aircraft (Avro RJ 85s and 100s) that were by then in service with the airline. Each sector had included a senior first officer in the crew (as observer), as well as the trainee captain or trainee first officer, and that provided a valuable insight into 'normal' THY operating procedures. THY flight operations were not immune to comment; I saw that a number of improvements were needed in the provision of pre-flight Met and NOTAM (notices to airmen) information, fuel policy, passenger loading and handling procedures and a couple of aircraft handling items. Nor were we in Avro immune to criticism, as there were also two ongoing and important deficiencies in two of our operating manuals.

The most worrying areas, however, were the deficiencies in aircraft maintenance within the airline. The two main issues were shortage of supervisory coverage by airline and Avro technicians and misinterpretation of the MEL (minimum equipment list). Those two issues often combined to cause long delays to rectification of minor defects in the aircraft. That amounted to something of a culture of neglect, a most unhealthy attitude to aircraft serviceability in an airline. There was a clear need to ensure that Avro should exert greater influence over maintenance practice and procedures and so help the airline to achieve a better standard of safety, serviceability and aircraft reputation. The only way to do that was to reinforce our technical representation in the country; at the time we had only one Avro engineer to oversee ten aircraft at two main hubs and three or four other overnight out-stations.

All of this sounds like a lot of problems but they were much the same issues that we had seen in several other countries that operated our ATP, 146 or RJ aircraft. They were, after all, the problems that we were there to identify and then to help operators to rectify, for the eventual benefit of both the airline and Avro and, indeed, to increase the prospects of further sales of our aircraft elsewhere.

Introducing new aircraft into an airline and flying the busy scheduled service whilst training new pilots was a very demanding business, but it wasn't all hard graft. The joy of being able to take advantage of the occasional day off, especially during a double night-stop when at an out-station such as Izmir or Antalya was much appreciated. From Izmir, for example, I went with a guide to visit the ancient (tenth century BC) Greek city of Ephesus and its famous Temple of Artemis. From Antalya, I hired a car and drove to the ancient ruins of Perge and to the great amphitheatre of Aspendos. Such visits provided great compensation and great interest after the busy days at work.

Compensation leads me to mention another subject. During the difficult preceding three years at BAe/Avro, when cash was tight, our management had chosen to impose a pay freeze without consultation with those affected. We pilots were contracted on a separate and specific scale that included annual salary increments according to years of service. Whilst we could understand and accept that the pay scale itself could be frozen for a short while, we were not at all happy that we could not at least progress annually up that frozen scale, as was part of our contract, and be able to look forward soon to a general elevation across the scale. However, two of the top people overseeing the pilot group were indeed quite unpleasant if approached on the subject. I was even directly threatened with being 'frozen out' of the company if I dared to raise the matter again!

Following three and a half years of salary freeze and after those two gentlemen had parted company with Avro, a much more approachable Head of Flight Operations (HFO) was appointed. I knew him quite well and I took it upon myself to raise the issue once more. This time, I was met by a far more mature and business-like reaction. I was encouraged by the HFO to put together a formal case for salary increases for pilots. Thankfully, I had quietly been a member of BALPA (the British Airline Pilots' Association) since before joining BAe. Though there was no company recognition of BALPA, I was at least able to gain advice from them on tactical (and tactful) presentation of the case that I began to put together. I had researched pay scales for pilots in airlines and at another manufacturer, Airbus, where, like us, their pilots had significant responsibilities in addition to those of ordinary airline pilots — as we of course had when carrying out line training with our customers. Also, most of us were accredited production and/or development test pilots, training captains and pilot examiners. We had fallen a long way behind the pay levels of Airbus, not to mention some of the major airlines.

Our particular, well-recognised 'X-Factors' included high risk operations and training in some very difficult areas, e.g. China, Bangladesh, Colombia and parts of Turkey, as I have described in some detail earlier. We often had to overcome or to accommodate significant environmental, language and cultural problems. Our overseas detachments amounted to four to five months per year or more, frequently in sessions of four plus weeks at a time, all of which were often subject to very short notice changes.

In terms of accountability, it wasn't difficult to argue that, in addition to our basic but vital, ultimate responsibility for the safety and preservation of aircraft and passengers, there were several other ultimate responsibilities that we shouldered or at least shared. They included: assessment and approval of aircraft design, modifications and production quality; management of the entry into operational service of the aircraft with new customers (to establish user success and thus further sales prospects); approval and release to service of candidate customer pilots and feedback of first-hand market intelligence. We were frequently ambassadors, on behalf of BAe/Avro, to top-level airline, government and other VIPs.

Now I mention all these highfalutin factors, not to imply that we factory pilots were somehow supermen of the aviation business but to illustrate that, with help from BALPA and my new high supporter in Avro, I was able to put together a convincing case. That soon won us all a very significant salary increase — and therefore a de facto subsequent pension increase, from which I happily benefit today! Yet there is another reason for mentioning that job evaluation exercise. It sets out the background and the definition of all the aspects that had to come fully together in my last, very long and very large project that I managed in Avro for most of the time until just before my early retirement five years later.

It was during a particular busy period in Turkey, when I was beginning to tire from the perpetual high demands of the operation and of the pay campaign, that my immediate boss, John Davies (then training manager, but later to be lost in a Hunter crash as mentioned earlier), asked me one day, in the airport terminal in Ankara, if I would take on the responsibility of running the very large, new project with Sabena. As I already knew, the Belgian national airline was to purchase 23 Avro RJ aircraft (two more were added later) for its domestic subsidiary, Delta Air Transport (DAT), based then at Antwerp and operating Fokker aircraft but scheduled to move to Brussels with the new jet operation. In due course, DAT would also take over Sabena's existing fleet of six BAe 146s.

A key point was that we would need to recruit many qualified and experienced BAe 146 pilots (for conversion to the Avro RJ), on contract from the outset, in order to put the first four new RJ aircraft into service immediately on delivery from December 1995, then to support the further expansion of the fleet over the next few years. Although a number of existing 146 pilots would come over to DAT two years later with the six aircraft from Sabena mainline, they too of course would have to be converted to the RJ. It was to be a massive task, soon becoming beyond even what I had anticipated at the time of being asked to take it on. The airline would receive thirty-one mostly new aircraft over a period of three years whilst moving its operating base. It would need to train a total of around two hundred and fifty pilots onto the RJ (around one hundred and fifty within the busiest eighteen-month period of the project), including the contract group, existing Sabena 146 crews and new recruits to DAT. My initial thought was "No, thank you very much! Could I please have the frontal lobotomy instead!"

However, I was of course trapped by my own hand and there was no escape route! Having taken the initiative to run a campaign for improved pilot salaries at Avro, I could hardly walk away from the new task that the company wanted me to take on in Brussels. As Avro's senior training captain by then, I really had no option. I demurred for a short while but reluctantly decided I had to say yes, at the same time trying to project more enthusiasm for the task than I thought I could muster at that early point. I will attempt to explain briefly what was to transpire over the period of the following, nearly five, years.

Once the decision was made, the game moved quickly onward. I flew back to the UK from Turkey for a brief few days at Woodford. On 7 September, John Davies and I had our first meeting with a senior Sabena training captain, Jacques Drappier, who had been appointed as the director of flight operations (DFO) at DAT to oversee the introduction of the new aircraft. We agreed the details of the training programme and the operational logistics required to meet the needs of introducing the first four Avro RJ 85s in the coming December. Jacques was a very professional and business-like individual as well as an amusing and friendly man; the rapport with him was excellent from the beginning and for the coming year in which he and I were to work closely together before he returned to Sabena mainline.

We used Parc Aviation in Dublin to find suitably qualified BAe 146 pilots. As project manager and ex-officio Chief Pilot for the contract group, I thankfully had the final say as to who should join the team. That was not possible for me to accomplish entirely from within my own knowledge so, where necessary, I was usually able to vet them through my BAe Hatfield colleagues who had trained BAe 146 pilots for many years and knew pretty well every candidate put forward by Parc and especially the captains. A key factor to add to their verified flying competence was the need for our contract pilots to fit in well as guests with our hosts in Belgium. We began with a group of eight crews, contracted for one year, who carried out RJ differences training at Woodford from mid-September and then joined the operation in Brussels in early December. The contract pilot group would eventually expand to nearly fifty pilots, many of whom would stay with us for nearly five years. They were drawn from eight different nations: UK, Ireland, Canada, USA, Germany, Sweden, Italy and South Africa. As you might imagine, managing that lot was interesting enough in itself! It worked out fairly well and we had to part company prematurely with only three individuals during the three plus years in which I was at the helm.

Meanwhile, DAT had nominated as their new chief pilot for the Avro RJ operation, Captain (and Baron) Nicolas d'Otreppe, an experienced Sabena 146 training captain. In October, Nic and four Sabena 146 crews, carried out their differences training at Woodford, comprising two days' ground school and three simulator sessions. The next month, I took DAT's first new RJ 85 aircraft through its two, production flight test schedule (PFTS) flights, its first six hours in the air after roll out from the factory.

On 30 November and 1 December, in the same aircraft, I flew the two customer acceptance flights (in which most of the test points in the PFTS schedule were demonstrated) with Nic at Woodford. Then, with Nic* as captain, he and I delivered it, in its new registration OO-DJK, to

301

Brussels (BRU) on 6 December. The very next day, with Nic as observer on the jump seat, I carried out base checks on two contract first officers, operating out of Charleroi. Nic and I began our years of close co-operation as they were to continue, i.e. in a very friendly and professional manner, understanding each other well and not afraid to challenge each other where required. Two days later, I set off in the evening with a contract pilot on the first revenue flight in DAT's second aircraft to Berlin Tempelhof (THF) for a night-stop. My contract colleague for the flight had been one of my mentors in Loganair six years earlier when I was gaining my first airline experience in the ATP.

THF was an unusual airport in many respects (though it closed on 30 October 2008) and it would have been useful to have had this, our first look at it, by day rather than by night. My colleague (under my supervision) flew the sector, arriving via an ILS approach to land on runway 27L(left), the southern of the two parallel runways. He was largely 'head-down' on instruments whilst I followed the standard operating procedure (SOP) of being 'head-up' to look for the runway. Reassuringly, I saw the runway lights clearly from a few miles out but I was certainly *very* surprised to see that the last half-mile before touchdown took us close between two blocks of flats, well-lit by the lights — in their rooms! I later discovered that the distance of the buildings to our right closed to less than seventy-five metres** away from my aircraft as we crossed the runway threshold! The runway was relatively short (one thousand, six hundred metres) so it was only a brief interval before we turned off at the end to follow the unfamiliar, circular taxi-track, crossing the northern runway and parking, uniquely, under the tall, over-hanging canopy that ran the length of the quadricircular airport terminal.

When we checked in the following morning for the return flight, we discovered that the weather at BRU was well below our limits for landing, as it was at neighbouring diversion airports in Belgium and Holland. Most unfortunately, that began a saga of delay that was very unwelcome on this, our first flight to Berlin.

The Avro RJ's greatest advantage over the BAe 146 was, of course, its Cat 3A autoland capability that allowed us to land in visibility down to two hundred metres with a decision height of fifty feet. Nevertheless, in common with all other operators and types at the time, national clearance for actual Cat 3 or Cat 2 (three hundred metres and one hundred feet) operations required general approval for a particular aircraft type, airfield and operator as well as specific training for the pilots. However, an operator could not be granted that clearance until it had first completed six months' operations to Cat 1 limits (five hundred and fifty metres and two hundred feet) with a new aircraft type. The fog at BRU stayed well below the Cat 1 limit for a further forty-eight hours.

From the outset, the Sabena station manager at THF — a German national — just would not understand or accept the situation as it was. He became livid that, on two successive days, we were unable to fly back with passengers from THF to BRU. It took all the tact and diplomacy that I could muster to deal with him — he gave me a very hard time. During many subsequent visits to THF, I did my utmost to avoid him. Meanwhile, we turned out to have an unexpected two days off in Berlin. By good fortune, one of the airport staff there had recently completed a written history of the airport and, having met and chatted with him, we were eventually able to have him give us a tour of the amazingly long arc of the terminal building that was — we were told and at the time anyway — the longest building of any kind in Europe, at one thousand, two hundred and thirty metres! He took us through the wartime aircraft factory under the terminal and through derelict, battle-scarred, internal rooms that had not been cleared of debris and amazingly still smelled of burnt structure, fifty years after the Russians had fought their way through them.

Within a couple of weeks, I was to spend my second and last Christmas 'away from home'. Until that day loomed, I honestly don't think I'd had much clue that airlines actually flew passengers around on Christmas Day. On that particular day, I flew four sectors, the first two to Milan and return and then to Frankfurt and return. I'd also flown four sectors on Christmas Eve, and took two more on Boxing Day then four sectors on each of the following two days — what an unexpectedly busy little assistant Santa I'd turned out to be!

As the months and years passed, I became totally immersed in the complex and highly demanding job with DAT. More and more aircraft arrived and more and more pilots were trained, both Belgians and contract pilots. A large number of airports were added to my repertoire; I was eventually to fly with DAT to over *fifty* airports in *thirteen* European countries. In addition, I found myself spending many hours in DAT's RJ simulator at BRU, including the hated slots from midnight to four a.m. and four a.m. to eight a.m., each preceded by a long walk in total darkness for several hundred yards to the simulator building — ugh!

A typical week began with me leaving my home near Harlech on Monday around seven a.m. to catch a ten thirty a.m. flight as passenger from Manchester (MAN) to BRU, arriving at lunchtime for a half day's admin and meetings, then flying off in the evening to one of the many destinations for a night-stop, mostly line training fresh pilots, lads and lassies, then four more busy days in aircraft and simulator interspersed with more management stuff. Usually, I could catch an early, Friday afternoon flight home to MAN, drive the two to two and a half hours home, change out of uniform then drive with my wife for twenty minutes to our favourite pub in good time for a Friday evening pint or two and a meal. Invariably, she kindly drove me home! Of course, there were also many weekends over which I was rostered to fly.

I commuted to Brussels from Snowdonia in much this way for almost all of the four and a half years, with only minor changes to the overall routine but with amazing variety and challenges during every week. I had a near-permanent room in the Brussels Airport Sheraton for the first three years. The period was very occasionally punctuated with short stays at Woodford, sometimes to test fly a new aircraft for DAT as it came out of the factory and then to take it on an acceptance flight with a senior DAT captain. In early 1999, as the training of pilots for DAT eventually began to tail off, I was able to hand over management of the project to a colleague. That produced breaks in my still busy ongoing involvement as a trainer with DAT to enable me to take each of five new Avro RJ crews from Mesaba Airlines (based at Minneapolis) through their thirty-six hour (nine x four-hour slots) full training course in the Woodford RJ simulator. Somehow, in the early January, I had found time to jet across to the USA for a day to fly with Mesaba in one of their new RJ 85s to familiarise myself with their operation on a passenger schedule from Minneapolis to Cedar Rapids and return.

Along the way with DAT, there were a few unusual items within the really hard intensity of the main passenger schedule in all weathers, the training schedule and the management of the project and of the contract pilot group. There were plenty of Cat 2 and Cat 3 operations (where I was able to exercise for real the procedures that I had myself written for the RJ) often into Lyon, where it appeared to me that most of the fog in Europe seemed to accumulate each winter. There were the special demands of approaches and departures at Florence, Bilbao, Amsterdam and Paris to be frequently enjoyed, either in close proximity to high terrain at the first two or on account of the traffic density or complexity of procedures at the second two. I operated the inaugural flight to Ajaccio in Sicily. I flew European Commissioner Neil Kinnock and his PA to Glasgow and was surprised to find what a pleasant fellow he was, despite press reports to the contrary.

There were two other short detours during my last eighteen months with DAT. I had a brief stay with Eurowings at Nuremberg in March 1999, where I flew as an observer in their BAe 146s to Berlin, Amsterdam and Paris, to evaluate their operation and produce a series of recommendations to improve it. The visit was very fruitful in both directions and I thoroughly enjoyed it.

On 30 April, I flew one of two new RJ 100s via Geneva to Athens for delivery to Aegean Airlines, an air taxi company that was taking the first steps into scheduled passenger services. I returned five weeks later to join colleague training captains from Woodford for ten days to fly the line from Athens to Chania, Heraklion and Thessaloniki. The new venture sparked off a most successful expansion of the small company to the eventual state where it became the largest Greek airline, with 36 Airbus aircraft, having taken over all of Olympics' public transport routes early in 2014.

On 2 July 2000, I flew what was to be my last sector with DAT, to BRU following a night-stop at Newcastle, having handed over the baton as project manager a few months earlier to another BAe colleague. A week later, I was in Sicily to join colleagues in another new start-up, National Jet Italia, a British Airways franchise operator, backed by Italian investors and an Australian company whilst operating under the British World Airlines (BWA) Air Operator's Certificate. During my planned ten-day stay, based at Palermo, I flew to Rome Fiumicino (FCO) during two return sectors each day, the only route used initially. On the last sectors of the planned last day, 20 July 2000, I was line training BWA's chief pilot whom I knew from years before. He was a former Cathay Pacific 747 captain and once a fellow RAF flying officer when he and I were in Singapore on our respective Canberra and Hunter squadrons in the mid 60s.

I chose to fly the aircraft back from Rome as the handling pilot. Perhaps with something of a premonition at the back of my mind, I wanted to do the last landing before my return to the UK where, amongst other things, I was due to attend the CAA HQ at Gatwick for an annual medical review. I made sure that the landing at Palermo was a really good one, thank heavens, for it was to be my last ever...

Nearly five years earlier (just before I started the DAT project), a cardiac 'anomaly' had been noticed on my routine ECG, so I had to go for an echocardiogram to enable further investigation. It transpired that I had a relatively common congenital heart defect, a bicuspid aortic valve. No big deal, I was merely instructed to get a further echo done every year to enable the CAA medics to monitor the leak rate across my valve. It was well within acceptable limits for quite a while. Unfortunately, two flaps on a heart valve get worn out faster than the normal three. At the test done prior to my CAA renewal in August 2000, the leak rate was found to be out of limits. I was medically grounded, summarily and permanently as it turned out, within a week or so. My wonderful career of forty years in aviation was over — for good.

It was a double whammy; I had just been appointed to be one of only three, full-time, development test pilots on the coming new Avro RJX programme, having been specially approved for that by the CAA. The aircraft was equipped with different engines from the RJ and that required some associated aerodynamic changes. In turn, that meant the new aircraft was to undergo a full certification test programme, as if it

306

were a totally new type. The programme would include hot and high testing and cold weather testing, in Arizona and Greenland respectively, including actual engine shut-downs at critical points of take-off. All those events would have been new and fascinating to me. It was a rare honour and a great privilege for someone like me, who had not attended a test pilots' school, to be fully approved as a development test pilot, qualified to captain aircraft during such demanding tests. It was a qualification to which I had aspired since first flying as an observer in flight tests in the Sea Vixen, Gannet and Meteor aircraft as a sixteen-year-old at RAE Bedford, forty years earlier. I was never to use it.

The test pilot approval from the CAA had been signed on 20 July, ironically the same date as my last flight. After being grounded on 1 August, I was offered, informally, the chance to take over as Head of Safety for British Aerospace Regional Aircraft (renamed once more); the holder of that position thought that my recent career demise would enable him to retire early! I was also offered the opportunity to continue as a flight simulator instructor at Woodford. I declined both and chose to retire to my home in Snowdonia, a happy situation that I have now enjoyed greatly for nearly twenty years.

I'd had a fabulous and a very lucky time as an aviator. I'd clocked up over ten thousand, five hundred hours flying during the thirty-four years that I'd been in full-time operation as a pilot. Half of those hours were packed into my eleven and a half years with BAe — *and* there was a total of nearly one thousand hours more in various military and civil simulators to add in! I had qualified and had become experienced in sixteen aircraft types, handled many others briefly and operated with eight air forces and seventeen airlines. I'd visited seventy-four countries, flown into and/or from one hundred and seventy-nine civil airfields and an uncountable number of military ones (of a similar order I would guess). Most of all, I had survived to write about it all, despite the various efforts of enemy action in the Dhofar War and the risks of training and operational accidents, in military and civil flying worldwide, that had claimed the lives of many of my friends and acquaintances (thirty seven in fact), along the way. Blessed with good fortune, I'm still here after the open-heart surgery that gave me a mechanical replacement valve in 2003 and seventeen years of romping around the local hills and valleys of Meirionnydd and enjoying various other activities.

A year later, Nic took over from Jacques Drappier as DAT's DFO then also returned to Sabena in May 1999 to fly the Airbus A330/340

**As first measured some time ago on Google Earth and still there*

Dear reader, thank you for indulging my wish to try to interest and entertain you with accounts of some of my exploits and of the aircraft, operations and countries in which they took place, along with the people whom I had the privilege to know along the way.

Roy Gamblin

Delta Air Transport (DAT) Avro RJ 100

Aegean Air RJ 100

Avro RJX Formation